D0463701

Freedom from Poverty

PENNSYLVANIA STUDIES IN HUMAN RIGHTS

Bert B. Lockwood, Jr., *Series Editor*

A complete list of books in the series is available
from the publisher.

Freedom from Poverty

NGOs and
Human Rights Praxis

Daniel P. L. Chong

PENN

UNIVERSITY OF PENNSYLVANIA PRESS

PHILADELPHIA · OXFORD

Published by
University of Pennsylvania Press
Philadelphia, Pennsylvania 19104-4112

Printed in the United States of America
on acid-free paper
10 9 8 7 6 5 4 3 2 1

Library of Congress Cataloging-in-Publication Data
Chong, Daniel P. L.
  Freedom from poverty : NGOs and human rights praxis /
Daniel P. L. Chong.
      p. cm. — (Pennsylvania studies in human rights)
  Includes bibliographical references and index.
  ISBN 978-0-8122-4252-2 (hardcover : alk. paper)
  1. Human rights. 2. Nongovernmental organizations.
3. Poverty. I. Title.
  JC571.C5535 2010
  362.5'57—dc22   2009048470

For Tyler and Owen,
part of the first generation able to achieve
freedom from poverty for everyone

Contents

Preface ‹   ix

1. NGOs and Freedom from Poverty   1

2. A Social Theory of Human Rights   17

3. Human Rights Organizations   31

4. Social Justice Organizations   71

5. Humanitarian Organizations   104

6. Using a Social Theory to Interpret NGO Efforts   131

Appendix: NGOs Working for Freedom from Poverty   143

Notes   159

Bibliography   197

Index   213

Acknowledgments   217

Preface

The research for this book began with a set of simple questions. If basic needs such as food, housing, and health care were so central to human survival and dignity, why were they discredited for so long in the West? Why, after all these years, were nongovernmental organizations (NGOs) beginning to accept the validity of freedom from poverty as a basic human right? Does this new trend have the potential to change the practice of human rights and our approach to extreme poverty?

Although existing studies regarding human rights and social movements provided some attempts to answer these questions, I was largely dissatisfied with the answers they suggested. Traditional human rights theory asserted that economic and social rights were inherently distinct from civil and political rights, a difference that resulted in their nonjusticiability or incompatibility with human rights methodologies. However, a number of human rights scholars dissented from the mainstream view, and I remained undecided entering my research. Constructivist theory argued that universalistic norms dealing in clear terms with vulnerable victims and physical harm were more likely to be effective; yet if these characteristics of subsistence rights remained constant, why did the historical acceptance of these rights vary? (Throughout the book, I use the term "subsistence rights" and "freedom from poverty" interchangeably, as a subset of all economic and social rights. See Chapter 1 for a more detailed definition.) Social movement theory explained that the political opportunity structure was hostile to subsistence rights in the West during the Cold War, but it was not immediately clear why subsistence rights advocacy has reemerged in the United States in a political environment that continues to be hostile. Finally, social movement theory suggested that issue framing is an important component of successful campaigns, but the details of how framing processes and contests operated in this case remained to be elaborated.

So in 2003 I embarked on a journey engaging with dozens of NGOs, using participant observation, interviews, and reviews of primary and secondary documents. One of my first research sites was the inaugural conference of the International Network for Economic, Social, and Cultural Rights in Chiang Mai, Thailand, in 2003. This conference, attended by several hundred activists from all regions of the world, represented the launching of the first international network of NGOs specifically devoted to the fulfillment of economic and social rights. At this conference, it became clear to me that activists were speaking different languages about human rights, depending on what kind of organization they represented and how they sought to use the human rights framework. Although human rights practitioners often spoke of a gap between lawyers and grassroots activists within the movement, these different approaches were largely unspoken understandings rather than explicit ones. I later labeled these two languages, which implied different understandings about what human rights really are, as the moral and legal approaches to rights.

Although there was some overlap between the languages, for the most part social justice groups and humanitarian organizations maintained a loose (if any) connection between human rights and international legal standards, while human rights organizations insisted that human rights are embedded within and defined precisely by those standards. These divergent approaches to defining human rights were linked to different ways that these organizations employed human rights to promote their strategic goals. Social justice NGOs used human rights in accordance with other moral discourses (equality, justice, responsibility) to mobilize their activist networks, appeal to donors, or advocate for local, national, or international policy changes. Subsistence rights served as a way of reframing public debate about poverty by reconstituting the poor as active subjects, and by asserting that extreme poverty is an issue of justice and systemic failure rather than charity and individual failure. Humanitarian organizations used rights language to reorient and guide their own relief and development work. For them, freedom from poverty became translated into moral principles of participation and accountability, which led humanitarian organizations to reconsider how they address the structural causes of poverty, how they can become more politically engaged, and how they can help empower the poor to claim their own rights. Human rights organizations, in contrast, used human rights to hold states (and increasingly other actors) accountable to their explicit legal obligations. For them, subsistence rights were a set of international legal standards that could be used to guide the writing of national legislation, take a violator to court, or publicly shame the violator into compliance.

These two approaches to subsistence rights, the legal and the moral, did not seem to hold equal legitimacy within the human rights movement. Social justice and humanitarian organizations were often viewed with an ambivalent mixture of support and suspicion by traditional human rights activists—support because the resources and constituencies they provided were essential to a strong movement, and suspicion because many people wondered whether their approach to subsistence rights genuinely qualified as human rights work. Human rights activists were also concerned that the adoption of rights-based approaches by social justice and humanitarian groups might not be a long-term, fundamental commitment. In the research I conducted, several human rights gatekeepers—representatives of the largest human rights organizations and their donors—advanced the notion that to *really* do human rights work, organizations must explicitly cite international documents and take advantage of the legal accountability that is ostensibly central to a rights-based approach. For these gatekeepers, organizations did not necessarily need to adopt specific legal strategies (litigation, treaty advocacy, and so on), but they did need to orient their approach to rights around a set of international legal standards and a notion of accountability and definitional clarity that accompanied them. In some cases, social justice organizations have matched their approaches to fit in with gatekeepers' strategies and have received funding and collaborative support as a result. In other cases, the suspicion about nonlegal approaches to rights may have closed off sources of support to some social justice and humanitarian groups adopting moral approaches to rights. Decisions on funding and support help to determine who is empowered to execute subsistence rights advocacy and what kind of advocacy will occur.

For my part, although I believe in an inherent right to subsistence, I began this project skeptical of the strategic value of human rights in achieving freedom from poverty and suspicious about the sincerity of the human rights rhetoric increasingly used by social justice and humanitarian organizations. However, I came to believe that these approaches, the legal and the moral, are valuable tools for the promotion of freedom from poverty. With this book, I hope to show that both legal and moral approaches to human rights can translate effectively into tangible strategic practice. Both approaches entail specific costs and benefits, appeal to different constituencies, and pursue different strategic pathways to reach equally valid goals. In the remainder of this study I hope to outline the tangible contributions that all of these organizations are making to the realization of subsistence rights, in both legal and nonlegal arenas, and in that way help legitimize the work of organizations previously at the margins of the human rights movement.

1

NGOs and Freedom from Poverty

Human rights advocacy in the West is changing. New issues are being promoted, which extend beyond the relatively narrow range of civil and political rights that nongovernmental organizations (NGOs) historically fought for. New organizations are joining in the fight, using concepts and methods not traditionally considered "human rights" advocacy. This book explains how the advancement of new rights—in particular, freedom from poverty—is redefining what human rights *mean* and how they can be used as tools for social change.

Since the early 1990s there has been a growing movement among NGOs, social justice organizations, UN agencies, and some state institutions in favor of using human rights rhetoric and strategies to combat extreme poverty. This is manifested by initial steps being taken in several domains:

- new international conferences relating to economic and social rights;[1]
- the mainstreaming of human rights approaches within UN development agencies;[2]
- an increase in national legislation and institutions (such as human rights commissions) that explicitly incorporate economic and social rights concerns;
- increasing reference to human rights in public education campaigns on poverty;
- an increase in funding for economic and social rights from private foundations and other donors;[3]
- increasing willingness of traditional human rights organizations to move toward advocating for the "full spectrum" of human rights;

- the proliferation of new organizations that focus exclusively on economic and social rights;
- increasing use of human rights language by grassroots social movements struggling against poverty, hunger, homelessness, and other social problems; and
- increasing adoption of rights-based approaches by humanitarian aid NGOs.

For the first time in history, then, extreme global poverty is being seriously considered in the West as more than just a personal misfortune, but as a human rights concern. Hundreds of NGOs are now involved in promoting the realization of economic and social rights in some fashion.[4] Yet even as they move to adopt a human rights approach to poverty, NGOs understand and approach the human rights framework in different ways. These different approaches to *subsistence rights*—that is, claims for social guarantees to guard against extreme poverty—represent differing avenues that organizations take to engage strategically in the politics of human rights. Studying this diversity in approaches to subsistence rights can help us understand how substate human rights politics is changing to adapt to new concerns.

At first glance, it is somewhat puzzling why the human rights framework was not employed earlier in Western NGOs' struggle against global poverty. Subsistence rights figured prominently in the Universal Declaration of Human Rights, and throughout the Cold War, rights language flourished as people began to "frame every social controversy as a clash of rights."[5] My research, therefore, tries to understand why Western NGOs have only recently begun to delve into freedom from poverty and what emerging NGO practice on subsistence rights implies for human rights politics more generally. I address this overall theme through three specific questions:

1. Why have NGOs begun to adopt subsistence rights—as part of a larger package of economic and social rights—in the past decade? Why do some organizations continue to resist subsistence rights?
2. How do different actors interpret and frame rights differently?
3. What does emerging NGO practice on subsistence rights imply, both for the politics of human rights and for efforts to eliminate extreme poverty?

This book focuses on three sets of actors who have increasingly adopted subsistence rights in the past decade: human rights, social justice, and humanitarian NGOs.[6] Human rights organizations are groups such as Amnesty International and Human Rights Watch, whose mission is explicitly focused on the realization of human rights. Within human rights organizations, subsistence rights have been promoted both by new organizations specifically devoted to issues related to poverty and by traditional human rights organizations expanding their mandates to include a limited range of economic and social rights. Social justice organizations include local constituency-based groups, national lobbying groups, interorganizational coalitions, and academic institutes that frame their social and economic advocacy campaigns in terms of social justice.[7] These groups are promoting subsistence rights by increasingly (though irregularly) employing human rights language as tools in their public advocacy campaigns against extreme poverty. Humanitarian organizations are groups such as Oxfam and CARE International, whose self-defined mission centers around providing goods and services to people living in extreme poverty around the world. These NGOs are promoting subsistence rights by increasingly adopting rights-based approaches in guiding the implementation of their project work among the poor. Although all of these organizations approach subsistence rights from different angles in different contexts, their work on subsistence rights is concerned with a similar goal: guaranteeing everyone the basic means for sustaining a minimum livelihood.[8]

I argue that these Western NGOs—human rights, social justice, and humanitarian organizations—that have adopted subsistence rights in the past decade have been motivated both by principled ideas and strategic organizational concerns. Subsistence rights advocacy is growing because of the way that NGOs express their fundamental values, anticipate the likely effectiveness of their methods, and interpret their organizational interests in responding to broader cultural, political, and economic changes that will be discussed below. In other words, the ongoing mutual interplay of principled ideas and strategic interests has led these organizations to increasingly adopt or resist subsistence rights. There is no characteristic inherent to the rights themselves that has led to this process, and there is nothing inevitable about the further expansion of subsistence rights advocacy. The interplay of normative ideas and strategic interests—which have been mutually congruent rather than contradictory—has also led these organizations to interpret and frame subsistence rights differently, leading to unique pathways toward the realization of rights.

Human rights organizations have adopted a predominantly *legal* approach to subsistence rights, which closely identifies rights with the international legal system and tends to privilege efforts that are focused on holding the state legally accountable. For decades, human rights organizations focused exclusively on civil and political rights because they operated under assumptions and within strategic environments in which human rights were defined as legal tools imposing negative obligations on states, which were only valid if they could be made justiciable. These organizations have increasingly accepted the legitimacy of subsistence rights and are incorporating them into their work. They are using their well-developed methodologies to realize important gains in the legal realm, thereby demonstrating that subsistence rights are indeed valid legal rights. Yet a legal approach to subsistence rights necessarily involves specific challenges, such as the reluctance of many courts to adjudicate economic and social rights claims, official U.S. opposition to legal subsistence rights, the inaccessibility of legal discourse and institutions to the people who matter most, ambiguity in the legal texts, and ideological controversies over the proper remedies for subsistence rights violations. Overcoming these hurdles, and instituting legal guarantees that protect poor people from severe deprivation, has become a major focus of the work of these human rights NGOs. In that sense, how an actor interprets rights strongly influences the strategic challenges they face and the pathway they must follow to achieve their goals.

Due in part to their own institutional histories and the challenges inherent in a legal approach, social justice and humanitarian NGOs—in contrast to human rights organizations—have adopted a predominantly *moral* understanding of subsistence rights. Moral approaches de-link human rights from their international legal sources, and typically interpret rights as basic moral principles synonymous with equality, justice, participation, empowerment, and dignity. Legal approaches to rights are also grounded in these same moral principles, but what makes a legal approach unique is its reliance on specific legal documents, discourses, authority, and procedures to define rights and their practical expression. Under a moral approach, human rights are claims that lead to social and political action, sometimes but not necessarily in the legal realm. Social justice NGOs use human rights language to mobilize their constituencies, most of whom have limited access to legal tools and are not interested in legal formulations of rights. The target of social justice groups' advocacy is typically a change in specific state policies (e.g., budget allocation), institutional reform, or broader changes in the cultural assumptions underlying societal responses to poverty. Similarly, humanitarian organizations employ a moral understanding of human rights to justify and guide organizational operations as they implement basic subsistence projects among the world's poor. Human rights principles act as a lens to reevaluate an organization's normative commitments, analyze the context in which it works, and reshape operations in the field.

Yet even as moral approaches to rights can resolve or circumvent some of the challenges inherent in a legal approach by simplifying the language and avoiding legal debates and institutions, they face unique challenges of their own in achieving their goals. Because moral approaches to rights are not grounded in a narrowly circumscribed set of positive laws, and because of the ideological heterogeneity within the social justice and humanitarian movements, there is considerable ambiguity about what a commitment to subsistence rights actually entails. Clarifying how notions of equality and dignity are implemented in practice becomes a major challenge in the work of humanitarian and social justice NGOs. Once again, actors' ideas and interests merge to construct a specific approach to subsistence rights, an approach that influences the challenges faced and the pathways taken in achieving their goals.

How is this emerging NGO advocacy for subsistence rights redefining human rights politics? Scholars have long noted that human rights are grounded in both legal and moral frameworks, yet due to the legalization of human rights politics, they have failed to outline how a moral approach to rights translates into tangible strategic practice. Scholars and practitioners often disparage moral approaches to subsistence rights as "soft," empty rhetoric, or merely a philosophical or historical precursor to enforceable legal rights. They also fear that promoting economic and social rights may dilute and damage efforts to strengthen civil and political rights. In contrast, I advance a social theory of human rights that argues that moral approaches to subsistence rights are valuable, because changes in culture, economic policy, the private sector, and political accountability are just as important to securing subsistence rights as legal enforcement. Even when legal enforcement of rights is the goal, there is no way to circumvent the discourse of politics, economics, normative values, and other extralegal debates in the process of advancing the law. Legal change is heavily influenced by political action and the cultural assumptions that resonate in society, and much of the work on subsistence rights must revolve around reframing those basic assumptions. A social theory of human rights validates both legal and moral approaches to subsistence rights as important tools that operate in a broader social context, each tool containing its own unique costs and benefits. Thus, I do not privilege either legal or moral approaches to rights; however, because legal approaches have been historically hegemonic in human rights politics, I attempt to restore attention to the strategically moral aspects of human rights.

Rather than trying to protect a core of certain rights or well-established methodologies, I argue that our notion of human rights (including what it means to *perform* human rights work) needs to be broadened. Rather than threatening to dilute the effectiveness of civil and political rights, emerging work on subsistence rights is demonstrating that economic and social rights are also valid legal rights. In addition, subsistence rights work has the potential to actually strengthen civil and political rights by causing us to reconsider the legal *and* moral strategies through which human rights can be made effective.

Freedom from Poverty: A Recent History

Because I focus on recent efforts by Western NGOs to fight extreme poverty through the promotion of subsistence rights, I should elaborate on what I mean by "subsistence rights," their relation to extreme poverty, and their historical place in human rights struggles. Subsistence rights are demands that a person's material survival be socially guaranteed—survival that depends on the ability to achieve a minimum standard of living and acquire goods such as nutrition, housing, and health care.[9] Among other sources, freedom from poverty is enshrined in the Universal Declaration of Human Rights, Article 25: "Everyone has the right to a standard of living adequate for the health and well-being of himself and of his family, including food, clothing, housing and medical care and necessary social services."[10] Similar wording has been included in the International Covenant on Economic, Social and Cultural Rights, Article 11, as well as in several other legally binding international treaties.[11] These rights have also been called "subsistence social rights," "the right to an adequate standard of living," and "the right to be saved from preventable death due to deprivation."[12] These, according to Henry Shue, are some of the most basic human rights, whose "enjoyment is essential to all other rights."[13]

Subsistence rights are therefore a subset of economic, social, and cultural rights. Other economic and social rights include, for example, the right to education, marriage rights, labor rights, and property rights. Economic and social rights have been labeled "second generation" rights, distinguishable from "first generation" civil and political rights such as freedom from torture, enslavement, or discrimination. Civil and political rights have been understood traditionally as negative rights that protect a person's freedom against oppression or interference by the state.[14] Conversely, economic and social rights have been considered historically positive rights that require a more interventionist state to promote social and economic equality. This distinction between two rigid categories of rights, and their association with positive and negative obligations, has recently been challenged by human rights scholars and practitioners, which will be discussed in more detail throughout the book.

Subsistence rights arguably stand at the core of all economic and social rights, or even at the core of all human rights, because no other rights can be exercised effectively by someone who is deprived of a minimum livelihood. As has been argued many times, people cannot participate in a political process or truly exercise free speech when they are dying of hunger or a preventable disease.[15]

There is an undeniable link between extreme poverty, defined as a deficiency in capabilities, and the inability to secure the right to subsistence.[16] As the UN Development Program states simply, "Poverty limits human freedoms and deprives a person of dignity." [17] The UN High Commissioner on Human Rights continues, "Indeed, no social phenomenon is as comprehensive in its assault on human rights as poverty. Poverty erodes or nullifies economic and social rights such as the right to health, adequate housing, food and safe water, and the right to education." [18] As such, efforts to promote subsistence rights are synonymous with efforts to establish social (and sometimes legal) guarantees against extreme poverty. This understanding of subsistence rights does not view poor people as passive recipients of goods that satisfy their basic needs; rather, it assumes that people should be active agents with the freedom to pursue their own livelihoods and the power to demand a social response if those efforts fail.[19]

Subsistence rights therefore deal with the fifth of the world's population who live in conditions of extreme material deprivation. One billion people in the world lack the ability to fulfill their basic physical needs, with roughly 1.4 billion lacking adequate housing, 700 million lacking adequate nutrition, and 1.2 billion lacking clean water.[20] Tens of thousands of people in these conditions die each day, largely from preventable diseases related to poverty and malnutrition—equivalent to an Asian tsunami occurring on an almost-daily basis. Extreme poverty is arguably the greatest ongoing human disaster in the world.

These facts need to be situated historically in order to better understand efforts to fight extreme global poverty. In the past fifty years, the world has witnessed tremendous progress in reducing the proportion of its people in poverty, due in large part to economic growth in China and East Asia.[21] But global progress in reducing the absolute number of people in extreme poverty has slowed since the early 1990s, prompting the UN Development Program to describe a "decade of despair."[22] This occurred despite the fact that the international community retains enough resources to meet all people's basic needs, and despite widespread public commitments to achieve that end. The funding task is not insurmountable; economists estimate that the additional $50–100 billion needed to address extreme poverty represents less than half of one percent of wealthy states' annual gross domestic product.[23] Thus, although the world has seen some success in reducing extreme poverty in recent decades, we are not close to reaching our professed collective goal, and with the recent global economic recession, we are quite possibly heading in the wrong direction. Few analysts would observe these achievements and conclude that the steps taken to eliminate severe deprivation have matched the scale of need.

It is somewhat ironic that subsistence rights have long been neglected within the West, given their centrality to basic dignity and to the realization of all other human rights. The most obvious historical reason for the neglect of nearly all economic and social rights is the Cold War. Shortly after the Universal Declaration was adopted, which spelled out all rights as indivisible and equal, the United States led an almost single-handed campaign to assign a secondary legal status to economic, social and cultural rights.[24] For example, in 1951, the U.S. Ambassador to the UN, Walter Kotschnig, argued that: "civil and political rights were of such a nature as to be given legal effect promptly by the adoption of such legislation or other measures as might be necessary. The economic, social and cultural rights while spoken of as 'rights' were, however, to be treated as *objectives* toward which States adhering to the [proposed] Covenant would within their resources undertake to strive, by the creation of conditions which would be conducive to the exercise of private as well as public action, for their progressive achievement."[25] Official U.S. policy on economic and social rights, despite some supportive rhetoric during the Carter administration,[26] has not changed substantially since that time. As a result of U.S. pressure, the planned UN covenant that would codify and make legally binding all human rights was subsequently divided into two covenants, each with different normative content and monitoring mechanisms. Economic and social rights were thereby perceived as the "poor

ErCR
— *as w.r.v. domestic law*

step-sister" in the increasingly legalized and professionalized field of international human rights,[27] and have been "wallowing in the relative purgatory of global efforts to secure human rights" ever since.[28]

The widening chasm between two sets of rights was reinforced by the growing cultural and political divide between the liberal democracies of the West and the socialist countries of the East. While the liberal democracies argued that protecting civil and political rights was the best pathway to economic prosperity, socialist governments claimed that by prioritizing economic and social rights, they were as human rights–compliant as the West. Socialist arguments failed to attract large numbers of supporters in the West, particularly among human rights activists in the United States, because these activists viewed Soviet support for economic and social rights as a sham that barely concealed the centralization of power, corruption, and misguided redistributive schemes common within the East.[29] Human rights activists in the West delegitimized Soviet governments and held onto their own notions of the priority of civil and political rights, on both strategic and ideological grounds.

In the context of the Cold War, the ideological arguments marshaled against subsistence rights typically took the following form. Human rights must be legally enforceable and justiciable (i.e., subject to review in courts and quasi-judicial arenas) to be legitimately defined as rights. States are only legally accountable for their negative obligations—obligations not to interfere with personal liberty—which were associated exclusively with civil and political rights. In other words, civil and political rights were justiciable, while economic and social rights categorically were not. Issues of basic material subsistence such as adequate housing, food, and health care thus were understood as "goals and aspirations" that are implemented voluntarily within the private sphere, but not subject to public scrutiny. As such, individuals should be held responsible for their own material well-being, and while the state was empowered to provide benefits to its vulnerable populations, it was not legally required to do so as a matter of individual right.[30] Subsistence rights, according to the predominant line of thinking in the West, required fundamental economic redistribution generated through massive governmental interference in the economy, which not only compromised other individual freedoms but also were impossible to monitor through the judicial process. In this manner, economic and social rights were perceived as *essentially* different from civil and political rights—a difference that involved extensive and expensive positive duties that were inherently nonjusticiable.[31]

   Once the constraints of the Cold War were lifted, an increasing number of human rights scholars and practitioners in the West began to argue that the East/West divide over human rights was the result of a historical coincidence rather than any essential differences between two sets of rights. Many have argued that the distinction between civil and political rights and economic and social rights is oversimplified, not only because of so much overlap in their practical implementation, but because both sets of rights impose positive and negative duties on other actors.[32] For example, the right to due process requires the state to spend a significant portion of its budget on courts and public defenders. Freedom from cruel and unusual punishment imposes a positive and expensive duty on the state to build and manage humane prisons. Similarly, many argue that realizing subsistence rights requires the state to implement reasonable measures of protection and some budget expenses, but not any massive redistribution or equalization of wealth.[33] Other experts have noted that civil and political rights began historically in much the same way that many economic and social rights stand today—as unelaborated norms with vague definitions that were subject to public debate, ideological controversy, and political struggle.[34] Gradually, over the course of many decades, civil and political rights such as freedom from torture and discrimination were accepted and elaborated more precisely through a web of judicial decisions, public policy making, and social practice.[35] Thus, many human rights practitioners in the West today believe that the divide between two sets of rights was primarily due to misperceptions about rights rather than any essential differences, and that there are no overwhelming barriers inherent within subsistence rights that would prevent their realization.[36] They argue that if the international community devotes the same amount of attention, resources, and effort to subsistence rights as they have devoted to civil and political rights, then with enough time subsistence rights would be just as embedded in our cultural, political, and legal institutions as civil and political rights are today.[37]

   This book, analyzing rights through the lens of a social theory merging constructivism and post-positivist legal theory, agrees with this new scholarship. A social theory claims that human rights are socially constructed ideas whose characteristics are historically and contextually dependent rather than essential, therefore rights are malleable and subject to ongoing interpretation.[38] It argues that the divide between two generations of rights was a result of particular interpretations of these rights and the ways that these ideas were strategically promoted.

This is not to say that there are no longer any practical differences among human rights. Instead, the differences arise from the historical attention given to and ideological positions taken on the rights rather than any essential qualities about the rights themselves or their subject matter. The legal and normative content of subsistence rights is weaker and more ambiguous than most civil and political rights,[39] which is manifested in the language and enforcement mechanisms attached to the International Covenant on Economic, Social and Cultural Rights. Article 2.1 in this Covenant contains considerably more equivocal language than the Covenant on Civil and Political Rights: "Each State Party to the present Covenant undertakes to take steps, individually and through international assistance and co-operation, especially economic and technical, to the maximum of its available resources, with a view to achieving progressively the full realization of the rights recognized in the present Covenant by all appropriate means, including particularly the adoption of legislative measures."[40] International legal experts have devoted many hours trying to discern and clarify exactly what state obligations are imposed by the phrases "taking steps . . . through international assistance . . . to the maximum of its available resources . . . achieving progressively the full realization of the rights." The definitional underdevelopment and relative weakness of legal institutions protecting economic and social rights, however, does not necessarily mean that these rights are inherently nonjusticiable and nonactionable. Ultimately, the question of justiciability regards whether an institutional actor (typically but not always a court or review body) is legitimate, competent, willing, and powerful enough to review a violation and ensure that a remedy is implemented.[41] Indeed, justiciability is socially constructed and varies among different contexts and across time.[42] Thus, there are no justiciable (or nonjusticiable) qualities *inherent* in civil and political rights or in economic and social rights; it depends entirely on the institutions that construct and interpret them in a particular time and place. These institutions are underdeveloped for economic and social rights in comparison with civil and political rights, which is evident both in the wording of treaties and the lack of monitoring and enforcement mechanisms.[43] Therefore, in realizing economic and social rights, the "question of justiciability is one of political and legal creativity,"[44] not an "automatic consequence of the 'nature' of economic and social rights."[45]

The indivisibility and interdependence of all rights has now become mainstream thought in the international system of human rights, a position expressed in the Vienna Declaration in 1993. This broad consensus over indivisibility, however, is noticeably thin.[46] Beneath the publicly expressed consensus, ongoing disagreements simmer about the nature and scope of economic and social rights and how they can be used as legal tools. Advocates for subsistence rights struggle to define more precisely what practices are required or prohibited by these rights, and how these rights should be balanced against other social needs when resources are scarce. Human Rights Watch's Kenneth Roth argues that economic and social rights, while morally valid, do not fit into Western human rights organizations' well-established methodologies, which entail the naming and shaming of clear legal violations.[47] Other influential human rights theorists continue to oppose economic and social rights on philosophical grounds, claiming that human rights ought to be exclusively negative protections of individual liberty, and that economic and social rights threaten to dilute the effectiveness of civil and political rights because they are inherently collective, positive, or programmatic rather than appropriately legal.[48] For example, the prominent human rights advocate Aryeh Neier argued:

> I think of rights as only having meaning if it is possible to enforce them. I don't think rights are an abstract concept—I think they are a contract between the citizen and the state or community, and the citizen has to be able to enforce his or her side of that contract. Enforcing that contract means that there must be some mechanism of enforcement, and judicial enforcement seems to be the mechanism that we have hit upon in order to enforce rights. Therefore, from my standpoint, if one is to talk meaningfully of rights, one has to discuss what can be enforced through the judicial process. . . . The concern I have about economic and social rights is when there are broad assertions which broadly speak of the right to shelter, education, social security, jobs, health care . . . then I think we get into territory that is unmanageable through the rights process or the judicial process. . . . So I think it's dangerous to the idea of civil and political rights to allow this idea of economic and social rights to flourish.[49]

Despite these arguments, which continue to serve as a restraint on NGO practice on subsistence rights, the movement toward expanding Western NGO work on subsistence rights is growing. The expansion of subsistence rights advocacy is welcome because these rights are fundamental to our survival and the exercise of all other rights. Indeed, this study explains that emerging NGO practice on subsistence rights is proving that the old distinction—between first and second generation, negative and positive, legal and programmatic, valid and invalid rights—is inaccurate in two respects. First, human rights organizations are winning important gains for subsistence rights in the legal realm, as these rights are increasingly subjected to monitoring by multilateral institutions, incorporated into national constitutions, and defended in courts throughout the world. This has demonstrated that economic and social rights can be valid legal rights when they are constructed and interpreted as such. Second, social justice and humanitarian NGOs have largely adopted a moral, extralegal approach to human rights, and are thereby demonstrating that human rights can be effective tools to develop norms, increase compliance, and guide internal practice even when they are not conceived as legal rights. Moral approaches to human rights, which were common in the early days of civil and political rights advocacy, have been partially restored to human rights politics; this is evident in the advance of economic and social rights. Instead of being an indicator of weakness or infancy, moral approaches to rights can serve as important tools to mobilize broad constituencies, change public discourse, reshape cultural assumptions about poverty, and accompany successful legal, social, economic, and political change. In that sense, emerging NGO work is redefining human rights politics in two ways, by validating economic and social rights within the human rights framework, and by reincorporating moral actors and moral approaches into the practical implementation of rights.

This work proceeds as follows. In Chapter 2, I develop a theoretical framework for understanding the emergence of subsistence rights and their political effectiveness. In brief, I argue that a social theory of rights persuasively explains how human rights stand at the intersection between international relations and international law. By merging constructivism and post-positivist legal theory, I develop a social theory that asserts that human rights are socially constructed ideas that must be strategically promoted (often by NGOs) in order to gain salience. Although legalization has been the predominant strategy pursued by human rights advocates in the past half-century, this choice of strategies is neither natural nor inevitable. Rights promotion depends on the nonlegal realm as much as legal institutions. Because both legal and nonlegal strategies occur in a broader social context, there is no way to avoid political pressure, rhetorical legitimation strategies, and cultural contestation in advancing either legal or moral rights.

I compare three different types of NGOs that have adopted subsistence rights—human rights, social justice, and humanitarian organizations—whose similarities and differences help me gain insight into the emergence of subsistence rights and its meaning for human rights politics. The next three chapters empirically examine the rise of subsistence rights within each of these three categories of actors. Chapter 3 discusses the role of human rights organizations, both the traditional civil and political rights NGOs who have expanded their mandates in the past decade and new organizations that have been specifically created to advocate for economic and social rights. I discuss the process by which organizations such as Amnesty International responded to pressures from the global South, their own members, and broader cultural shifts by expanding their mandates to include work on subsistence rights. I describe the predominant legal approach that human rights organizations have carried over from their work on civil and political rights, and outline some of the important accomplishments for subsistence rights that these groups have achieved. While legal approaches to subsistence rights have demonstrated the potential for their justiciability and legal enforcement, they are also limited in effectiveness, implying significant challenges for the human rights movement to overcome. These challenges are rooted in cultural assumptions and political interests aligned against subsistence rights, therefore successfully addressing these challenges requires activism within the moral, cultural, and political realms as well as the legal realm.

In Chapter 4, I describe how social justice organizations, primarily in the United States, have increasingly adopted human rights language in their struggles against extreme poverty. Although the overall trends facilitating the expansion of subsistence rights advocacy are similar, social justice groups tend to invoke human rights language more irregularly and infrequently than human rights organizations, and in a broadly moralistic way that is synonymous with equality, dignity, and justice. By de-linking human rights from legal texts and institutions, groups such as the Center for Economic Justice, the One Campaign, and the Jubilee Network have used a moral approach to mobilize public constituencies to change public policies. Framing poverty through human rights lenses helps these groups work to change public discourse and broad cultural understandings about poverty, moving away from a charity-based understanding and toward a justice-based approach. Moral approaches to subsistence rights allow social justice groups to circumvent some of the challenges inherent within a legal approach, by making the language accessible and empowering, and engaging debates with a broad set of institutions over their policy making rather than on their interpretation of legal texts. Moral approaches can also complement legal approaches by providing deeper cultural and political support for legal reforms and progressive legal decisions. Yet moral approaches also necessitate certain challenges that social justice movement members must overcome if they hope to advance subsistence rights effectively. Because moral understandings of rights are not grounded in specific legal texts and because a diverse range of social justice organizations hold widely divergent understandings of justice and equality, social justice movements must deal with this heterogeneity to develop a unified and unifying message.

In Chapter 5, I examine the process whereby Western humanitarian NGOs (i.e., international relief and development organizations) have increasingly adopted a rights-based approach to development. For many of these groups, human rights has become an umbrella term that encapsulates many of the recent trends within the international development industry, such as becoming more politically engaged, analyzing the root causes of poverty, working toward structural solutions, being accountable to stakeholders, and promoting local participation and empowerment. Although rights-based approaches vary among humanitarian NGOs, most of the major organizations such as Oxfam, CARE and ActionAid have adopted a moral approach to subsistence rights that translates international law into basic principles to guide internal practice. I argue that while there are some reasonable grounds for suspicion about the meaningfulness of new rights-based approaches, the adoption of subsistence rights is beginning to result in important changes within humanitarian organizations at the normative, analytical, and operational levels. Rights-based approaches require humanitarian organizations to reconceptualize development as involving political contestation rather than merely a technical/logistical process, and urge these NGOs to take sides on behalf of the most vulnerable people. Rights-based approaches to extreme poverty also require humanitarian organizations to fundamentally reexamine their relationships with "beneficiaries," asking for a radical transformation in decision-making power and participation in project implementation. Thus, humanitarian organizations are likewise demonstrating that moral approaches to subsistence rights can be effective in changing widespread behavior without any recourse to legal texts, institutions, and remedies. Yet, as in the other two cases, adopting a specific approach to subsistence rights imposes significant challenges for humanitarian NGOs to overcome, particularly with regard to clarifying the requirements of a rights-based approach and balancing political advocacy and service provision amid a scarcity of resources.

Chapter 6 concludes with a recapitulation of my main arguments and a discussion about the implications of emerging NGO work for human rights politics. I explain how NGOs have drawn on both principled ideas and strategic interests in adopting subsistence rights, how they have approached rights through legal and moral lenses, and how these lenses entail their own unique costs and benefits. I suggest that NGO efforts on subsistence rights have opened up space for reinstating moral approaches to all human rights, potentially including civil and political rights. Although legal approaches remain valuable, perhaps even central tools in the advancement of human rights, we should not underestimate the importance of moral tools in reorienting cultural assumptions, generating public constituencies, supporting legal change, and guiding the implementation of subsistence rights on the ground. In sum, I argue that a social theory of human rights allows us to redefine rights according to a broadened notion of what counts as strategic and effective human rights practice.

2

A Social Theory of Human Rights

In Chapter 1, I briefly described the historical process whereby subsistence rights (and indeed, nearly all economic, social, and cultural rights) were assigned a secondary status within the Western human rights movement during the Cold War. I discussed the ideology behind separating human rights into two categories—that economic and social rights were inherently positive, expensive, and nonjusticiable in contrast with civil and political rights—and I argued against the essentializing and naturalizing distinction between two sets of rights. The remainder of this book examines the reemergence of subsistence rights in the past decade, their manifestation in NGO practice, and their implications for human rights politics. This chapter provides a theoretical framework for understanding NGO advocacy of subsistence rights by advancing a social theory of human rights, a theory that challenges rationalist, positivist, and legalistic scholarship on rights.

Theorists of international relations and international law have had much to say about the emergence of human rights—and other formal and informal norms—and their meaning for international politics. Surprisingly, however, international relations has not engaged in much dialogue with international legal theory, and thus theories on the successes and failures of human rights are not particularly well integrated.[1] The disjuncture between international relations and international legal theory has been a result of the dominant paradigms operating in each discipline, which have largely marginalized study of the other. Realism and rational choice theories in international relations argue that actors (almost exclusively states) have a predetermined, static interest in increasing their power or maximizing utility. Norms, laws, and human rights tend to emerge only when they serve the interests of the strongest actors. Powerful states comply with norms only when the norm happens to be congruent with their interests, and weak states comply only when they anticipate coercion or have similar interests. In any decision-making situation, an actor will calculate the costs and benefits of the action in terms of maximizing his or her own interests.[2]

For realists and rationalists, international law—and all normative ideas—are epiphenomenal and merit attention only insofar as they reveal the distribution of interests and power.[3] The real motivation for decision making is not the legitimacy of a norm, but the way in which a norm masks or facilitates the expression of more fundamental interests and power relations. As Hans Morgenthau stated: "Governments . . . are always anxious to shake off the restraining influence which international law might have upon their international policies, to use international law instead for the promotion of their national interests, and to evade legal obligations which might be harmful to them. They have used the imprecision of international law as a ready-made tool for furthering their needs."[4]

While realism in international relations has tended to minimize the causal role of international law, the historical dominance of positivism in legal theory has equally marginalized the study of international relations and the political, social, cultural, and ideological contention contained therein. Legal positivists define the law in terms of formal texts, institutions, and proceedings that ostensibly separate legal interpretation and enforcement from other nonlegal processes.[5] Therefore legal positivists either downgrade international law as too soft (because only "hard" domestic law can be defined as law), or they view political, moral, and cultural contention as largely irrelevant to the national application of law.[6]

Within a political realist and legal positivist understanding, then, law only matters when states' interests converge in voluntarily adopting formal legal frameworks, establishing legal institutions, and enforcing the law through coercive measures. The historical Western bias toward civil and political rights, which are ostensibly "hard" law as opposed to economic and social rights, arises from this theoretical understanding of the role of law and the status of human rights as law.

Human rights stand at the intersection of international relations and international law, but I argue that a social theory of rights provides a different, and more illuminating, connection between the two disciplines. More recent scholarship in both international relations and international law has expanded our understanding of the emergence of human rights and their influence on widespread behavior. *Constructivist theory* in international relations asserts that ideas—expressed in the context of rhetorical, political, moral, and cultural contestation—help to shape an actor's identity, interests, and behavior. Constructivism grants a central role to both legal and nonlegal norms in influencing behavior, argues for the importance of nonstate actors such as NGOs in world politics, and describes some of the ways in which these actors strategically attempt to shape norms and institutions. Constructivist scholars have demonstrated that NGOs and activist networks promote new norms and identities,[7] pressure actors to modify their behavior,[8] and change states' understanding of their national interests.[9] Likewise, *post-positivist legal theory*[10] (e.g., critical legal studies, feminism, and the New Haven school) argues that the law does not, in fact, operate in a realm separate from politics, therefore rhetorical, political, moral, and cultural contestation is just as important in the interpretation and implementation of so-called "hard" law as it is with soft law and nonlegalized norms.

In contrast to realist, rationalist, and legal positivist understandings, this book is grounded in the marriage of constructivism and post-positivist legal theory. This theoretical framework—which I label a social theory of human rights—explains the importance of both legal and nonlegal norms by situating them in their social context, a context that shapes actors' identities, interests, and behavior.[11] A social theory of human rights explains the reemergence of subsistence rights in the West by referring to the ways in which contests over ideas and interests find expression in organizations' behavior. A social theory accounts for the potential effectiveness of subsistence rights in both formal institutions and informal environments, by arguing that both of these pathways attempt to lead to the same goal—a change in widespread behavior—within a broader social context. In this chapter, I seek to elaborate a social theory of human rights by describing how it speaks to the interplay of ideas and interests in motivating behavior, the strategic considerations involved in promoting normative ideas, and the legalization of human rights politics.

Do Principles or Interests Guide NGOs' Actions?

There is a well-known and long-standing debate between those who argue that human behavior primarily involves actors expressing their predetermined interests, and those who argue that behavior is the manifestation of ideas shaped through discourse. This rationalist-constructivist debate has significant implications for how we understand the emergence of NGO work on subsistence rights. Rationalists would claim that Western NGOs have increasingly adopted subsistence rights because they have a strategic interest in doing so, based on their essential natures. Likewise, rationalists would claim that states and other powerful actors would adopt subsistence rights only when they calculated a benefit in doing so, based on their inherent interests and in a manner congruent with those interests. Since most rationalists believe that states have a predetermined interest in maximizing their own material resources and autonomy, they would tend to be skeptical about powerful states making deep commitments to subsistence rights and introducing policies that may limit their sovereignty or reduce their wealth.

Constructivists believe that ideas themselves—about who an actor is, who can legitimately act, how to define a situation, and what actions are appropriate in certain situations—play an important role in guiding behavior. Yet constructivists themselves differ about the extent and depth at which principled ideas or interests shape behavior. There is a tension within constructivism between so-called postmodernists or thick constructivists, who suggest that the world is comprised of ideas "all the way down,"[12] and modernists or thin constructivists, who claim that there is some essential reality underlying ideas that generates a handful of predetermined human interests.[13] While this is ultimately an unsolvable ontological question, this book is grounded in thin constructivism because it assumes a limited set of basic human interests arising out of our material needs and our essential status as human beings. At the very least, these interests include the capability to survive physically and live in dignity.[14]

From this starting point, behavior is always the result of the mutual interplay of ideas and interests, or the result of the contestation of ideas built on an ontological foundation of interests.[15] As Alexander Wendt states, "The material force constituting interests is human nature. The rest is ideational."[16] This is slightly different than how many thin constructivists treat the interplay between ideas and interests, or principles and power. Most thin constructivists attempt an integration of ideational and interest-based explanations of norms by applying them within different contexts or at different stages of a process; in other words, they tend to bracket one factor at a time. For example, Keck and Sikkink explain that NGOs and transnational advocacy networks play a major role in promoting principled ideas and pressuring states to change their human rights policies, but that states tend to calculate their interests or respond to coercion in implementing changes.[17] Risse, Popp, and Sikkink's "spiral model" of norm socialization similarly posits that states adopt human rights initially for instrumental reasons, then are pressured to conform to their normative commitments or internalize those beliefs at later stages of the process.[18]

A social theory of human rights grounded in my ontological understandings cannot separate interests and ideas so neatly into stages or different contexts. Rather, there is an ongoing mutual interplay among ideas and interests, such that one constructs and constitutes the other. Interests are primarily generated from and expressed through ideas, and ideas are built upon a foundation of essential interests and promoted through strategic, often calculated, practice.

My constructivist framework therefore understands the growth of subsistence rights work among Western NGOs as resulting from the way in which these organizations (and new groups entering the field) have defined their interests, interpreted the human rights domain, and calculated the anticipated effectiveness of new practices in accomplishing their self-defined goals. Thus, as will be shown in subsequent chapters, when human rights NGOs such as Amnesty International expand their mandate to promote subsistence rights, they are responding to an idea based in an essential human need (physical survival), in a manner that strategically pursues their organizational interests (organizational survival, membership growth, effectiveness, geographical balance, and so on)—interests that are themselves constructed through the exchange of ideas. When social justice groups adopt human rights language to promote antipoverty policies, they are strategically appropriating an idea that they fundamentally believe in (the inherent dignity of people) to appeal to particular constituencies that further the groups' normatively driven mission. The explanation required by a social theory of human rights is not ideas versus interests, but a complicated story of how ideas and interests are inextricably intertwined.

Why Are Some Ideas More Successful Than Others?

Human rights are one kind of idea—a norm that expresses expectations about appropriate behavior. Given that a social theory of human rights affords an important role to ideas in guiding political and social change, it should attempt to explain why some norms, and the groups that promote them, are more successful than others. Ideas and interests are malleable, and they are subject to ongoing contestation among actors with unequal power.[19] Norms are influential but always arise within a competitive context. Constructivists and theorists of social movements have attempted to provide answers to the question of why some ideas, and therefore some human rights, have been more successful than others in terms of generating support and motivating compliant behavior.

Some theorists point to intrinsic characteristics of the norms themselves that they argue may explain their strength or weakness. One of these characteristics is the clarity or specificity of the norm. They argue that norms that are clear, specific, unambiguous, and parsimonious are more likely to survive challenges and be effective.[20] Norms that are formalized into clear rules and expectations are more likely to elicit compliant behavior than norms that allow a wide range of interpretations. Another characteristic of a norm that may lead to broader support and success is its claim to universal applicability.[21] According to these scholars, norms making universal claims about what is good for all people in all places (such as human rights) have a better chance of enduring and generating compliant behavior than a particularistic norm claiming to be applicable only to a narrow population. Norms that have an emotional appeal to a population are also more likely to gain legitimacy. Norms that involve bodily harm, innocent or vulnerable victims, and basic ideas of human dignity are likely to be shared widely across cultures and situations.[22] Thus, for example, activists were successful at persuading transnational corporations like Nestle to adopt a code of conduct in marketing infant formula in the Third World (despite the corporations' perceived better interests) because norm promoters used universalistic language to call attention to the bodily harm directly inflicted on vulnerable children.[23]

These explanations may be accurate, but these theorists fail to provide an account of *why* these characteristics are ostensibly so powerful, in what contexts they are powerful, or to argue persuasively that they are intrinsic to certain norms. A social theory of human rights explains these normative characteristics as powerful when they appeal to a particular dynamic cultural milieu as much as when they appeal to certain universal, predetermined human interests or rationality. Likewise, a social theory of human rights would suggest that these characteristics are not intrinsic to certain norms, but that norms are strategically constructed, framed, and interpreted with these characteristics (and sometimes others) for particular purposes.[24]

Contestation over the framing of norms with particular characteristics that attempt to appeal to particular populations is what much of politics is about. The battleground is largely rhetorical, and the prize for victory is legitimacy.[25] When an actor is able to frame an idea rhetorically in such a way that it resonates with existing social practices and cultural assumptions, then the idea is more likely to be perceived as legitimate, adopted, and complied with.[26] These cultural/political processes of legitimation may be more important in ensuring the strength and durability of a norm than whether the norm is embedded in legal institutions.[27] NGOs, operating in the realm of civil society, are important purveyors of this legitimation rhetoric as they compete against other actors in shaping ideas.

Researchers of social movements have examined these contests over issue framing in some detail.[28] They argue that since normative ideas emerge within a cultural context of existing norms, successful "efforts to promote a new norm take place within the standards of 'appropriateness' defined by prior norms."[29] This context consists of society-wide understandings that influence a movement's strategies by supporting or conflicting with the norm being promoted.[30] Thus, norm promotion that can appeal to existing cultural assumptions, yet simultaneously challenge and reform them, has a greater likelihood of effectiveness than norms perceived as entirely new or foreign. The success of frames depends more on how broader themes resonate culturally—how general ideas are "activated" for certain constituencies—than on the detailed substantive content of the norm.[31] Many of the themes mentioned above, such as universalism, bodily harm, clear rules, and vulnerable victims, are culturally resonant in a wide variety of contexts and easily applicable to human rights issues. An important framing strategy for the subsistence rights movement is therefore to "redefine as unjust and immoral what was previously seen as unfortunate but perhaps tolerable."[32] In the U.S. context, however, subsistence rights must also be promoted in a manner that is roughly consistent with and speaks to dominant cultural norms such as individual liberty, patriotism, and respect for private property. The fact that economic and social rights were framed in precisely the opposite way in the United States during the Cold War, as discussed in the previous chapter, suggests a reason why they may have been rejected during this period.

For the subsistence rights movement, this raises the question of whether a human rights approach is the most effective way to promote an end to extreme poverty, considering the plethora of available alternative frames that the movement could draw on. Advocates can, and often do, frame poverty issues in the language of charity, national security, religious obligation, or basic needs.[33] All of these discursive approaches to poverty have strategic implications different than those of a rights frame. Yet organizations appear eager to use the human rights discourse to advocate for an end to poverty. It is not that a human rights frame is incompatible with, or mutually exclusive from, other frames. In fact, organizations often employ a variety of frames simultaneously or at different times. But a focus on a particular strategic frame, such as human rights, tends to lead organizations toward particular action strategies with different implications than their alternatives.

The cultural, political, and material context[34] also helps to define who is a legitimate actor, the degree of public support an actor can rally, and the kinds of tactics that will be perceived as appropriate. Powerful, well-funded, and legitimate norm-promoters are more likely to be successful than illegitimate, hypocritical, underfunded, or weak ones.[35] In the field of human rights, NGOs such as Amnesty International and Human Rights Watch, and donors such as the Ford Foundation, have been described as "gatekeepers" who have the power to certify and support some human rights claims and not others, because they have gained legitimacy, respect, resources, and the capacity to spread information widely.[36] Efforts to promote subsistence rights are therefore more likely to be effective if they can garner the support of these main gatekeepers (or develop new ones to replace them). As Clifford Bob describes, this is not necessarily a simple process, because in the "Darwinian struggle for scarce resources," support often goes to the "savviest, not the neediest" norm promoters.[37] Normative contestation occurs in a marketplace consisting of actors with unequal power who are justifiably concerned about their organizational survival. Thus weaker groups must often frame their issues in a way that matches a gatekeeper's "goals, tactics, ethics, culture, and organizational needs" in order to gain an audience.[38]

Thus, a social theory of human rights argues for the power of ideas, but suggests that ideas must be promoted strategically within a competitive environment to gain the attention and support of powerful actors with similar ideas and methodologies. Although subsistence rights arguably deal with bodily harm suffered by vulnerable people on a global scale, they must still be promoted through savvy methodologies that take advantage of existing institutional and cultural resources in order to be effective. Historically, the primary expression of strategic human rights promotion has been through the framework of *legalization*; in other words, legal approaches have been viewed as the most effective and the only legitimate way to promote human rights.

The Legalization of Human Rights

Human rights experts, both critical and supportive of legalization, almost universally agree that the practice of human rights politics and scholarship in the past half-century has become increasingly legalized.[39] While most scholars define human rights as both legal and moral instruments, they describe a historical process whereby the moral, philosophical foundations of rights have evolved to become codified, interpreted, and implemented through legal frameworks.[40] Thus scholars have come to accept this supposed division of labor for human rights expression: morality providing the normative ideals and the law providing virtually all of the practical implementation of those ideals.[41] For most human rights practitioners, legalization is seen as the primary or even exclusive route through which rights will be made effective; thus even politically or morally grounded arguments tend to be made in legal terms.[42]

While definitions of legalization vary somewhat, most scholars understand the term to mean that positive law, both international and domestic, has become the primary means through which human rights are defined, expressed, and implemented. As a process, legalization involves imbuing norms with features characteristic of formal law: making rules legally obligatory, clarifying the content of rules precisely, and delegating the monitoring and implementation of rules to a neutral third party.[43] Rules that contain all of these features represent "hard" law, and rules that fail to display any one of these features are "soft" law or nonlegalized norms.[44]

The authors of a special issue of *International Organization* devoted to the concept of legalization concur that international institutions, including those governing human rights, are becoming increasingly legalized.[45] While these authors state that hard law is not necessarily or always preferable to soft law, they tend to see greater advantages in the legalization of norms and the mechanisms of accountability and enforcement that ensue.[46] For them, hard law helps to concretize normative consensus by sealing it in tangible legal documents, and to remove controversies from the realm of political contention by placing them in the courtroom.[47] The more that rules are defined precisely and delegated to a third party, the less an actor can engage in "deliberate self-interested interpretation" and unilateral implementation of rules.[48] This should help to ensure that rules are complied with and enforced. For those who support the legalization of human rights, then: "Law aspires to provide a process which is accessible, and simple in structure: one that does not depend on an ability to debate and 'prove' difficult or controversial moral standpoints—but rather on a different kind of authority and validity. The coercive component, characteristic of law, gives the prospect of real, practical solutions to problems. The structure of requirement (provision) and sanction makes law a predictable medium with which to work. Furthermore, as a locus of decision-making, difficult problems concerning conflict claims can be resolved in detail: case-by-case." [49]

These advantages of legalization are drawn from a particular theoretical understanding of the law: legal positivism. For legal positivists, the effectiveness of the law depends on the issuance of formally binding rules by a sovereign authority, reviewed within autonomous institutions, and backed by coercive sanctions. [50] Positivism asserts "the strict separation of the law in force, as derived from formal sources that are part of a unified system of law, from non-legal factors such as natural reason, moral principles and political ideologies. . . . Extra-legal arguments, e.g., arguments that have no textual, systemic or historical basis, are deemed irrelevant to legal analysis; there is only hard law, no soft law." [51] By focusing on formal law implemented by autonomous institutions that interpret, monitor and enforce the law, positivists attempt to separate and protect the law from the messy and often violent realm of political conflict. The best way of advancing human rights amid cultural, political, and moral diversity is by "sticking close to concrete rules" and ensuring that their interpretation is carried out by legal experts independent of the political process. [52]

Positivists argue that legal discourse and rationality are distinct from, and preferable to, political or moral discourse. Legal institutions have a set of accepted procedures for determining violations and prescribing remedies typically designed to ensure that all parties to a conflict engage in a fair process. [53] For positivists, "establishing a commitment as a legal rule invokes a particular form of discourse. Although actors may disagree about the interpretation or applicability of a set of rules, discussion of issues purely in terms of interests or power is no longer legitimate. Legalization of rules implies a discourse primarily in terms of the text, purpose, and history of the rules, their interpretation, admissible exceptions, applicability to classes of situations, and particular facts. The rhetoric of law is highly developed, and the community of legal experts—whose members normally participate in legal rule-making and dispute settlement—is highly socialized to apply it." [54]

Thus, for legal positivists, international human rights law is not really law unless it is written into national legislation, interpreted by judges, and enforced by a sovereign authority. This is one of the main qualities that civil and political rights have gained throughout the world, which economic and social rights still mostly lack. In the second half of the twentieth century, civil and political rights were increasingly enforced through national legislation as larger sections of the world embraced democratic institutions. At the same time, in the West civil and political rights also came to represent all human rights, supported by a human rights movement increasingly led by legal experts. Civil and political rights have successfully appealed to and even defined the dominant political culture in the West, which is individualistic, legalistic, and comfortable using the language of rights.[55] Meanwhile, economic and social rights became defined as inherently nonlegal aspirations.

As a result of the legalization of human rights in the past half-century and the lower legal status of economic and social rights, advocates for subsistence rights have two strategic options for gaining legitimacy for them. First, as mentioned in the previous chapter, they can argue that subsistence rights are valid legal rights, because there is nothing inherent about these claims that prevents their legalization. Legalizing subsistence rights would involve building a higher level of obligation into these norms (e.g., by getting more states to ratify relevant international covenants or holding states accountable to their legal commitments); making rules more precise (e.g., by litigating cases in courts or supporting UN General Comments that elaborate norms); and delegating enforcement authority to third parties (e.g., by creating an individual complaints procedure at the UN or encouraging more domestic courts to review violations). Western human rights organizations have primarily followed this first path, and as will be described below, they have successfully demonstrated the potential effectiveness of legalizing subsistence rights.

The second strategic option is to question the very idea that legalization is the only way to make human rights practically effective. Everyone agrees that legalization provides tremendously important tools for the realization of human rights, and if it is viewed as one part of an overall human rights strategy, legalization has valuable advantages.[56] Yet legalization is not the only or even the most natural way of understanding and engaging in human rights politics, and the emphasis on legal approaches in human rights may prevent alternative approaches from becoming effective.[57] Social justice and humanitarian organizations are taking this second path, by adopting moral approaches to subsistence rights that do not seek legalization as their end. They are demonstrating that subsistence rights, as moral claims that are expressed through simple principles, can be effective in mobilizing public constituencies, changing the terms of public discourse, or guiding the implementation of antipoverty work in the field.

This second path finds support in *post-positivist legal theory*, a set of perspectives on law that questions legal positivism's assumptions about the determinacy of legal texts, the independence of the legal realm, and the importance of coercive enforcement in ensuring compliance with human rights norms. Post-positivist theorists range from the policy- and process-oriented legal scholars in the New Haven school to the more radical approaches to the law contained in critical legal studies, feminism, and linguistic theory.

New Haven scholars approach the law not as a corpus of positive rules, but as a process through which a particular community pursues its common interests.[58] The law is a "stream of authoritative decisions" within a community, but the authority to influence decisions is variable, dependent on the context.[59] Legal discussions arise as much in the process of policy making as in the courts.[60] Although they acknowledge the uniqueness of the legal process, New Haven lawyers argue that the process is much more infiltrated by politics and other extralegal factors than positivists admit. Thus, rather than relying on a unique form of rationality to objectively interpret a formal text, these legal practitioners attempt to "expand the scope of legal inquiry" by addressing all of the political, cultural, moral, and other factors that will determine whether a legal process promotes certain overarching values.[61]

All legal theorists claim that the law and politics are connected. Positivists acknowledge that political actors create laws and institutions, appoint judges, and execute legal mandates.[62] Yet a post-positivist critique notes that this represents only one possible connection between law and politics: between formalized law and formal political institutions. They point us to the discursive aspects of processes that merge the law with policy making, the informal contexts in which the law is executed, and how this informality affects how we define the "law." [63]

New Haven scholars see the law and politics as deeply intertwined, and they encourage us to pay attention to social movements, cultural trends, and other factors that determine whether a norm is legalized, and even when it is not legalized, whether it is complied with. For these scholars, the law is only the tip of a "social iceberg," and the effectiveness of the law depends upon a complex set of social relations as much as the formal provisions of the law itself.[64] For example, Ellen Lutz and Kathryn Sikkink examine three norms that have achieved varying levels of legalization in Latin America: prohibitions against torture, against disappearances, and support for democracy. They find that the least legalized norm (democracy) has been the most effective.[65] They attribute this to broader cultural changes and states' political commitments to democracy, and to the informal, extralegal pressures put on states when they deviated from the democracy norm. The lesson here for subsistence rights promoters is that although legalization can provide important tools for human rights, there are informal mechanisms available for making these rights effective, absent a high degree of legalization.

Critical legal scholars and other linguistic analysts take the New Haven critique of positivism a step further, by problematizing the privileged status of the law itself. Beyond saying that the law is affected by politics, theorists such as David Kennedy and Marti Koskenniemi argue that the law *is* politics under the guise of something unique.[66] For them, the law is literally insepara-ble from politics, public discourse, and social practices.[67] Legal processes are nothing more than "argumentation, 'language-games,' rhetoric—a linguistic practice oriented toward social reality."[68] Positive legal texts do not determine their own interpretation, or even adequately limit the range of possible in-terpretations; therefore the personal biases of a judge, the political pressures surrounding the courtroom, or the deeper cultural assumptions underlying the legal process influence the implementation of the law as much as the text itself. All of these extralegal processes *are* the law insofar as they attempt to inscribe explicit or implicit rules to constrain social behavior.

Many critical legal scholars are suspicious of the supposed objectiv-ity inherent in legalization and the ways in which it imposes costs on some populations or excludes alternative social practices.[69] They argue that legal institutions, posing as neutral and objective monitors of society, often serve to reinforce the marginalized status of the poor, racial minorities, women, and other social groups who do not have privileged access to legal institu-tions or discursive power within them. Feminist legal theorists such as Hilary Charlesworth note that legal experts are overwhelmingly male and legal ra-tionality is largely masculine; thus a practice defined as objective is actually gendered and deeply political.[70] Again, the lesson in this for human rights practice is not only that political contention affects how hard law is produced and implemented, but that given the significant social costs of legalization and the impossibility of separating law from politics, it might be more effec-tive to promote subsistence rights outside of formal legal institutions alto-gether. Post-positivist legal theory points to the importance of human rights as moral tools, and to the importance of cultural and political discourse in strengthening legal instruments. Even if subsistence rights are promoted through legal processes, there is never any reason to believe that they can be protected from the muddle of political and social contention. Social move-ments engaging in political struggles help to determine which legislatures are put into place, which laws are enacted, and even how those laws will be later interpreted by the courts.

Radical critics of legal positivism are themselves often criticized for not providing concrete alternatives to existing forms of legal practice—for example, the editors of a recent book critical of the legalization of human rights acknowledge that they make no attempt to discuss and defend alternative ways to promote human rights.[71] While scholars have long noted that human rights are both legal and moral tools, research that empirically investigates the use of human rights as moral tools and outlines the tangible implications of alternative rights strategies remains sparse. This is precisely what this book intends to accomplish—to highlight the concrete ways in which NGOs are effectively walking both traditional and alternative strategic pathways, the legal and the moral, to advance subsistence rights.

In sum, the contours of a social theory of human rights are made possible by the marriage of constructivism and post-positivist legal theory. A social theory of human rights argues that norms and ideas play an important role in guiding behavior, and that NGOs play an important role in shaping and spreading those ideas. A social theory argues that NGOs must frame ideas strategically in the context of ongoing political contestation if they hope to be effective. It claims that there are both costs and benefits to the legalization of human rights, but that legalization is neither natural nor inevitable. It suggests that rhetorical, political, moral, and cultural contestation is central in the interpretation and implementation of subsistence rights, whether or not legalization is the ultimate end of NGOs' efforts.

3

Human Rights Organizations

The purpose of this chapter is to trace efforts in recent years by Western human rights organizations[1] to redeem economic and social rights, particularly subsistence rights, from their decades-long status as the "poor stepsister" to civil and political rights.[2] I will discuss the increasing adoption of subsistence rights by the human rights movement, ongoing resistance to subsistence rights, the way in which human rights organizations interpret subsistence rights and translate them into practice, and the strategic implications of this trend on the politics of human rights and its application to extreme global poverty.

This chapter focuses on groups that identify themselves specifically as human rights organizations—such as Amnesty International, Human Rights Watch, Human Rights First, and the World Organization Against Torture—that for decades worked exclusively on civil and political rights, but whose mandate has been in the process of expansion to include a limited range of economic, social, and cultural rights, including the right to subsistence. As Leonard Rubenstein notes: "International human rights organizations that have been so prominent in promoting adherence to civil and political rights and to the laws of war have taken tentative first steps to support [grassroots] organizations and movements and to take independent steps to realize economic and social rights."[3] To cite just a few examples, the International Commission of Jurists was one of the first human rights organizations to devote significant attention to economic and social rights, convening a meeting of international experts as early as 1986 that led to the Limburg Principles, which seek to clarify and elaborate international law on economic and social rights. The World Organization Against Torture has retained its focus on preventing torture, but in recent years has established a program on economic and social rights that seeks to link extreme poverty to an increased vulnerability to cruel and degrading treatment. The International Federation for Human Rights, a network of over 140 French organizations, expanded its mandate in 2001 to include a focus on making international law applicable to global trade and the activities of transnational corporations.[4]

New human rights organizations have also been founded within the past two decades whose mission is directed primarily toward subsistence rights. These include issue-specific organizations, such as the Food First Information and Action Network and the Centre on Housing Rights and Evictions, which advocate specifically for rights related to basic subsistence. It also includes new organizations created to promote economic and social rights more broadly, such as the Center for Economic and Social Rights, the National Economic and Social Rights Initiative, the International Centre on Economic, Social and Cultural Rights, and many more.[5] These groups were established to fill some of the gaps left by the major human rights organizations that have historically moved very slowly toward economic and social rights. They focus on strengthening domestic legislation and building the capacity of local organizations to monitor and enforce economic and social rights.[6]

The increasing adoption of subsistence rights by human rights organizations is evident in their growing participation in international arenas in which subsistence rights are discussed. For example, in 2003, hundreds of human rights organizations and other groups came together to launch the International Network for Economic, Social and Cultural Rights (ESCR-Net). This network is the first of its kind, devoted exclusively to advancing economic and social rights in all regions of the world. Human rights organizations have also increased their involvement in UN mechanisms such as the Committee on Economic, Social and Cultural Rights since the early 1980s, conducting research, presenting alternative country reports, and collaborating on monitoring functions.[7]

Amnesty International's recent history[8] is instructive in understanding the shift toward subsistence rights, both because of its prominence within the human rights community and its historically narrow mandate in working on torture and political prisoners. Amnesty has been described as one of the main human rights gatekeepers that maintain the resources, personnel, reputation, and political access to define and certify the international human rights agenda.[9] Amnesty's work "is often equated with the worldwide human rights struggle," [10] and its shift toward subsistence rights is somewhat indicative of the process in other organizations.

As Curt Goering notes, Amnesty's history has been marked by a process of "gradual incrementalism, that is, a cautious expansion of the boundaries of AI's work." [11] Around the early 1980s, several debates began within Amnesty about expanding its mandate beyond the focus on a limited range of civil and political rights. These discussions included whether Amnesty would denounce violations committed by nonstate actors, or against persons because of their sexual orientation, or whether Amnesty would adopt a position on the use of force to protect human rights.[12] Thousands of members within Amnesty were also debating whether the organization should move into the promotion of economic and social rights. Dissatisfied with Amnesty's progress in this regard, several Amnesty activists broke off and eventually formed Food First, an organization devoted specifically to the right to food. However, by the 1990s Amnesty's mandate allowed it to refer to economic and social rights in its educational and promotional materials, thus Amnesty began to include economic and social rights more in its work.[13] Researchers who realized that these rights were intimately tied to violations of civil and political rights often "snuck in" economic and social rights into their background reports. Thematic reports on indigenous people (1992), women (1995), and children (1998) made increasing reference to economic and social rights as part of the context of Amnesty's main concerns over civil and political rights violations. However, as recently as Amnesty's 1997 International Council Meeting (ICM), a formal policy of expanding into violations of specific economic and social rights was rejected.

By the early twenty-first century, however, there was a growing conviction within Amnesty's membership that the organization should get more involved with economic and social rights. Amnesty officially expanded its mandate at its 2001 International Council Meeting in Dakar, Senegal, allowing its chapters to mobilize against "grave abuses" of economic and social rights. Amnesty chapters, particularly from the global South, demanded that the organization adopt a "full spectrum" approach involving equal attention to both civil and political and economic, social, and cultural rights. Others cautioned against such a leap beyond Amnesty's traditional core concerns. Ultimately the ICM adopted a "messy compromise" extending the organization's traditional emphasis on nondiscrimination from the political to the economic sphere.[14] Since the ICM in 2001, however, Amnesty has developed a long-term strategy on economic and social rights, engaged in research and reporting on specific violations, created advisory bodies within the organization, and produced promotional materials on economic and social rights.[15] It officially adopted a mission statement in 2007 that reflected the "full spectrum" approach to human rights.[16] Amnesty describes their expanded work in these terms: "We are integrating the new emphases on economic[,] social and cultural rights into our work gradually and carefully. We prioritize according to the severity and pervasiveness of the human rights abuse concerned, the potential for Amnesty International to make an impact and the relationship this has with our previous work."[17]

Amnesty also retains a strong promotional aspect to its work, and it recently expanded its work on subsistence rights by launching a global campaign specifically related to this theme in 2009.[18] The Global Campaign for Human Dignity comprises a four- to six-year commitment to specific poverty-focused goals, similar to the global campaign to stop violence against women that Amnesty launched in 2004. This represents a deeper, long-term, and more integrated approach to freedom from poverty, and Amnesty chapters are in the midst of shaping the specific contours of this campaign. The Global Campaign for Human Dignity contains three main demands: (1) accountability, or making economic and social rights legally enforceable; (2) access, or ensuring that the most vulnerable can attain basic services; and (3) agency, or respecting the right of the poor to control their own livelihoods. The Campaign focuses on two strategic areas of subsistence rights work—health and housing—by initiating advocacy projects in key countries, which will enable Amnesty to "campaign for individual remedies for those abuses while building momentum for broader policy and legal changes at the national and international level."[19]

As one of the few human rights NGOs with strong grassroots support, Amnesty has the flexibility to adapt its methodologies in accordance with new campaigns. This adaptation is beginning to occur as Amnesty is moving into economic and social rights.[20]

Other traditional human rights organizations have not moved as far down the path toward economic and social rights as Amnesty has. For Human Rights Watch, this is partly due to its leaders' conception of human rights, and partly due to the methodologies it has developed over time. For example, Kenneth Roth, the director of Human Rights Watch, and Aryeh Neier, the former executive director, have expressed in public forums their hesitancy about economic and social rights.[21] They argue that, unlike Amnesty, Human Rights Watch does not have a strong base of grassroots activists and therefore relies more heavily on media campaigns and lobbying actions that involve shaming a specific perpetrator for a clear legal violation. They are wary of what Roth calls the "sloganeering" of economic and social rights, or broad moral assertions of rights, which they believe would limit the effectiveness of rights strategies.[22] As a result, Human Rights Watch's work on economic and social rights was initially limited to situations in which it reinforced or flowed from its already existing work on civil and political rights.[23] After a process of internal debate, Human Rights Watch in 2003 expanded this policy to include all economic and social rights, but its work on these rights remains methodologically restricted to situations in which a clear legal violation, identifiable violator, and achievable remedy exist—most commonly in the case of arbitrary or discriminatory governmental conduct in the context of a civil and political rights violation.[24]

The entry of the main human rights gatekeepers such as Amnesty and Human Rights Watch into subsistence rights has been perceived by subsistence rights activists as a mixed blessing.[25] On the one hand, these organizations provide the resources and the sense of legitimacy to certify subsistence rights as valid and worthy of promotion. They are the organizations that have been empowered to essentially define what constitutes a human rights violation; thus, only with their participation is the expansion of economic and social rights widely recognized.[26] On the other hand, as traditional organizations expand their mandates, it will inevitably spread their resources more thinly. And because they are the most powerful players, they consume a large proportion of the overall funding for human rights work, and they shape how these rights are understood and the dominant methodologies used to pursue them. Some advocates have noted that the large organizations therefore have the potential to drown out the capacity-building work and intensive research often done by smaller, local human rights organizations.[27] Therefore many are ambivalent about the participation of the larger human rights organizations, even as they welcome the advance of subsistence rights advocacy overall.

Why Have Human Rights Organizations Adopted Subsistence Rights?

It is well known that when the Universal Declaration of Human Rights was adopted in 1948 there was no distinction made between categories of rights. The subsequent history of government opposition to economic and social rights in the West during the Cold War, particularly in the United States, is well-traveled terrain. The question, however, remains: Why was there such silence on economic and social rights even within civil society, specifically among human rights organizations, in the decades that followed the Universal Declaration? Why have they only begun to incorporate them into their work in the past decade or so?

In part, the absence of economic and social rights advocacy in the West during the Cold War is due to the fact that the human rights gatekeepers— leading human rights organizations and their institutional donors—adopted methodologies that were consistent with the notion that civil and political rights were the core human rights, and that human rights were best defended by legal experts.[28] Phillip Alston, former Chairman of the UN Committee on Economic, Social and Cultural Rights, lamented during the early 1990s, for example: "Human Rights Watch has had an ideological or philosophical objection to economic and social rights, and does not participate in any way [in the Committee]. Hundreds of NGOs send representatives to the U.N. Commission on Human Rights to protest violations of civil and political rights. At our sessions, you'll find just one representative, a fellow from the Habitat International Coalition, sitting rather quietly. Lawyerly NGOs, accustomed to traditional legal argument, cannot accommodate economic and social rights within their comfortable framework."[29] These groups therefore reinforced the distinction between two generations of rights by narrowing their mandate to civil and political rights. Aryeh Neier continues to the present day to oppose economic and social rights as valid rights because he believes that they are not the proper objects of judicial review.[30] He is joined by human rights scholars and practitioners such as Michael Ignatieff, who argues that human rights must be confined to a minimal, defensible core of individual, justiciable, negative rights, which he associates with civil and political rights.[31] Despite this philosophical opposition to them, a portion of the membership of all of these NGOs have always been supportive of subsistence rights as valid legal rights.

Yet the barriers to involvement in these rights were not only ideological, but also institutional and material. There was no funding for economic and social rights work from Western governments due to their philosophical opposition, and NGOs refused to take money from Eastern states because they could be tagged as communists and their work perceived as a "sham."[32] Because there was minimal interest in, and no funding for, this kind of advocacy during the Cold War, the major human rights organizations survived and thrived precisely by defining their mandates so narrowly.[33] Amnesty, for example, grew from a small office in London in 1962 to one of the most far-reaching and influential NGOs on the planet.[34] Although all of these organizations were dedicated to the universal principles of the Universal Declaration of Human Rights, they justifiably recognized the need to be strategic about their institutional survival. As such, one of their biggest concerns about adopting subsistence rights has been "overstretching" in terms of organizational resources, staff expertise, and membership loyalty, which would ultimately reduce their effectiveness.[35] Amnesty has been concerned that if they venture too far into subsistence rights, it would create dissent among members who believe they are too controversial, confusing, or outside of Amnesty's original mandate. There was also a fear that promoting them would dilute Amnesty's well-guarded public image as an impartial protector of political prisoners.[36] One of the most fundamental concerns, therefore, has been that the major human rights organizations do not have the *internal capacity* to advocate for subsistence rights effectively.

According to academics and activists within the human rights movement, there are several reasons why Western NGOs have recently begun to expand their work into subsistence rights despite these barriers. Most prominently, the end of the Cold War in the early 1990s provided an historic opportunity to bridge the ideological divide over human rights that had stifled their expression in the West for half a century. Because economic and social rights were associated with the socialist policies and rhetoric of the Soviet bloc during the Cold War, there was little political and cultural space for human rights organizations in the United States and Europe to advocate for those rights.[37] In at least one sense, then, the end of the Cold War de-linked the struggle for human rights from the geopolitical conflict between East and West. This provided an opening for economic and social rights to be promoted without being associated with the policies of an actual enemy. Despite the U.S. government's ongoing opposition to economic and social rights, human rights and humanitarian organizations were able to reframe these rights as being consistent with a liberal state, rather than requiring a form of totalitarian socialism in their implementation. The end of the Cold War also allowed funding organizations to provide support for economic and social rights without being labeled as communists.[38]

Not coincidentally, at the same time that socialist regimes were being dismantled, states throughout the world began to liberalize their trade and investment policies, privatize public services, and "divest themselves of the

responsibility to provide social services and ensure adequate living and working standards" for their populations.[39] Poverty and economic inequality also
increased in many places in the 1990s, which resulted in increasingly urgent
calls coming from the global South for human rights organizations to take
subsistence rights more seriously. Thus the end of the Cold War and continu-
ing global poverty were the structural conditions that facilitated, but certainly
did not determine, the increasing adoption of subsistence rights.[40] In the early
1990s, the end of the Cold War and the expansion of economic globalization
were seen as potentially threatening to the rise of subsistence rights because
they reinforced the neoliberal ideology of official U.S. policy.[41] Their expansion occurred when the human rights community acted as if these new developments were opportunities to engage in economic and social rights work
rather than barriers to entry.

A deeper explanation of the rise of subsistence rights requires attention to
the dynamics within human rights organizations and to agents within those
organizations. Antipoverty activists in the North and South, "freed from the
ideological and material constraints of the Cold War," [42] began to advocate for
them despite the hesitations of the human rights community.[43] Groups within
the South, especially in Latin America and Eastern Europe, who had pressured their own governments for years on civil and political rights, heard this
call early on and incorporated subsistence rights into their daily work.[44] The
end of the Cold War and the resulting democratization in former Soviet-bloc
and authoritarian countries also allowed many new human rights organizations to form in the South.[45] Many of these local and national groups, such as
the Centro de Estudios Legales y Sociales in Argentina, the Programa Venezolana de Educacion y Proteccion de Derechos Humanos in Venezuela, and
the Asociacion Pro Derechos Humanos in Peru, were very active on these
rights and collaborated with the emerging organizations in the United States
and Europe that were devoted exclusively to them.[46] Increasingly these organizations published reports on economic and social rights violations and the
right to subsistence, often related to access to land.[47] It is not surprising that
these national organizations in the global South have historically been more
concerned with subsistence rights than groups in developed countries, given
that they were often located within areas of extreme poverty and had personal
connections with people suffering from economic deprivation.[48] For many
years, however, these smaller groups were not able to influence the largest
human rights organizations in the West that had historically focused on civil
and political rights, for the reasons mentioned above.

Eventually the leading human rights organizations began to hear the call to expand their work.[49] Organizations like Amnesty and Human Rights Watch, which originally feared that economic and social rights advocacy would "dilute their core mission," realized that their relevance and legitimacy as global human rights organizations increasingly depended on expanding that mission to include a focus on extreme poverty.[50] Senior staff members came to believe that adopting economic and social rights was the best way to respond to a number of trends occurring both within and outside the organization—such as the ongoing salience of global poverty, young people's involvement in human rights activism, and the critiques of the Western human rights regime in the global South.[51] Numerous discussions took place within Amnesty over whether to adopt economic and social rights, and a fragile consensus emerged that, despite the methodological difficulties, these rights were too important to ignore. Within Amnesty, this process was led by Secretary General Pierre Sané, who initiated a process in 1993 to reevaluate Amnesty's role in the world and adapt to current trends.[52] In addition, Western human rights organizations had been seeking to expand their membership (and thus their base of funding and activism) among youth and among new regions of the world such as Asia and Africa. Amnesty, for example, was concerned about its reputation as a "white middle-class organization" and sought to be "relevant in developing countries."[53] When the so-called antiglobalization movement ignited in the late 1990s, and young people marched in Seattle, Bangkok, Genoa, and elsewhere carrying signs demanding economic and social rights, the message was reinforced that the global legitimacy of human rights organizations depended in part on finally getting involved in issues of poverty.[54]

The increasing interest among the leading human rights organizations was bolstered by a growing willingness among institutional donors to fund economic and social rights.[55] These donors, such as the Ford Foundation and the Mertz Gilmore Foundation, were themselves influenced by the growth of these rights strategies in the global South. Donors witnessed a "dramatic increase in requests for funding" in the late 1990s from organizations focusing on economic and social rights, most of whom were local and national groups based in the global South.[56] Ideological and logistical barriers that had hindered Western organizations from promoting them at the international level were less relevant to human rights organizations in the South. As one donor describes, when she had conversations with members of human rights organizations in the Philippines and Venezuela about their economic and social rights work, "I was blown away because the issues that had stuck conversation at the international level were almost—not completely, but almost—beside the point at the national level. It was as if having people come to you as a human rights organization on the ground with issues of food, housing, whatever . . . then you just figure out ways to do this. It was like, they couldn't say, 'No, the standards are too vague,' or 'No, there's this issue of justiciability.' You just have to do it. So they were sort of breaking through some of [these barriers]." [57]

Given the impetus from Southern groups, activists in human rights NGOs and grant-making foundations began to push the economic and social rights agenda forward within their own organizations. These norm entrepreneurs seized the opportunity to translate their long-held personal beliefs in subsistence rights into organizational policy. Contact between Southern groups, norm entrepreneurs in Western NGOs, and other decision makers within gatekeeping organizations was facilitated by their participation in a number of UN development-related conferences in the 1990s, including in Rio de Janeiro, Vienna, Cairo, Copenhagen, Istanbul, Rome, Beijing, and elsewhere. Institutional learning and socialization about subsistence rights also occurred through intraorganizational meetings (such as Amnesty's annual ICMs) and through private donor-supported NGO conferences organized specifically to study economic and social rights. For example, the Ford Foundation sponsored a series of conferences in Mexico beginning in 2002 to develop the use of budget analysis in the implementation of economic and social rights, which led to the formation of the International Budget Partnership.[58] This general diffusion pattern of economic and social rights from South to North is somewhat surprising, given our expectations about how the power of ideas is related to the strength and resources of the actors promoting them.

In sum, both principled ideas and strategic interests have interacted in the decision-making process within human rights organizations to push them to adopt subsistence rights. The largest source of philosophical opposition to economic and social rights has revolved around the argument that they are not "really" human rights because they are not valid legal instruments, or that they are not effectively adaptable to human rights methodologies. However, scholars and practitioners have increasingly adopted a position that subsistence rights are valid legal tools, that all human rights impose both positive and negative duties on states and other actors, and that subsistence rights obligations are not overly burdensome.[59] Therefore, there is clearly an ideational basis for these organizations to adopt subsistence rights, yet the timing of the trend cannot adequately be explained without reference to these organizations' strategic interests and concerns. Human rights organizations began to expand their mandate when it became clear that their legitimacy and credibility were at stake; yet their engagement with subsistence rights remains limited by concerns over organizational capacity, overstretching resources, and the effectiveness of the new advocacy.

The Legal Approach to Subsistence Rights

The concept of human rights as a social construction requires interpretation in order to translate into strategic practice and be realized on the ground. Therefore, this book investigates both the rise of subsistence rights and the political implications of interpreting rights in a certain way. How, then, do human rights organizations understand and interpret rights in the context of promoting freedom from poverty?

Human rights organizations have largely carried over their methodologies from decades of working on civil and political rights into subsistence rights work, which has resulted in a *legal* approach to rights. A legal approach closely associates human rights with legal processes, institutions, and texts. Although human rights practitioners understand that human rights express moral principles and ideals, they believe that the practical implementation of those principles should be grounded in international law; therefore they privilege efforts to strengthen international law, incorporate it into domestic legislation, and use legal standards to hold the state accountable to its actions. Morality is typically viewed as the philosophical basis for human rights that provided a historical precursor to the actual implementation of legal rights.[60] In practice, human rights are conceived primarily as legal instruments.

For human rights organizations, subsistence rights thus are understood as legal claims that cannot be "reduced to developmental or social principles."[61] Under this approach, effective rights are those that are "specified under a valid legal rule and enforced by legal sanctions."[62] Human rights are entitlements whose strongest source of power is the authority of the law and "enforcement backed by a punitive legal structure."[63] Activists with a legal interpretation of human rights do not deny the validity of moral appeals, but they typically argue that human rights, in referring to concrete legal obligations, involve "*more* than just a moral declaration."[64] Therefore the law exists to fill gaps in protection left behind by moral appeals, political processes, and social movements; and in some sense the law stands above and apart from morality and politics. As Amnesty USA's former director William Schulz argued, "When morality is not enough—well, then, there is always the law."[65] Establishing a legal right makes it less "vulnerable to political whim" and the vagaries of policy making,[66] and ensures that solutions to injustice are legal and rule based.[67] While political and moral tools of accountability may be important, legal accountability remains "an essential aspect of the defense of economic and social rights."[68] Therefore, the central focus of a human rights strategy is the "use of international human rights standards and law as a point of departure."[69] According to the UN High Commissioner on Human Rights, the "express linkage to rights . . . as legally enforceable entitlements is an essential ingredient of human rights approaches."[70] Subsistence rights therefore are by definition spelled out in the Universal Declaration of Human Rights; the International Covenant on Economic, Social and Cultural Rights; and other legal texts.

Under a legal approach, human rights advocacy is not limited to drafting laws and litigating them in courts. Subsistence rights can be promoted through public education, budget work, media campaigns, grassroots movement building, and many other methods. However, all of these methods point back to rights explicitly enumerated within specific legal documents and institutions. By grounding all of these efforts in an understanding of rights as legal instruments, employing a legal approach to subsistence rights tends to lead to unique rhetoric and strategies.[71] Legalization implies a different kind of discourse from political or ethical reasoning, in that it focuses on a particular text, the history of its drafting, various interpretations, exceptions, and relevant facts.[72] As Tony Evans states, "The legal discourse focuses upon the internal logic of the law, its elegance, coherence, extent, and meaning, which the application of legal reason is said to reveal."[73] Debate about the validity of subsistence rights tends to center around whether international texts are clear enough and whether the rights are legally enforceable. This takes human rights organizations onto a particular kind of terrain that influences the strategies they pursue and the solutions they recommend.[74]

The legal approach to subsistence rights tends to lead human rights organizations into two kinds of strategies. The first set of strategies is to pursue "some sort of judicial or quasi-judicial process" in implementing rights; the tactics most often used within this strategy are lobbying for international treaties, working for the incorporation of international law into domestic legislation, and litigating individual cases in courts or other review bodies.[75]

Because human rights organizations define subsistence rights primarily as legal rights, and because they have historically developed particular competencies in the law, then judicial bodies often properly become the target of their work. Within this approach, subsistence rights must be made *justiciable*, meaning that individuals can demand them in courts or similar arenas and receive an appropriate remedy.[76] In that sense, ensuring that everyone can attain an adequate standard of living is a necessary but not sufficient condition for subsistence rights fulfillment. To be called a right, this guarantee must also be reviewable in a judicial proceeding that can grant an effective remedy for a violation.

A second set of strategies that human rights organizations follow is to use international law to hold states and other actors accountable for their actions, typically through public education and the "naming and shaming" of specific violations of international or domestic law.[77] For example, Amnesty mobilizes its grassroots constituency to write letters to public officials and shame them into compliance. Although this methodology is not court based, it still assumes a legal understanding of rights because the target of shaming actions must be a violation of international law with a clear perpetrator and a legal remedy. Amnesty's researchers in its London headquarters have the responsibility of deciding who qualifies as a prisoner of conscience or a victim of a violation, based largely on their interpretation of international law.[78] Identifying human rights violations is central to this work, and "violations language should only be utilized when a legal basis and a corresponding legal obligation exist."[79] When human rights organizations conduct educational work, it typically involves trying to foster a greater understanding of the international legal standards among local communities or grassroots activists.

Not all human rights organizations adopt a legal understanding, but the legal approach to rights has been hegemonic within the international human rights movement and the Western discourse surrounding rights.[80] States, international organizations, interest groups, NGOs, and intellectuals act as if the global human rights regime were primarily a legal construct.[81] Thus, for example, human rights practitioners tend to be legal professionals, and human rights scholarship occurs predominantly in law schools.[82] According to a former staff member at Amnesty, "the crucial thing is legal accountability and the legal framework. That's absolutely essential, and that's why human rights organizations are full of lawyers. It's natural."[83] Because of the dominance of legal approaches in human rights, nonlegal approaches are often relegated to the so-called "footnote phenomenon: the idea that so long as the putative non-legal foundations for rights are cursorily stated, one can quickly move on to the important discussions of specification and implementation, which are primarily legal."[84]

How Has a Legal Approach Translated into Tangible Progress?

The adoption of subsistence rights has required some institutional restructuring within human rights organizations, such as the creation of new staff positions, training in economic and social rights law, and the use of different research techniques and informants in the field.[85] Organizations are strengthening their research and analytical capabilities to specifically understand and promote economic and social rights.[86] However, the leading human rights organizations argue that they continue to employ essentially the same "spectrum of actions" that they have utilized for decades with civil and political rights—including naming and shaming, lobbying national legislatures, litigation in courts, work in international bodies, and some public education.[87] This is because their interpretation of what human rights essentially *are*— entitlements based in international legal standards—has remained fairly constant even as their focus has expanded beyond civil and political rights to include economic and social rights. Has this legal approach resulted in tangible progress for subsistence rights?

Thanks to the efforts of human rights practitioners around the globe, we are witnessing advances in the construction and interpretation of legal subsistence rights in several different arenas. In general, subsistence rights continue to have a lower legal status than civil and political rights in most national constitutions. If they exist at all, they are typically relegated explicitly as "directive principles" to guide the political process rather than "fundamental rights" subject to judicial enforcement.[88]

But exceptions to the rule are increasingly evident.[89] For example, the South African constitution, adopted in 1996, explicitly incorporated economic and social rights using language making them more precise and justiciable. The European Social Charter was also revised in 1996, which expanded the list of protected economic and social rights, established a collective complaints procedure, and initiated one of the world's most rigorous mechanisms to monitor states' reports.[90] In Northern Ireland, the national human rights commission recommended a new Charter in 2008 with a broad Bill of Rights that expands on the European Social Charter.[91] Northern Irish commissioners expect that this Bill of Rights will be "the strongest national legal document to protect [economic and social rights] in the world."[92] And the Scottish parliament passed new housing legislation in 2003 with additional protections against evictions that may prove to be the "most progressive anti-homelessness law in Europe."[93]

Based in part on nascent national legislation providing increased protections for economic and social rights, human rights organizations are finding and creating opportunities to litigate subsistence rights cases successfully before the courts. To date, the case law is "embryonic, . . . disparate and uneven," but a "global body of jurisprudence does exist" that demonstrates the possibility of making subsistence rights enforceable in judicial systems.[94] The International Network for Economic, Social and Cultural Rights maintains a database that details dozens of cases adjudicated in the past decade that have advanced these rights through national, regional, and international legal mechanisms.[95] The argument that economic and social rights are not and cannot be made into valid legal instruments is therefore highly dubious.

Typically, human rights NGOs utilize two sources of leverage in litigating subsistence rights cases: (a) using civil and political rights in national constitutions, such as the right to life or nondiscrimination, to litigate cases involving basic subsistence issues; and (b) using progressive national constitutions such as those mentioned above to litigate subsistence rights cases directly.[96] A successful and far-reaching example of the former is *People's Union for Civil Liberties v. India* in 2001, in which a local human rights organization sued the government of India for failing to provide food for its malnourished populations amid a surplus of state-owned food stocks. The Indian Supreme Court drew from the right-to-life provision in the Indian constitution to order the state to introduce midday meals in all primary schools, provide subsidized grain to 15 million poor households, and double its resource allocations to India's largest rural employment program.[97] An example of the latter is *Grootboom v. Oostenberg Municipality* in South Africa in 2000, in which approximately 900 squatters who had been forcibly evicted from their informal settlements petitioned the state to provide them with alternative housing. The Constitutional Court referred to the right to housing provisions in the South African constitution to order the state to provide relief to the claimants who were destitute and homeless.[98] The court judged the government's housing policy according to a "reasonableness" standard, and held that even though the state showed overall statistical improvement in the provision of housing, it was still obligated to provide relief to this destitute population. The developments in South Africa prompted one constitutional court justice to remark,

"I think we are entering a new kind of era now, and the question is ceasing to be whether or not one can enforce social and economic rights through the courts, the real question is how can it best be done?"[99]

Thus the foundations for successful subsistence rights litigation have been laid in many places. The issue now is the extent to which courts are willing to "get into social policy" and use the reasonableness standard such as the one used in *Grootboom* and many previous cases involving civil and political rights.[100] According to the reasonableness standard, the state is allowed a wide range of discretion to determine specific housing, food, health, and other social policies, but the courts maintain the power to determine whether these policies, or the decision-making process that led to them, were reasonable.[101] Likewise, when courts order a remedy, they have tended to provide the state with wide discretion in what specific policies it chooses to implement their order (particularly when the remedy is more costly or far-reaching).[102] In sum, the role of the courts in enforcing subsistence rights has been to require the state to implement some kind of minimally reasonable policy immediately, which the state has the discretion to design.[103]

Litigation of subsistence rights based on national law is therefore "not a panacea" but has certainly provided remedies and influenced policy.[104] One of the most successful attempts to influence public policy with litigation was *Treatment Action Campaign v. Minister of Health* in South Africa's Constitutional Court in 2001, which compelled the South African government to provide medication to all HIV-positive mothers to prevent mother-to-child transmission of the disease.[105] The legal and political pressure created in South Africa by the Treatment Action Campaign also led to price reductions on HIV medications, increased national spending on HIV treatment, and a new national strategic plan on HIV in 2007 that is explicitly rooted in human rights terms.[106]

Human rights activists hope that judicial decisions like this will "reverberate around the world"[107] because "there is nothing like success to breed emulation."[108] Because courts are able to "clarify the content of the right for a [specific] group of people,"[109] as successful and precedent-setting legal decisions spread, the hope is that momentum will develop, and the content of these rights, including states' positive obligations to fulfill them, will become more precise.[110] As Flavia Piovesan argues, "the idea that [economic and social rights] are not legal rights is completely outdated"[111] because human rights organizations have demonstrated their justiciability in concrete settings.

Human rights organizations' work in national legislatures and courts has been buttressed by advances in clarifying and enforcing subsistence rights at the regional and global levels. For example, the UN Committee on Economic, Social and Cultural Rights has issued several General Comments that clarify states' obligations on particular rights; it has investigated the status of several states' economic conditions on request from human rights NGOs; and it has issued highly critical and forward-looking reports on some states' subsistence rights policies. The influence of human rights NGOs in this regard is clear, in part because the Committee openly welcomes NGO input and collaboration. For example, in drafting a General Comment on the right to food, the Committee worked with NGOs like Food First over the course of a decade, and eventually adopted about 85 percent of the language supplied by NGOs.[112] Recent efforts by human rights NGOs to advance economic and social rights at the international level include promoting voluntary norms and codes of conduct for transnational corporations, voluntary guidelines on the right to food, and an Optional Protocol to the International Covenant on Economic, Social and Cultural Rights that would create an individual complaints mechanism.[113]

Finally, human rights organizations are advocating for subsistence rights through traditional naming and shaming campaigns, a technique that human rights and many other organizations have used effectively for decades. Although generating public outrage and shaming states into action is a common strategy, for human rights NGOs that adopt a legal understanding of subsistence rights, shaming involves identifying the specific violation of domestic or international law for which the state is culpable. In this vein, organizations like Human Rights Watch have issued dozens of reports condemning specific violations of subsistence rights in the areas of housing, food, and health.[114]

In sum, human rights organizations are using their legal approach to rights to prove that subsistence rights are indeed valid legal rights and to enforce those rights in specific cases. Subsistence rights can be used as important tools both within and outside of courts to hold the state and other actors accountable to their legal obligations to people living in poverty. The extent to which these tools are effective does not depend on any essential characteristics in the rights themselves, but on how they are constructed and interpreted by the institutions designed to protect and promote them.

Challenges Inherent in a Legal Approach to Subsistence Rights

As can be seen from the discussion above, the increasing incorporation of subsistence rights into the work of the human rights community has led to some very promising signs of progress toward clarifying and enforcing subsistence rights around the globe. And yet, adopting a legal approach to human rights necessarily leads to certain strategic barriers to the effective implementation of subsistence rights, based on their political, cultural, and institutional context. These challenges demonstrate that even within a legal approach, the law cannot be used to trump political, moral, cultural, and economic concerns. Attention to these concerns, and the extralegal arenas in which they reside, continues to be central to making the enforcement of subsistence rights effective. The remainder of this chapter discusses several of the challenges triggered by a legal approach to subsistence rights.

Reluctance within the Courts to Adjudicate Subsistence Rights

Relatively few countries have accorded subsistence rights equal status in their national legislation; within these contexts, legal progress for subsistence rights remains distant. In addition, even when states have incorporated aspects of economic and social rights into their national legislation, courts have generally been unwilling to "get into social policy" and adjudicate them.[115] This is not because these rights are inherently nonjusticiable, but because of the way rights have been conceptualized in public discourse and interpreted by the courts. This challenge is well understood by human rights practitioners. According to Piovesan, litigation of economic and social rights is limited by: "1) the still-timid acceptance by civil society of economic and social rights as legal rights that can be claimed through the courts; 2) the limited familiarity of the juridical agents when litigating on these rights (for instance, lawyers are more familiar with the guarantees offered by *habeas corpus* for protecting freedom of movement than with the public civil action; 3) the largely conservative profile of people implementing the law, insofar as the law is viewed more as a tool for conserving the social order than as a springboard for social transformation."[116]

In general, courts tend to show deference to the judgment of the state and are reluctant even to adjudicate civil and political rights; but they have shown special hostility to adjudicating subsistence rights as well as a narrow interpretation of what actions these rights require. Ran Hirschl analyzed the status of economic and social rights litigation in three capitalist democracies—New Zealand, Israel, and Canada—all of which underwent constitutional reform that gave the judiciary more authority to review state policy.[117] In all three countries, high courts held to a "predominantly neoliberal conception of rights," which prohibited most state intervention in the economy except to protect property rights. As such, subsistence rights that require positive actions by the state "have been effectively deprived of their binding force by judicial interpretations." For example, the New Zealand Court of Appeal gave an opinion that it would be "less inclined to intervene" in subsistence rights because "complex social and economic considerations and trade-offs were involved." In Israel, the right to property is virtually inviolable, as the Israeli Supreme Court has argued that property serves as the basis for human dignity and individual freedom. Hirschl concluded that courts in these countries provide "very limited capacity to advance progressive notions of social justice."

Even in those few cases in which courts have made progressive pronouncements on subsistence rights, the effects in terms of the actual alleviation of poverty have been limited by the relevant population addressed and the scope of the intervention required of the state. Legal solutions may protect the poor, but tend to do so in a manner that is least disruptive of the status quo.[118] "Indeed, . . . specific judicial remedies may solve the problem of an individual group, but leave all those in a similar situation unsatisfied. In other words, although legal intervention can secure the rights of a group of people, it is generally unable, at least on its own, to bring about sufficient change in public policy."[119] For example, the *Grootboom* case in South Africa led to immediate compensation for the 900 squatters who faced eviction, but critics contend that the government has largely failed to comply with the constitutional court's order to implement a comprehensive program to progressively achieve the right to housing for millions of other South Africans.[120] Judgments in favor of one group of people may actually result in a deterioration in the condition of other groups if they do not have the same access to the justice system or leverage over the state's scarce resources. Even when there are formal guarantees that are unambiguously interpreted, the poor often cannot take advantage of their rights because of their lack of access to legal institutions, or because seeking legal redress is too costly.[121]

Thus, focusing on the justiciability of subsistence rights in legal systems may reinforce social and economic inequality and concede legitimacy to governments that use the courts to serve the elite.[122] Conceptualized as justiciable entitlements, subsistence rights may not be well built to address structural violence and economic vulnerability.[123] As antipoverty activists have stated, "Of what use is the human rights struggle to the poverty-stricken if it does not liberate them from hunger, from homelessness, from ignorance, from disease?"[124] These limitations are why human rights activists themselves have said that litigation "falls significantly short of actual implementation" [125] and described the courts as "particularly weak mechanisms" for subsistence rights enforcement.[126] The legal application of human rights "risks being more of a band-aid, than a tool for systemic social and political change." [127]

The challenge for human rights organizations is not only to litigate subsistence rights cases successfully, which helps to clarify the content of rights, but also to choose carefully cases that affect a broader population either through setting precedents or directly affecting state policy making. In addition, human rights organizations are tasked with making the legal process itself empowering for vulnerable communities, as different groups can collaborate on education, research, documentation, and other roles in the legal process.[128] Given the difficulties inherent in coordinating like-minded organizations to accomplish all three goals, the strategic choice facing human rights advocates using litigation as a primary strategy is whether to focus their limited resources on more winnable cases (such as more extreme, discriminatory violations of "negative" obligations) or on precedent-setting, far-reaching ones (such as those that would require positive actions by the state that affect large populations), since the two goals are often in conflict. For that matter, if courts tend to be weak mechanisms that affect subsistence rights implementation in very limited ways, there are real trade-offs that organizations must consider when deciding whether to commit their institutional resources toward litigation in the first place, given that it is a "laborious and lengthy and expensive process." [129]

However, judging from the evidence of recent progress in national legislation and case law discussed above, there is good reason to hope that momentum will gradually develop over time and that judicial decisions around the globe will increasingly recognize states' obligations to take positive steps to fulfill subsistence rights. Optimists within the human rights community hope to continue to "create positive jurisprudence, which will enable continual progress towards the complete enforcement of all economic and social rights." [130] While this hope may be unrealistic, there are some signs that we are inching slowly in that direction.

Official U.S. Opposition to Legal Protections Against Poverty

Although the United States was undeniably a central actor in the 1940s in creating the international system that promotes economic and social rights, it is no secret within the human rights movement that "skepticism about the full international human rights agenda has been strongest" in the United States.[131] A sense of U.S. exceptionalism seems to pervade most of its foreign policy on human rights,[132] and U.S. opposition to economic and social rights has been particularly intense ever since the end of the Carter administration.[133] The end of the Cold War changed nothing about the official U.S. position. In the international arena, the United States has stood alone, or nearly alone, in blocking the extension of economic and social rights in international law, such as its rejection of the right to housing at Istanbul in 1996;[134] voting against a UN General Assembly resolution on economic and social rights in 1998;[135] actively opposing any mention of the right to food in Rome in 2002;[136] and trying to block the work of the UN Working Group on the Optional Protocol to the International Covenant on Economic, Social and Cultural Rights.[137] Domestically, U.S. courts have never recognized any positive legal obligations to ameliorate poverty,[138] and the 1996 welfare reform law officially ended the (at least implicit) acknowledgement that each U.S. resident had an entitlement to a minimum livelihood.[139]

The U.S. government argues against the legal enforceability of subsistence rights on the basis of a neoliberal rationale similar to courts that deny them—namely, that the only rights that are justiciable are those that impose negative duties on the state and do not interfere with the legislature's budgetary authority.[140] The U.S. government also argues that subsistence rights are the appropriate terrain for "qualified experts" like economists, not politicians and judges.[141] The official U.S. position remains unchallenged by the U.S. public, that has a limited understanding of economic and social rights despite the saturation of rights language throughout the society. Paradoxically, the American people claim rights to nearly everything, but they still conceive of rights very narrowly in terms of negative freedoms, civil rights, and private property.[142]

Thus, human rights activists have well-founded doubts about whether the U.S. federal government will adopt and enforce any legal subsistence rights anytime in the near future.[143] The U.S. government has some grounds to fear being sued over its roughly 40 million citizens who lack food security or health insurance, or its lingering racial disparities on a range of economic and social indicators within its own borders.[144] To date, human rights activists have tended to either circumvent the United States by trying to strengthen subsistence rights internationally without U.S. support, or use nonrights-based approaches when advocating for antipoverty issues within the United

States itself. For example, the initiation of the UN Human Rights Council in 2006 led human rights practitioners to strategize about how they might newly advance the subsistence rights agenda in the UN, given the absence of U.S. membership on the Council.

This results in another strategic choice for subsistence rights advocates. They can largely continue to circumvent and ignore U.S. opposition and devote precious institutional resources to areas that hold much greater promise of success. As one antipoverty activist stated, "We live in a conservative country, let's face it," [145] and there is no benefit in taking on such a Sisyphean struggle. Few have adopted the strategy advocated in 1990 by Philip Alston, who recommended a major new effort to directly confront the United States on its legal obligations by promoting its ratification of the International Covenant on Economic, Social and Cultural Rights. [146]

Alternatively, human rights activists, bolstered by an Obama Administration that is at least more rhetorically supportive of subsistence rights, could make a major new push in the United States of the kind Alston suggested. The launching of the U.S. Human Rights Network, which advocates that the full spectrum of rights be fully applicable within the United States, is evidence that organizations are attempting to hold the American government accountable to its economic and social rights obligations. Given the U.S. government's opposition to legal subsistence rights described above, the risk of failure inherent in this approach is apparent. However, the risks associated with circumventing, ignoring, or writing off the United States may be less apparent, but even more dangerous. Besides being the only global superpower, the United States maintains a $14 trillion economy that touches every corner of the globe. No single state's economic policies—ranging from the management of trade and investment to domestic interest rates—come close to matching U.S. policies in terms of their impact on global poverty. In that sense, it may not be very practicable to try to ignore the 800-pound gorilla in the global economic room.

The leading human rights organizations already have a history of confrontation with the U.S. government on civil and political rights on issues that range from the death penalty to arms transfers to voting rights to torture. [147] If human rights activists decide to confront official U.S. antipathy to subsistence rights more aggressively, their primary challenges will be to: (1) collaborate with and build on the energy of an extremely broad range of social movements; and (2) reframe legal subsistence rights in such a way that they are not only palatable, but perceived as vital to the U.S. public. The difficulties involved in these tasks lead to a third challenge for human rights activists.

The Inaccessibility of Legal Rights Discourse and Institutions

Legal language can be confusing to nonpractitioners, and this is no different in human rights law. All legal discourse can seem foreign to nonlawyers, and while this is equally true for civil and political rights, it is worse for economic and social rights because of the difference in legal texts and historical lack of attention given to elaborating economic and social rights. Civil and political rights have become embedded in U.S. (and perhaps global) cultural understandings in a way that economic and social rights have not, which is expressed and reinforced through the proliferation of detective- and attorney-focused programs on television. Most average citizens in the West understand what due process and equal protection require because they watch these themes play out regularly in popular media.[148] For most laypersons—who obviously constitute the majority of social justice organizations, humanitarian NGOs, and other groups devoted to antipoverty work—the discourse and institutions of international law can seem much more unfamiliar and inaccessible.[149] For many groups carrying out local struggles, human rights are often perceived as UN connected, elite oriented, and therefore quite distant from the realities they work with on the ground. Louise Arbour once described international law satirically as something "practiced by people in limousines being polite,"[150] which divorces legal discourse from the experiences and needs of the poor.[151] As Larry Cox contends: "as the human rights effort has moved from a cause to a professional career, it has increasingly employed an exclusive, legalistic language that fails to resonate with people's lives and daily struggles. Its link to what is human and universal has been diminished, if not lost, and correspondingly, so have its power and appeal."[152] If this is true in the developed world, it is even more accurate in the global South. Chidi Anselm Odinkalu describes a situation in which the poor

> feel that their realities and aspirations are not adequately captured by human rights organizations or their language. The current human rights movement in Africa—with the possible exception of the women's rights movement and faith-based social justice initiatives—appears almost by design to exclude the participation of the people whose welfare it purports to advance. . . . In the absence of a member-

ship base, there is no constituency-driven obligation or framework for popularizing the language or objectives of the group beyond the community of inward-looking professionals or careerists who run it. Instead of being the currency of a social justice or conscience-driven movement, "human rights" has increasingly become the specialized language of a select professional cadre with its own rites of passage and methods of certification. Far from being a badge of honor, human rights activism is, in some of the places I have observed it, increasingly a certificate of privilege.[153]

A legal approach to human rights, if implemented narrowly, can restrict participation by the poor in their own emancipation by confining them within a lawyer-client relationship or identifying them merely as a single documented illustration of a broader violation.[154] Historically, then, human rights language has been "used for exclusionary purposes" even within human rights movements, which has created "wounds that need to be healed."[155] In fact, human rights experts themselves admit to a great deal of confusing terminology within economic and social rights law.[156] Human rights lawyers are doing tremendously important work and often do collaborate with grassroots actors. However, the inaccessibility and elitism of the legal human rights system works against the two related goals mentioned above: building broad alliances among social movements, and framing subsistence rights so that they resonate with a mass audience.

Social justice organizations could be given a standard two-week training in the legal aspects of subsistence rights so that they have a basic ability to use the language and understand legal mechanisms. However, the more fundamental issue is whether the legalistic human rights rhetoric itself, as currently constructed, is clear and comprehensible enough to resonate with and mobilize a broad range of social movement actors, and whether human rights mechanisms are accessible enough for local groups to take advantage of them. For social movements to be successful, activists in the streets must be able not only to understand the issues clearly, but also to employ the language fluently enough to persuade and activate others.

This has not happened yet, and most activists recognize the need to include more grassroots social justice groups in human rights work.[157] There is, however, no consensus within the traditional human rights community about *how* to accomplish this. It could be done by trying to provide more training in human rights law to social movements; or by trying to make legal language more accessible to ordinary people; or by reconstructing the human rights discourse itself so that it speaks directly to poor people's experiences.[158] Taking the latter path would cause human rights organizations to rethink the primacy of the legal approach altogether and incorporate alternative approaches. It would begin to redefine what legitimately counts as "human rights work."

But first, it is a reasonable question to ask, *why* are the language and mechanisms of subsistence rights perceived as being so inaccessible to non-lawyers? I believe it is not only due to the inaccessibility of legal language, but also because economic and social rights issues, as currently constructed, are more controversial and more complex than human rights advocates tend to acknowledge.

Controversies About the Obligations that Freedom from Poverty Imposes

Human rights activists frequently decry states' "intransigence" or "lack of political will" in failing to implement subsistence rights.[159] While there is certainly an element of truth in these critiques, there is also a distorting aspect. Governments may be unwilling to enforce subsistence rights, but it is more analytically useful to conceptualize their "lack of will" in terms of *alternative interests* the actors have, the ideas that generate those particular interests, and the *rhetorical legitimation strategies* actors use to justify those interests instead of protecting subsistence rights.[160] For example, scholars must ask, why are Western governments able to promote trade liberalization, or subsidize their own agricultural industries, or increase their military spending, or end their own welfare entitlements? And how do they successfully gain public support for those policies?

One reason why states can justify their existing policies is because the legal obligations inherent in subsistence rights are not yet sufficiently clear and specific. Most human rights advocates openly acknowledge that the legal content of subsistence rights is relatively imprecise.[161] The International Covenant on Economic, Social and Cultural Rights, while in theory a legally binding treaty, contains moderating language, particularly in Article 2.1, that provides for an unusually wide range of interpretation. Thus advocates are reduced to speaking about the responsibility for subsistence rights implementation as being "spread across nations," or "everyone's responsibility," or the responsibility of the "international community." Again, while these statements are technically correct, they do not require or guide individual states or other actors to do anything concrete.

Because legal obligations are imprecise, there is a similar lack of clarity about what constitutes a violation of those rights except in the most egregious cases. Yet identifying specific violations has been a central methodology for human rights organizations. When a government arbitrarily or maliciously discriminates against a particular group of people in providing social services or otherwise protecting subsistence rights, then almost everyone would count this as a violation.[162] Most court cases that have successfully upheld subsistence rights have focused on these kinds of discriminatory and arbitrary violations of "negative" obligations.[163] Yet the overwhelming majority of the billion people in extreme poverty are probably not in their condition because of specific and discriminatory state violations of their negative duties to the poor. Most live in extreme poverty due to a complex combination of familial, local, national, and global factors that include social, political, and economic relationships.

In fact, human rights activists themselves disagree about whether the mere existence of extreme poverty constitutes a rights violation. Those who take the maximalist position argue that poverty itself is a human rights violation, and that basic needs themselves create obligations typically held by whoever is able to provide the necessary resources.[164] As Hertel and Minkler state, "Anyone anywhere who suffers from severe poverty not of their own choosing is having their economic rights violated. If we were to actually enforce economic rights, there would be no involuntary poverty anywhere in the world."[165] Others take the minimalist position and argue that a violation implies the need to identify a specific act (or omission) by a specific actor or set of actors.[166] While the chances of success in individual cases are increased when obvious violations can be specified,[167] the problem, again, is that this strategy would cover relatively few of the billion people who live in extreme poverty.

Imprecise legal language is not always an impediment to the strengthening of the human rights system and the realization of rights. In fact, vague legal norms can be beneficial in facilitating consensus on basic principles or in allowing duty-bearers the flexibility to determine how they will comply with norms when compliance behaviors are relatively uncontroversial.[168] In the early stages of the movement for civil and political rights, activists often referred to "soft, vague definitions" of rights in order to build mass acceptance of the basic moral principles involved, and precision in the application of law took decades to develop.[169] However, when the imprecision of legal texts is successfully used by the state to avoid any obligation whatsoever, it presents a major challenge in implementing rights. Human rights organizations therefore often perceive their task as seeking precise, binding legal obligations that can be independently reviewed and enforced.[170]

Thus, the challenge that a legal approach to subsistence rights raises is to argue persuasively that specific policies and actions, by both public and private actors, deny subsistence rights to large segments of the global population. Activists tend to be more influential when they can vilify a specific actor and when there is a clear, direct causal connection between the violator and victim.[171] The question for human rights organizations is whether this targeting process is facilitated or harmed by the legal discourse of economic and social rights.

The list of possible legal violations that advocates of subsistence rights have generated is extensive. In the domestic context, these actions include appropriating land without adequate compensation, state corruption, maintaining social services below a subsistence level, privatizing social services, signing onto trade agreements that disadvantage the poor, failing to provide sufficient security in situations of violent conflict, failing to have a national plan for poverty reduction, failing to prioritize social spending in the national budget, and failing to collect adequate taxes from the wealthy. In the transnational context, possible violations might include providing aid to a rights-violating state, exporting hazardous waste, economic sanctions that deprive poor countries of basic resources, financing development projects that displace people, subsidizing agriculture in wealthy countries, enforcing restrictive patent laws, requiring debt repayment from the poorest countries, or otherwise maintaining "economic and trade policies that exacerbate global inequality."[172]

Given the wide range of possible violations and the structural nature of poverty, it is certainly a difficult task to link specific actions to specific instances of extreme deprivation. In addition, an initial glance at the list above shows that while some of the policies are fairly clear violations, others are extremely controversial and could reasonably be argued to be rights-enhancing. The lists of potential subsistence rights violations are extensive; the problem is that they are sufficiently debatable so that virtually all states are arguably violators, and at the same time, every state could generate a reasonable and complex justification to call its actions legal.[173] To take one example, human rights activists frequently contend that more priority be given to economic security in national budgets, and so they make a claim for more resources accordingly. While most activists recognize that spending more on vulnerable populations would require trade-offs with other social services or socially beneficial programs, they tend to downplay the trade-offs or categorically deny funding to disfavored programs like "unnecessary" military spending.[174] For example, Leonard Rubenstein argues that advocacy for greater resources for subsistence rights "tends to enlarge the pot" of state resources, rather than trading off with other important needs.[175] He cites the Bush Administration's new funds for HIV/AIDS via the PEPFAR program as a supporting example.[176] The Bush Administration is an interesting case, however, to support the notion that you cannot avoid trade-offs in setting budget priorities. For years the United States borrowed its way into higher spending and tax cuts across the board, but subsequent budget deficits and an economic recession showed that eventually, priorities have to be set (in this case, against almost all nondefense discretionary spending before 2009).

Aside from the fact that the majority of U.S. citizens believe military spending to be the most important priority of government, spending on national security does protect human rights (the right to life and physical integrity) as well. The International Monetary Fund even argues that the level of national spending on basic needs is not correlated with outcomes on health and other social indicators, therefore the proportion of the national budget directed to social programs should not be used as an indicator of legal compliance with subsistence rights.[177] As such, the argument that a particular social program is a legal obligation rather than "just one good idea among many"[178] will fall short because, at best, each program is just one legal obligation among many.

It becomes clear why legal rights language framed as politically neutral, nonnegotiable entitlements that lead to precise state obligations does not comfortably fit into situations of scarce resource trade-offs and distributional justice.[179] Decisions to allocate public resources can only come under legal review in a very limited range of cases, and thus the legal discourse of subsistence rights does not deal well with distributional justice.[180] Legal rights language is "adversarial and adjudicatory" in the context of budgetary decisions that require "inclusive and communal" reasoning.[181] There is therefore the danger that a judicial approach to these rights will "displace reasonable legislative judgments about sensible priority setting."[182]

Identifying precise obligations on behalf of the state is further complicated by the fact that so many actors besides an individual state have a direct or indirect effect on the realization of subsistence rights. Poor states, even those who have ratified international treaties and have demonstrated willingness to implement subsistence rights, are dependent on the aid, trade, debt, and other policies of the wealthy states.[183] The activities of transnational corporations and international financial institutions have a tremendous effect on extreme poverty, but neither type of actor has been captured adequately within international human rights law. With the expansion of the power of global capital that has accompanied economic globalization, even wealthy states have limited options in dealing with poverty.[184] The causes of extreme deprivation are often systemic rather than the result of any individual perpetrator,[185] and any given policy will likely have both positive and negative effects on poverty for different populations.[186] The realization of subsistence rights requires a "complex interaction of policies and programs in a wide range of sectors and institutions." [187] Although human rights NGOs attempt to sift through the shared responsibility for rights violations, whether they can use legal texts to do this effectively in the face of structural causes of subsistence rights violations remains an open question.

Paradoxically, then, a legal approach to subsistence rights is in danger of overcomplicating rights, by grounding basic normative ideas in inaccessible legal discourse, at the same time as it is oversimplifying rights, by assuming that violations of legal obligations can be identified in a relatively noncontroversial or technical manner. As mentioned earlier, human rights advocates have good reason to hope that the legal content of subsistence rights is elaborated gradually through an expanding web of legal decisions and interpretive comments across the globe, thus concretizing a state's basic obligations. Ideally, "further clarity will emerge, both with respect to what is prohibited and what behavior is considered conducive or mandatory to ensure the full realization of these rights." [188] The question is, how will that clarity emerge? It will require further elaboration of the legal texts, but also the resolution of debates that occur in the political, economic, and cultural realms. As such, even in promoting the law, the more difficult ideological questions that surround states' legal obligations (including what constitutes a subsistence rights violation) preclude human rights organizations from taking the high ground through legal discourse and its ostensibly objective reasoning.

One option for human rights advocates may be to use the human rights discourse to emphasize solutions and remedies to poverty rather than focus solely on violations.[189] Rather than conceptualize rights as entitlements whose violation triggers a remedy, it may be better to think of rights as a legal framework that guides the design of policy solutions.[190] This is an important point that could lead to effective public action on extreme poverty even when the root causes are unknown, and violations are nonexistent or controversial. However, it also leads to the next challenge for legal rights advocates.

Controversies over Policies that Would
Achieve Freedom from Poverty

While there is considerable controversy over the content of international law and the obligations it imposes, an equally intense debate exists over the policies that would actually lead to the elimination of extreme poverty. The International Covenant on Economic, Social and Cultural Rights was framed in language that attempted to be ideologically neutral—that economic policy should be specifically targeted to meeting basic needs—yet ideological debates about how to meet basic needs inevitably arose and took center stage.[191] It is not just that eliminating poverty requires a complex mix of policies from a range of actors; it is that so many policies can be argued to be either rights violating or rights enhancing.[192] These ideological debates make it more difficult for human rights organizations to do what they have historically done best: public shaming, education, lobbying, and legal action. When no clear policy solutions exist in situations of complex needs and scarce resources, shaming the state over its legal obligations is not likely to prove effective.[193]

Controversy is nothing new to human rights practice. Even in the realm of civil and political rights, debates rage over the proper balance between liberty and security, whether the death penalty constitutes inhumane punishment, or when interrogative techniques cross the line into torture. Yet the controversies over economic and social policy are more fundamental and severe than debates over civil and political rights, largely because civil and political rights have attained a taken-for-granted status within Western political cultures. In contrast to subsistence rights, there is a broad and deep consensus about the validity of the core content of civil and political rights. Thus, debates over civil and political rights tend to be concerned with how these rights are balanced with other public goals, or when a particular practice crosses the line into a rights violation. With economic and social rights, there is little agreement about whether specific policies (e.g., land reforms, privatization, trade liberalization) are actually violations or paths to realize subsistence rights. The controversy over economic and social policy is analogous to a debate over whether torture in fact helps or hurts the prisoner, not about whether a particular practice constitutes torture or whether it is allowable in extreme circumstances.

One debate over solutions to extreme poverty surrounds the primacy of economic growth versus redistributive policies. For many years the so-called Washington Consensus dictated that growth was the almost exclusive path to poverty reduction. However, Jean Dreze and Amartya Sen convincingly argued that, at least in the short term, societies could achieve tremendous improvements in the livelihoods of their poorest members through either "growth-mediated" or "support-led" policies (i.e., even when there is low or negative GDP growth).[194] There is now a consensus (or at least a sense of détente) among economists that both growth and the redistribution of wealth are important goals that, if pursued properly, can even reinforce each other.[195] This two-pronged goal of economic policy is often called "pro-poor growth." [196]

Nevertheless, the controversy arises over the specific policies that states tend to implement in pursuit of pro-poor growth, which are often contradictory or mutually exclusive. "Pro-growth" policies tend to include low taxes on entrepreneurs and businesses, easing labor and environmental regulations to keep businesses profitable, focusing state resources on industries that are the most economically productive (and not necessarily socially beneficial), privatizing social services, maintaining the primacy of private property rights, minimizing government intervention in the economy overall, placing good governance conditions on foreign aid, and lowering barriers to trade and investment. This is what economists often refer to as "getting the macroeconomic fundamentals right." [197] On the other hand, "redistributive" policies typically include higher taxes on the wealthy, more government spending on basic social services, land reform, strong labor laws, more foreign aid, ensuring that development projects do not displace vulnerable populations, and some social or environmentally based restrictions on trade and investment. The problem is not that these two sets of policies cannot be balanced or mixed successfully in some cases; some advocates promote the idea of balance. The main challenge is that experts who support each set of policies often argue that the other set of policies is counterproductive and will hinder poverty reduction. Thus the human rights movement does not lack ideas about solutions (e.g., welfare states, debt relief, a Tobin tax, removing agricultural subsidies), but the solutions are so controversial and explicitly ideological that they limit the legal force behind their claims.

In pressing for redistributive policies, as subsistence rights activists typically do, they run into economists and other "technical experts" who claim that these policies are actually counterproductive—that redistributive policies not only stifle growth, but they fail to help improve the lives of the destitute over the long term. Pro-growth economists argue that free-market capitalism is "unique in its ability to raise the living standard of every person on earth," [198] and the majority of people (at least in the United States) agree. In fact, using the language of legal rights may actually exacerbate the backlash against even limited redistributive policies, because of the perception that economic and social rights are a "Soviet, Third World creation" that "encourages unlimited government meddling of the sort on which dictatorships thrive." [199] This threatens to "entrench the very problem it purports to address." [200]

The controversy is not just over technical policy details, but also over fundamental philosophical issues such as the role of government and the market in the economy, and the "rival cultures" of individualism and communitarianism. [201] These philosophical differences involve not only a culture war, but also one with class-based implications, and one with a political history rooted in the Cold War and anticommunism. This is why the debate is not just a disinterested conversation among technical experts, but a passionate fight with invectives often lobbed by both sides. Free marketers are often maligned as greedy capitalists with no social conscience, and social justice activists labeled as unreformed and unrepentant Marxists.

In most capitalist democracies, promoters of market liberalization are currently winning the ideological, rhetorical, and policy-making battle. At the level of ideology, "the virtues of the market mechanism are now standardly assumed to be so pervasive that qualifications seem unimportant." [202] Rhetorically, human rights themselves have come to be associated with individual liberty, which is equated with free market democracy and the inviolability of property rights. [203] Thus, when George W. Bush extolled the virtues of freedom in his second inaugural address, there was very little doubt that he spoke of freedom in a way that left little room for economic and social rights. The rhetorical and ideological victories for free markets become reflected in policy-making and institution-building processes, as can be seen from the relative strength and enforceability of international trade law compared with human rights law. [204] As Baxi notes, "Global trade relations now stand invested with the resonance of the rhetoric of the moral language of human rights. . . . The paradigm of the UDHR is being steadily, but surely, *supplanted* by that of trade-related, market-friendly human rights." [205]

This could be a significant threat to the implementation of subsistence rights, because if free markets maintain normative priority, then subsistence rights must fit within that framework to be recognized as valid. As Kerry Rittich states:

First, the perceived demands of markets can be expected to feed back
into the way that human rights are conceptualized and reshape the
definition of a human rights-respecting society. The attempt to construct a version of human rights that is consistent with the project
of market reform seems destined to set limits on the use of the discourse; at minimum, it is likely to reestablish a hierarchy within the
corpus of human rights. This process of recognition, prioritization,
and exclusion of rights in turn might be expected to place limits on
the social and economic policies, as well as the resources, that can be
legitimately marshaled to further transformative political objectives.
Second, the discourse of human rights may lose much if not all of its
critical bite against the "normal" institutions and practices of liberal
market societies. Third, as the concepts of markets and human rights
become more closely interwoven, human rights complaints are likely
to be leveled [only] at those practices that are perceived to be "market
deviant." [206]

In other words, if the validity of subsistence rights is dependent on their compatibility with free markets and other pro-growth policies, it can severely limit
the reach and effectiveness of those rights. Rittich continues: "What does it
mean to be in favor of human rights . . . when market reformers also claim to
be in favor of human rights? Human rights activists have to confront the fact
that the discourse of human rights can be and is being used to support varied
agendas, some of which may run directly counter to transformative goals.[207]

Human rights organizations tend to turn to international law, and their
interpretation of it, to resolve these economic arguments. They claim that an
economic policy is legitimate to the extent that it is congruent with international law. But critics have described international law as unhelpful in this
regard, because legal discourse is subject to "eviscerating qualification" that
closes off other discourses about solutions to poverty.[208] Rights claimants are
forced into discussing difficult legal quandaries such as: Who is obligated to
do what? Subject to what resource constraints? With whose assistance? Immediately or progressively? How operationalized? Thus the profusion of legal
discourse surrounding economic and social rights can allow states to participate in the international human rights system to improve their public image,
but avoid being deeply challenged on their economic and social policy.[209]
This opens up strong incentives for actors to use human rights discourse and
mechanisms to justify the pursuit of their narrow self-interests.[210]

In sum, because of the complexity, imprecision, and ideological controversy involved in promoting the full range of economic and social rights, states
and other actors have too many reasonable excuses for failing to implement
these rights.[211] When confronted with a claim that they have violated rights,
states have a range of justifications at their disposal: they can deny the causal
link between their policies and extreme deprivation, claim that existing policies already address the problem, shift responsibility onto other actors, plead
for more time to implement rights progressively, claim an overall lack of resources, or claim the priority of other state obligations that must be balanced
with subsistence rights.[212] For example, the U.S. government, which was earlier described as hostile to these rights, claims with some justification that it is
in fact the world's most friendly state to those in extreme poverty—citing the
fact that it is the world's largest consumer, produces the most food for export
and donation, gives the most foreign aid in absolute terms, its citizens tend to
have adequate livelihoods, it promotes poverty reduction through democracy
and the expansion of free markets, subsidizes global security, and so on.[213]

In the face of this daunting challenge, it seems that human rights activists have the following strategic options. First, they can concede the normative battlefield to free market advocates and claim that subsistence rights are
entirely compatible with the expansion of pro-growth market policies. Those
who follow this strategy would try to implement subsistence rights with
the "least possible interference with the market place,"[214] typically through
minimum social safety nets provided by the state to "compensate [for] the
imbalances created by the market."[215] The danger here is that economic globalization has put pressure on the state to lower taxes and transfer responsibility for social services onto private actors, thereby weakening the state's
capacity to ultimately provide adequate safety nets. To the extent that a state
privatizes its traditional functions, disavows responsibility for regulating the
economy, and requires itself to respond to the demands of global investors, its
safety net is likely to become smaller and thinner.

Second, human rights practitioners can attempt to avoid the confrontation by staying above the ideological fray—either by focusing attention only
on the clearest and most egregious violations[216] or by claiming that international law sets basic standards and then leaving it up to policy makers and
"technical experts" to decide on the details of implementation.[217] The problem with focusing on egregious violations, as mentioned earlier, is that the
clearest violations of subsistence rights may not affect the overwhelming
majority of people who live in extreme deprivation. The problem with del-

egating implementation to technical experts is that policy makers currently understand their subsistence rights obligations in the narrowest sense, and the experts themselves have wildly divergent opinions about what economic policies would adequately realize subsistence rights. There is a largely unspoken assumption among legal rights advocates, which I believe to be incorrect, that if states would only base their development practices on international human rights law, then consensus on economic policy would automatically follow and political debates would be avoided.[218]

Human rights advocates have been pursuing each of these strategies with some limited success, but they appear increasingly willing to adopt a third path that differs altogether from the first two: to confront these ideological debates head on. They do this by arguing that subsistence rights obligations require states and other actors to implement specific regulative, tax, trade, investment, and other economic policies—in essence, saying that subsistence rights are *not* compatible with certain pro-growth policies.[219] The goal of human rights is not to prescribe a specific policy; it is about restricting the range of policy options a state may pursue in advancing its interests, and international law has not progressed to a point that it is able to restrict states' (or other actors') behavior sufficiently.[220] Human rights does not mandate a particular economic policy, but it should be able to recognize that some policies are "more pathogenic than others and should be denounced as such."[221] Narrowing the range of options a state may pursue to implement subsistence rights requires speaking the language of political economy, distributional justice, and public policy, which is not a central feature of the legal discourse of human rights as it is currently constructed.[222] To fill this gap, the Ford Foundation has funded meetings between progressive economists and human rights advocates beginning in 2004 to explore ways that they can work more closely together and link human rights law with economic policy critiques.[223]

The risks inherent in this strategy are significant: not only may human rights advocates fail to win the economic and political arguments, but in adopting positions perceived as more "ideological," human rights organizations may also lose their credibility among policy makers that was previously based on their reputation as legal experts who provided objective information. As mentioned earlier, Western human rights organizations have historically survived by moving beyond broad moral claims and narrowing their mandate and their methodology in order to foster their reputation for providing reliable, accurate data on specific rights violations. Therefore they are understandably hesitant to make broad claims about global poverty, political economy, or power relations and risk losing the quality of their research or the effectiveness of their methodology.[224] As Alicia Ely Yamin notes, "To argue that certain economic models structure systematic violations of human rights is of course politically contested; it seems somehow ideological in contrast to the ostensible neutrality that the human rights movement has historically attempted to maintain. The strict separation between the political and economic realms has been both a decisive and a limiting factor in traditional human rights work, which reflects its origins in the Western liberal tradition."[225] Despite these risks, the increasing engagement with controversial issues in the global economy simply cannot be avoided if human rights organizations intend to take subsistence rights implementation seriously. If human rights organizations lack clear policy positions on the most important ideological issues, their role and effectiveness is destined to remain limited in the area of subsistence rights, and the law will remain indeterminate on economic policy. As Neil Stammers argues: "We must develop a very different strategy for the establishment and protection of human rights, one that is rooted in, and clearly accepts the legitimacy of, political and social demands generated in popular struggles and social movements that directly challenge the legitimacy of existing relations of power. The alternative, trying to set human rights above the fray by abstracting the concept . . . is simply an error. A socially constructed concept such as human rights can never be put beyond context and power. Attempts to do just this have enabled the idea of human rights to be ideologically redeployed to sustain existing power relations."[226]

Adapting Human Rights Organizations' Capacities and Identities to New Strategies

If human rights organizations fully engage the ideological debates discussed above, how will this affect their identities, their legal understanding of rights, and the unique skills and methodologies they have developed? Do human rights organizations, and the human rights framework itself, have anything of real value to add to debates over the global economy that has not already been argued by social justice movements for decades?

Human rights organizations have developed skills, capacities, and methodologies that they tend to rely on, which include legal expertise, research and reporting on rights violations, and naming and shaming campaigns. Human rights organizations are adept at analyzing responsibility for violations, and publicizing it accordingly.[227] As a result, they have gained a strong reputation for the quality of their analysis and their expertise, which has given them access to governments as well as a base of donors. However, with the possible exception of Amnesty International, human rights organizations are generally weak at mass mobilization and the grassroots organizing skills that are common among social justice groups.[228] Human Rights Watch, for example, eschews grassroots mobilization in favor of media and Internet campaigns, lobbying government officials, and legal work that it claims is a more effective use of its limited resources.[229] It seems reasonable for human rights organizations to build on their existing skills and competencies. But what additional skills, structures, and capacities do human rights organizations need in order to meet the requirements of subsistence rights advocacy? As one practitioner notes, "We're still a long way from having the methodology that we need" to advocate for legal subsistence rights effectively.[230]

At the very least, human rights organizations need to develop new expertise in order to strengthen their research and analytical capabilities on subsistence rights issues.[231] For example, the Center for Economic and Social Rights in New York has adopted an almost exclusive focus on developing and disseminating a rigorous methodology for identifying violations and measuring progressive realization of these rights.[232] Amnesty International's London headquarters has hired new researchers to focus on economic and social rights.[233] However, the new expertise should not be limited to international law, but should include a "sophisticated understanding of the design of social programs"[234] as well as a more refined understanding of the global economy. In other words, perhaps human rights organizations need to hire more economists, grassroots organizers, political scientists, and public policy advocates rather than, or in addition to, more lawyers. Amnesty is beginning to do this, as it is increasingly consulting with town planners, agronomists, public health experts, and people with interdisciplinary expertise, as well as collaborating with organizations involved in free trade, debt, aid, and other issues.[235]

Some of the smaller human rights organizations are also beginning to move away from the traditional violations-based methodology of naming and shaming because structural violence and economic injustice is often too complex, indirect, unanticipated, and unintended to shame effectively.[236] The leading human rights organizations are currently debating the extent to which they will follow in their footsteps. Amnesty appears to be moving toward a broader thematic approach with its Global Campaign for Human Dignity; it will be interesting to see where this develops. Because the leading human rights organizations are often based in cities where global economic policy is determined—New York, London, Washington, D.C., and elsewhere—they can take advantage of their location to focus on the policies generated closest to home. If they do take a broader approach, they can still avoid overstretching their own institutional resources by focusing on a limited range of issues and collaborating with a wider range of social movement actors.

If human rights organizations do enter more fully into the ideological and policy debates, they certainly cannot expect the recitation of human rights law to be a magic bullet that persuades actors to live up to their legal or moral obligations. Human rights law can, however, add a sense of universality and legitimacy to policy advocacy. Promoting subsistence rights in this way can redefine the Western human rights movement's central concerns, and it can move the normative discourse away from the neoliberal claim that human rights are adequately fulfilled through electoral democracy and free markets.

Conclusions

The implications of taking a legal approach to subsistence rights demonstrate what a social theory of human rights argues: that promoting subsistence rights through legal mechanisms is no less "political" than other methods, because the law is deeply embedded in politics, not a separate realm.[237] Legal approaches to rights cannot "get above politics" because "speaking law to politics is not the same as speaking truth to power."[238] Power, political process, and ideological debates are embedded in the implementation of subsistence rights even if they are largely missing from the legal discourse of subsistence rights. As post-positivist legal scholar David Kennedy suggests, the traditional conception of human rights:

> promises a legal vocabulary for achieving justice outside the clash of political interest. Such a vocabulary is not available: rights conflict with one another, rights are vague, rights have exceptions, many situations fall between rights. The human rights movement promises that "law"—the machinery, the texts, the profession, the institution—can resolve conflicts and ambiguities in society by resolving those within its own materials, and that this can be done on the basis of a process of "interpretation" that is different from, more legitimate than, politics. And different in a particularly stultifying way—as a looser or stricter deduction from a past knowledge rather than as a collective engagement with the future. . . . The human rights movement suggests that "rights" can be responsible for emancipation, rather than people

making political decisions. This demobilizes other actors and other vocabularies, and encourages emancipation through reliance on enlightened, professional elites with "knowledge" of rights and wrongs, alienating people from themselves and from the vocabulary of their own governance.[239]

Legal reasoning about subsistence rights, therefore, cannot be separated from the political pressures, judicial biases, and cultural assumptions inherent in debates over economic and social policy. Legal approaches to subsistence rights, while presenting tremendous advantages, also have significant costs. At their best, legal approaches are demonstrating and expanding the justiciability of subsistence rights. At their worst, legal approaches crowd out practical policy discussions of how to free people from poverty by entangling rights in thorny debates over legal concepts, definitions, and implementation mechanisms.[240]

Because of this, any approach to subsistence rights, even one that takes international law as its grounding point, must focus as much on political, economic, and cultural legitimation strategies as on the creation, elaboration, and implementation of formal law. Advocates must pay attention not only to the elaboration of international law and its enforcement, but also to the cultural assumptions, economic debates, religious norms, customary law, and local customs and living practices that determine whether and how a rights regime is implemented.[241] Human rights advocates certainly understand that educational and cultural work are important in promoting human rights; but they may not fully recognize what this implies for the human rights discourse itself, what counts as "human rights work," or how the movement can shape the development of subsistence rights. Success in promoting subsistence rights is dependent on changing the terms of public discourse—for example, framing subsistence in terms of justice or equality rather than charity or efficient economic growth—as much as it is dependent on a clearer elaboration of states' legal obligations. The "real potential of human rights lies in its ability to change the way people perceive themselves" and its ability to reframe economic deprivation as a violation that cannot be tolerated.[242] Some of the other organizations described in this book have focused their moral rights strategies on precisely that—changing basic perceptions about poverty.

All of the legal strategies mentioned in this chapter—litigation, promoting legislation, naming and shaming, monitoring and reporting, and more— must therefore be accompanied by political and cultural strategies in order to impact the nonlegal, intangible environment in which positive law is developed and interpreted. The process can be mutually reinforcing: legal strategies can be used to educate and mobilize constituencies to "build culture," and cultural strategies can be used to influence legal outcomes.[243] In that way, the human rights movement has the opportunity to redefine human rights to recapture the power of rights both inside and outside of the legal realm.

4

Social Justice Organizations

While the adoption of subsistence rights among traditional human rights organizations has been well publicized, the increasing incorporation of human rights rhetoric into the campaigns of social justice groups represents a quieter but equally significant trend.[1] The importance of the social justice movement should not be surprising, as Neil Stammers argues, because "many of the key innovations in the socio-historical development of human rights were constructed and articulated, in the first instance, in the context of social movements seeking to challenge extant relations and structures of power."[2] Economic and social rights "are given meaning primarily through actual struggles around access to resources, demands for recognition and voice, and social justice."[3] Because the recent trend is unique in several important regards, social justice movements are the focus of this chapter's analysis.

After a brief discussion of basic concepts, I trace the development of this trend, explaining why social justice groups in the West, particularly in the United States,[4] have increasingly integrated human rights into their public discourse and action strategies in the past decade. I then discuss how human rights have taken shape in organizational practice through the different interpretive lenses that the social justice movement applies to rights. Finally, I investigate the strategic and political implications of the moral approach to rights that predominates within the social justice movement. I analyze these implications from both sides of the human rights/social justice equation: What value does a human rights framework provide to a social movement's efforts to combat extreme poverty? What does current social movement practice imply for our understanding of human rights?

I argue that social justice organizations increasingly have adopted human

Why do they use the language of rights?

rights language in their public campaigns against extreme poverty, but they tend to use human rights in limited contexts where it suits their strategic goals. The majority of social justice organizations interpret human rights in a broadly moralistic way that is synonymous with equality, justice, and dignity. They have used this moral approach to mobilize their constituencies and lobby public institutions, drawing on the strengths of human rights rhetoric to transform public discourse and cultural assumptions about poverty. Moral approaches to rights allow these groups to avoid some of the challenges inherent in a legal approach, yet by divorcing themselves from legal discourse and institutions, moral approaches contain their own set of challenges to making subsistence rights advocacy effective.

Definitions

SJ = poverty

I define the social justice movement as the sustained, collective efforts to combat extreme poverty through both institutional lobbying and extrainstitutional organizing. The movement includes lobbying groups, think tanks, academic institutes, labor unions, religious groups, indigenous groups, and influential individuals. While organizations that explicitly self-identify as human rights organizations would certainly be part of this broad movement, they have a distinct history and identity, therefore were the focus of the previous chapter.

Social movements are not neatly bounded entities, but are ongoing phenomena whose activity ebbs and flows, and whose parameters are largely defined by the observer.[5] Social movements are often comprised of heterogeneous groups with different and conflicting goals, which change throughout the course of a movement.[6] Thus, language that describes social movements as unitary actors with fixed goals, a consistent repertoire of actions, and a single trajectory should be considered problematic.

Nevertheless, the broad parameters of the social movement for economic and social justice have been defined, even if loosely. While definitions of social movements differ, Doug McAdam and David Snow note that most include sustained, organized collective action for social change that includes at least some "extrainstitutional protest."[7] This distinguishes social movement groups from humanitarian NGOs, whose primary or exclusive role tends to be service delivery or project implementation on a global scale.[8] Activists themselves also make similar distinctions between human rights, social justice, and humanitarian organizations. For example, the International Network for Economic, Social and Cultural Rights (ESCR-Net) distinguishes traditional human rights organizations from "social movements" or "grassroots social justice groups," the latter typically being defined as more closely rooted in local communities.[9]

While the terms "social justice" or "economic justice"[10] do not lend themselves to a single, unambiguous definition either, these are terms commonly used by activists and organizations within the antipoverty movement to describe their own work.[11] Paul Farmer explains that "people who work for social justice, regardless of their own station in life, tend to see the world as deeply flawed. They see the conditions of the poor not only as unacceptable but as the result of structural violence that is human-made."[12]

A sample of organizations in the United States that explicitly identify their work in these terms includes groups like Public Citizen, the Bank Information Center, the Center for Economic Justice, the Women's International Coalition for Economic Justice, Bread for the World, the Center of Concern, the One Campaign, the Kensington Welfare Rights Union, and the Women's Economic Agenda Project.

Explaining the Social Justice Movement's Increasing Use of Human Rights

For centuries, aggrieved groups of all kinds have been framing their struggles in terms of rights. As Philip Alston notes, "Proclamation of the existence of human, natural or other forms of inalienable rights as a means by which to mobilize public support through the invocation of high moral principles in a given cause or struggle is a time-honored and proven technique."[13] Likewise, groups have struggled for centuries under the banners of social justice, economic equality, the elimination of poverty, and similar goals. However, even as human rights became more institutionalized and internationalized by the mid-twentieth century, there was a notable lack of social justice groups, particularly in the United States, applying a human rights framework to their work on extreme poverty.

This situation has changed over the past decade. Clifford Bob argues that "today grievances rooted in identity, ethnicity, disability, occupation, poverty, homelessness—all are framed in rights terms."[14] The trend "seems to be cropping up in different areas all across the United States simultaneously."[15] For example, the Poor People's Economic Human Rights Campaign, a national coalition of grassroots groups fighting for basic subsistence, grew from a

handful of organizations to more than sixty within a five-year period.[16] When
Food First, a national antihunger research and advocacy group, organized
congressional hearings on U.S. food policy as part of its 1998 "Economic
Human Rights: The Time Has Come" campaign, over 180 local social justice
groups participated nationwide.[17]

Other examples of the reconnection of human rights and social justice
movements in the last ten years are too numerous to mention, but a few
cases may serve to illustrate the trend. Local constituency-based groups
have begun to frame some of their mobilizing campaigns in rights-based
terms, such as the Kensington Welfare Rights Union in Philadelphia, the
Women's Economic Agenda Project in Oakland, the Coalition to Protect
Public Housing in Chicago, and the Coalition for Immokalee Workers in
Florida. National advocacy groups and coalitions based primarily in Washington and New York, such as Public Citizen, the Bank Information Center,
the Center of Concern, the Center for Economic Justice, the Washington
Office on Latin America, the One Campaign, and the National Mobilization
Against Sweatshops, are similarly using rights language to lobby policy mak-
ers or raise public awareness about poverty. All of these groups occasionally
receive assistance from legal-aid programs such as Legal Momentum, the
NAACP Legal Defense Fund, the Urban Justice Center, and the National
Law Center on Homelessness and Poverty, who are themselves increasingly
willing to apply international human rights law in addition to national law
to the issues that affect the poor. Academic institutes, such as the Center for
Human Rights and Global Justice at NYU and the Center for Health and
Human Rights at Harvard University, are supporting this trend by conducting research and publishing reports on the links between human rights and
social justice issues. Finally, networks have emerged in the past decade, such
as the U.S. Human Rights Network and ESCR-Net, whose explicit goals are
to facilitate communication and collaboration between social justice and
human rights organizations.

The reasons why this trend has emerged in the past ten years are closely
related to the trend among human rights organizations. During the Cold
War, any economic and social rights claims were associated with communism, which for decades stifled any expression of social justice goals in those
terms. Social movements such as the civil rights movement in the 1960s that
attempted to move the rights debate into issues of economic subsistence "got
attacked for being Commies and red-baited to death," and therefore abandoned this approach.[18] As Carol Anderson notes:

The struggle [for African American economic rights] was ultimately destroyed, however, by the Cold War and the anti-communist witch hunts, which compromised the integrity of the black leadership, twisted the definition of human rights into the hammer and sickle, and forced the NAACP to take its eyes off the prize of human rights. . . . The Southern Democrats and isolationist Republicans joined together and denounced rights, such as housing and health care, as foreign to all liberty-loving Americans and inspired by the scourge of Marxist dogma. . . .

The Cold War had obviously transformed human rights into an ideological battlefield between the Soviet Union and the United States and engulfed the struggle for black equality. The Cold War identified in stark, pejorative terms entire categories of rights as antithetical to basic American freedoms. It punished mercilessly those who advocated a more expansive definition and a more concrete commitment to those rights. And it demanded unconditional loyalty.[19]

Yet the successes that African Americans achieved through the courts in protecting a narrow range of civil rights simultaneously led to a "rights revolution" in the United States, as advocacy groups of all kinds began to frame their goals in terms of individual rights and look to the judiciary for similar protections.[20] For decades, however, the proliferation of rights claims did not address questions of extreme poverty.

In the early 1990s, there was a collection of events that led to a ripe moment for using human rights to frame struggles to combat extreme poverty. At roughly the same time that the end of the Cold War took the geopolitical edge off the old debate over human rights, and the "triumph of neoliberalism was being exalted" as an economic model, many human rights and social justice groups around the world were becoming increasingly disconcerted about growing economic inequality and the dismantling of the government's role in providing a social safety net.[21] Severe global poverty became one of the main themes of the so-called antiglobalization movement in the late 1990s; that theme was often expressed in terms of rights to basic subsistence. Young protestors marched for economic and social justice in Seattle and around the world under the banner of human rights, among other slogans.

Meanwhile, the maturation of the human rights movement meant that many legal practitioners were warming up to economic and social rights, therefore human rights experts were increasingly providing training for social justice groups interested in taking a rights-based approach to poverty. Major private foundations, particularly the Ford Foundation, which had previously failed to provide financial support for economic and social rights, began in 1995 to fund these groups.[22] With the support of these major human rights gatekeepers, economic and social rights began to emerge in the mainstream of the U.S. social justice community.

The adoption of rights-based approaches by social justice groups has also been a manifestation of more general trends that have reverberated throughout the social justice movement in the United States. Local groups involved in service delivery among the poor have been increasingly willing to take an active role in political debates and focus on the systemic causes of poverty.[23] In addition, activists have argued that a "powerful new politics of social justice is emerging" that transcends single issue campaigns or single identity-based movements, and focuses more on building horizontal coalitions across traditional fault lines.[24] Human rights has become one of the uniting themes that links these movements.

Still, compared with the total field of social justice work in the United States, the proportion of work explicitly incorporating human rights approaches is fairly small. This is due to the sheer number of social justice groups (which reaches into the thousands), to the newness of the recent trend, and to the fact that the employment of human rights rhetoric and strategies within organizations has been uneven. Many groups still find "a deep resistance to framing their work in human rather than single-identity/issue terms."[25] The majority of social justice organizations rely occasionally on human rights language when it fits a particular campaign strategy, or frame a particular program consistently in human rights terms while other programs within the same organization are not explicitly rights oriented. For example, Public Citizen frames its Water for All program fairly consistently in human rights terms, including advocacy around international law, but much less so in its other programs on food, energy policy, democracy, or global trade.[26]

Likewise, Bread for the World, a national Christian antihunger advocacy group, began its work in 1975 with a human rights orientation (through lobbying for the Right to Food resolution in Congress), but has since mostly abandoned an explicit rights-based approach for various reasons.[27] Even though many of Bread's 50,000 members are personally motivated by human rights principles, the organization has found that framing hunger primarily around religious themes is much more effective for its particular constituency. Staff members at Bread tend to associate human rights with legal strategies, such as lobbying for U.S. ratification of international treaties, and feel that taking on such an approach would be impracticable because it would "totally change Bread's structure and mission." Additionally, Bread's organizing strategy is centered around pragmatic, short-term, tangible goals that make an immediate difference in the lives of poor people, and human rights strategies are perceived as ill-suited to this approach. Finally, Bread's staff members understand the U.S. government's historic antipathy toward legalizing economic and social rights, thus have made the decision to apply their limited resources to other approaches when trying to change U.S. policy.

Other groups have avoided using the human rights framework for reasons that "do not appear to be conceptual or ideological; rather they are structural and pragmatic."[28] For example, a global housing movement called Slum Dwellers International found resistance to human rights among local women's cooperatives largely because human rights were interpreted as legal instruments requiring a confrontational approach. Because the poor have had very little access to these processes and institutions, they determined that they had a greater chance for success through adopting a collaborative approach with state officials in lobbying for housing reforms, which they did not interpret as a human rights approach.[29] Thus the adoption of human rights by social justice groups has been variable, depending on their organizational identity, their strategic context, and what they understand the human rights framework to entail. *hr is not uniformly adopted by NGOs*

A report from the Ford Foundation explains the trend toward economic and social rights in the United States in this manner: "The shift to employing human rights in social justice work in the United States means different things to different groups. For some, its use is largely instrumental, helpful in limited contexts for a specific purpose. For others, its value is more fundamental, engendering a profound rethinking of their work from which, as one activist put it, 'there is no turning back.' Most practitioners fall somewhere in between these two positions."[30] This statement implies that some social justice organizations are motivated by strategic interests and others by principled ideas. However, these two motivating factors, the strategic and the principled, can coexist within the same organization and can be mutually supportive. Organizations that adopt human rights language because of fundamental philosophical beliefs still think strategically about how to use them; likewise, groups that utilize human rights instrumentally are unlikely to use them if they disagree with the basic principles that the rights framework implies. This is evidenced by the way in which many social justice activists re-

Figure 1. Legal Versus Moral Interpretations of Human Rights

Human rights as primarily rooted in international legal documents		Human rights understood primarily as basic moral principles

◄──►

| (Legal aid organizations) | (Kensington) | (One Campaign, Jubilee Network) |

spond derisively to the question, "What value does human rights add to your work?" They essentially reply: Of course human rights should add strategic value to our work, but of course we believe fundamentally in the principles as well.[31] When they find it advantageous, social justice organizations are strategically appropriating human rights ideas and language to serve their purposes—purposes that are encompassed by these very ideas.

Perhaps a better way to conceptualize the diversity of human rights approaches among social justice groups is to describe the extent to which each group incorporates international legal standards[32] into its rhetoric and practice (Figure 1).

At the left end of the spectrum[33] are social justice groups that embrace an understanding of human rights as primarily rooted in international legal standards. These groups tend to refer more explicitly to the international standards, such as the Universal Declaration of Human Rights and the International Covenant on Economic, Social and Cultural Rights, and tend to make greater use of legal and quasi-legal mechanisms in their work. They work with communities to "anchor local abuses in specific international human rights law."[34] As such, "the incorporation of human rights among these groups has not so much expanded their substantive focus, but rather added an international element to their existing domestic rights advocacy."[35] For example, the National Law Center on Homelessness and Poverty is increasingly incorporating international human rights law into their training programs for housing activists, adding it to their existing training agenda on local and national law.[36]

To the extent that social justice groups adopt this kind of approach, they come to resemble traditional human rights organizations more closely. For the human rights gatekeepers, who also associate human rights with international legal standards (and who were the subject of the previous chapter), these are the social justice groups that are "really doing human rights work."[37] Like human rights organizations, these groups do not focus exclusively on legal strategies or understand human rights exclusively in legal terms. In fact, for social justice groups there is often a different motivating logic underlying their legal campaigns; they tend to use legal approaches to "lend credibility to organizing efforts"[38] rather than to build an expanding web of legal practices and institutions that can be enforceable on the state. Nevertheless, in these efforts, the moral power of human rights cannot be unhinged from their tangible manifestation in positive international law.

In the middle of the spectrum are organizations that often straddle the legal/moral divide. Largely due to the support they receive from human rights gatekeepers and other organizations, these social justice groups have occasionally matched tactics with their donors in particular campaigns. For example, the Kensington Welfare Rights Union, which began as a group of women organizing around local poverty issues, eventually spearheaded the Poor People's Economic Human Rights Campaign in 1997 in response to the welfare reform law enacted the year before. That campaign is explicitly premised on the Universal Declaration of Human Rights, and organizing strategies have revolved around documenting and publicizing economic rights violations against the poor across the country. The campaign is also making use of courts and quasi-legal mechanisms, collaborating with other organizations in suing the United States at the Inter-American Commission on Human Rights for its alleged violation of the right to housing.[39] But for Kensington as well, even its legal strategies are directed toward the goals of public education, alliance building, and grassroots mobilization, more than judicial enforcement itself. This is what Michael McCann calls the "legal mobilization" approach, wherein the law is defined as a set of cultural symbols that can give social movements power to shape public policy as much as, or more than, the power of legal accountability.[40]

The vast majority of social justice groups that have adopted human rights language in fighting extreme poverty fall on the other side of the spectrum; I argue that they are "really doing human rights" as well. These are myriad social justice groups that use human rights language to define their work, but tend not to associate human rights directly with international legal standards.[41] They can use human rights either consistently or occasionally, and can be motivated both philosophically and strategically, but their interpretation of what human rights *are*—that is, what is important about the human rights framework—differs from the legal understanding. They tend to understand human rights as basic moral principles that may have a historic connection to international legal standards, but the connection is secondary in importance to the underlying principles. For example, the One Campaign is a national coalition of religious, humanitarian, social justice, and other organizations advocating an end to extreme global poverty. Human rights language is used rarely in the One Campaign's own literature and public statements, but many of the member groups use human rights rhetoric to promote the campaign. The Irish rock band U2, whose lead singer Bono is the founder of DATA (Debt, Aid, Trade, Africa), explicitly linked social justice to human rights in its 2005 concert tour in an attempt to enlist supporters to the One Campaign. At a critical point in each concert, the Universal Declaration scrolled down the large screen behind the stage, and the band made an appeal to the audience to join the One Campaign by arguing that "everyone is equal under the eyes of God." [42] Through this appeal to human rights, U2 played a major role in enlisting over two million people to join the One Campaign over the course of several months.

Likewise, through my own work with the Ecumenical Program on Central America and my resulting contact with many of our coalition partners, I got a sense of how social justice organizations use human rights language morally to activate their constituencies and work for policy change in a variety of institutions. For example, I participated in a public demonstration in Washington, D.C., organized by the Poor People's Economic Human Rights Campaign, led by the Kensington Welfare Rights Union. This demonstration advocated for changes in U.S. antipoverty policy (e.g., affordable housing, income support, health care) using human rights language (e.g., "Poverty is a human rights violation"), with sparse and very loose reference to international legal standards. By speaking with some of the participants in the demonstration, I learned that many had very limited knowledge of, and interest in, international legal documents. Activists at both the leadership and grassroots levels were guided by a set of basic religious and moral principles that were congruent with human rights language, rather than the international legal standards that most analysts associate with human rights.

How Do Social Justice NGOs Employ a Moral Approach to Human Rights?

As the discussion above indicates, moral approaches to subsistence rights delink human rights rhetoric from its international legal sources, interpreting rights in terms of basic moral principles such as equality, dignity, and justice. Within the moral approach to human rights, "it is best to see rights as a set of ethical claims" that can lead to political action.[43] According to Cheri Honkala of the Kensington Welfare Rights Union, these claims are a "set of very basic concepts" that are based on the "essence of being human."[44] As Fernando Garcia of the Border Network on Human Rights has stated, "Human rights are about equality and dignity."[45]

Even when activists refer to international documents in this context, they often refer to the Universal Declaration of Human Rights (UDHR) rather than binding international law because the Universal Declaration spells out rights in their preinstitutionalized, nonelaborated form. Thus, even experienced and knowledgeable activists within this perspective tend to use rights language via more general slogans. A typical example of this interpretation of human rights is found in Paul Farmer's *Pathologies of Power*, a book that urges the reader to understand public health as a basic human right.[46] "Human rights" is in the subtitle of the book; rights rhetoric is ubiquitous throughout; and human rights is clearly a central organizing theme of the book. Yet in the nearly four hundred pages, international human rights law (primarily Articles 25 and 27 of the UDHR) is referred to exceedingly sparingly, and "human rights" is used interchangeably with social justice, equity, ethics, and the principles that underlie liberation theology.

Another example of the moral use of human rights language is when documentary filmmaker Michael Moore appeared on the *Oprah Winfrey Show* in September 2007 to discuss his film *Sicko*. Oprah Winfrey maintains an extremely loyal audience of millions of Americans, and having an issue discussed on her show is something of a cultural litmus test of mainstream legitimacy. This program investigated the gaps in the American health-care system, and centered around the question, "Do we believe that everyone has the fundamental right to health care?"[47] The participants in the show made several powerful arguments throughout the program that health care should be considered a basic right, and should be guaranteed as a public good in the United States, without once mentioning international law or legal strategies.

The principles that underlie this conception of human rights are generally the same as those that underlie legal standards, but they are typically expressed in a form that avoids legal language. When applied to subsistence rights, these principles include, for example, that the most vulnerable should be protected from suffering, the poor should be empowered to participate in the decisions that affect their lives, government should be held accountable for its policies to provide basic needs, and the poor should be protected from discrimination on the basis of their identity.

This kind of moral rights rhetoric can often precede legal institutional-ization and enforcement,[48] but legalization is not a necessary later step for human rights to retain their power as important tools for social justice. Human rights become a set of claims that lead to social and political action, sometimes but not necessarily in the legal realm. Making subsistence rights justiciable and legally enforceable is undoubtedly good, but it is not the focus of their work. Therefore, the debate about subsistence rights does not revolve around whether they are valid legal instruments, but whether they are use-ful tools for social action. Policies and practices are critiqued based on their deviance from these basic moral principles rather than their illegality.

A moral approach to rights focuses on the social power of the claiming process itself, rather than the formal institutional sources of the claim. Social justice advocates often stress the need for the poor to define their own rights. Thus, for the social justice movement, the moral approach focuses primar-ily on the power of human rights language to resonate with and mobilize particular constituencies—nonlawyers, nonprofessional activists, the con-cerned public, and most important, the poor themselves. As Farmer argues, human rights is "best understood (that is, most accurately and comprehen-sively grasped) from the point of view of the poor."[49] As such, human rights language "can be a powerful organizing tool" to motivate political activism, because "human rights standards of economic and social justice give every human being and every community a powerful tool of struggle."[50] As one U.S. housing advocate describes, rights-based arguments about basic subsistence "appeal to populations we work with to organize themselves."[51] According to the Ford Foundation report: " 'Most people have no idea how isolated and unsupported poor people are, or how powerless, unimportant, and small they are made to feel,' said Chris Caruso, founder of Human Rights Tech, a Phila-delphia nonprofit organization that counsels grassroots anti-poverty groups on using the Internet. According to Caruso, human rights language empow-ers poor people by offering a vision for a better life and a better future. 'It gives them a reason to speak for themselves and fight back,' Caruso said."[52]

Is This Approach "Merely" Rhetorical?

If so many social justice groups are adopting human rights language in a form that is virtually interchangeable with "equality, dignity, and social justice," what difference does human rights make? Some practitioners worry that social justice organizations are using human rights as "mere packaging" for their preexisting goals related to economic redistribution.[53] Private foundations review grant applications and often come away with the impression that many groups are framing their grant proposals in human rights terms just to get funding. In that sense, is the shift to human rights just empty rhetoric?

There are two answers to this question. The first is that for most social justice groups the shift to human rights has been more than rhetorical, even though they still use human rights language less often and less systematically than traditional human rights organizations. Even when they do not explicitly draw from international standards or use legal mechanisms, a human rights approach engenders a profound change in practice for some groups, away from a service delivery or charity model and toward more participatory, empowering advocacy strategy. For example, the Border Network for Human Rights has developed a rights-based approach to organizing, whereby communities on the Texas-Mexico border participate directly in training leaders, identifying problems, and making decisions about the abuses that happen to immigrants. Despite the fact that they often cite legal documents, their "philosophy is not that rights come from the Constitution or the United Nations; rather, rights are understood to arise from communities themselves."[54] Human rights approaches also lead to new documentation strategies and other tactics to help the poor address the economic policies and institutions that affect them.[55] While some of these tactics require an orientation toward international legal standards (such as documenting violations of international law), others do not.

The second answer is that even when the human rights shift is primarily or exclusively rhetorical, it is misleading to describe this change as empty or meaningless. Scholars of social movements, agenda setting, and political communication frequently note that there are strategic implications to framing, naming, or branding an issue in a particular way. "Mere" rhetoric can serve important purposes to strategic actors, whether it is to attract public attention, inspire sympathy, gain funding, enlist new members, or guide an organization's internal decision-making process. Mary Ann Glendon argues: "The way we name things and discuss them shapes our feelings, judgments, choices, and actions, including political actions. History has repeatedly driven home the lesson that it is unwise to dismiss political language as 'mere rhetoric.'"[56] As an example, Glendon points to the contrasting ideas about social responsibility that are weaved into the rights language of European and American legal systems. She concludes that the specific attributes of rights rhetoric "seems related importantly to the shape of the welfare system in each country—its basic commitments, the spirit in which it is administered, the degree of support and approval it receives from taxpayers, and the extent to which it disables or empowers those who depend on it." [57]

Rhetoric provides the central weapon in battles to legitimize ideas and the actors who hold them. Therefore a better question to ask than "Is it empty rhetoric?" is, "What actors and actions does this rhetoric legitimize?" Social justice organizations use human rights rhetoric to legitimize not only their own existence, but also an understanding of poverty that would profoundly change our cultural assumptions. In that sense, human rights language has important implications for how extreme poverty is framed and understood. Additionally, a moral approach to human rights has different implications in terms of how we understand poverty and its alleviation than a legal approach does. Both of these claims will be explored in detail in the rest of this chapter.

How Human Rights Rhetoric Changes
Public Discourse About Poverty

Using human rights rhetoric to make claims for guarantees against extreme poverty has particular kinds of political implications. It legitimizes some kinds of activities and condemns others. It activates certain actors and provides them with a basis for acting.

The first, and perhaps most obvious, strength of rights-based approaches to poverty is that human rights principles are nearly universally recognizable and broadly perceived as legitimate—they are the "lingua franca of global moral thought." [58] This is not to downplay the ideological debates over human rights, it is simply to say that despite those debates, the basic principles underlying human dignity "bite in a way that other things don't" because of their broad appeal. [59] As one practitioner explains, people "mostly get excited about human rights because it gives them a legitimacy they didn't feel they had. That the whole world recognizes that their claim is valid means a lot to them." [60] Invoking any claim as a human right implies that the right is applicable to all persons equally and individually, by virtue of their human identity rather than their membership in a territorial, ethnic, gender, or other identity-based community.

Human rights are also described as the only antipoverty framework that is fundamentally rules based, and any solutions arising from rights discourse ought to be principled and consistent. This is true whether speaking of rights as general moral standards or as concrete legal obligations. Human rights language goes beyond earlier notions of social justice and equality based in socialism because it restricts the actions that challengers are allowed to take, and requires them to redirect their energy into principled, nonviolent reform leading to social guarantees for the poor.[61] Thus human rights language tends to delegitimize violent revolution as an appropriate response to extreme poverty.

Another strength of the rights discourse is that it explicitly addresses political and legal institutions, particularly the state, by demanding accountability for each individual.[62] Invoking rights implies a corresponding duty for other actors to respect, protect, or fulfill the right. Human rights rhetoric demands that powerful actors be accountable to everyone, but particularly the most vulnerable, the worst off, and the most marginalized sectors of a population. As such, human rights discourse identifies different policy priorities than other frameworks might, and it places the individual person at the center of any justifying strategy.[63] Growth in GDP or other national-level statistics are therefore inadequate measures of whether social obligations are being fulfilled; rather, the state has the duty to ensure, to the best of its ability, that every person has access to an adequate standard of living. The human rights framework provides "powerfully incisive normative critiques" when a state or other actor fails in its basic obligations.[64] In fact, human rights discourse has been criticized for being too state-centric, and certainly legal human rights frameworks have historically concentrated on the state. One advantage of a moral approach to human rights is that it is immediately and clearly applicable to all actors at all levels.

Promoting individual well-being as the state's raison d'être provides tremendous leverage for activists to demand certain policies from the state.[65] Because of this, human rights can become a tool of power that the poor and marginalized use against states that fail to fulfill their legal, political, and/or moral obligations. In addition to the potential of human rights strategies to change legislation or policy, the process of invoking rights can be empowering in itself, as claimants do research, get educated, mobilize others, and speak out on their own behalf.[66] While human rights may not be the most powerful weapon, "human rights languages are perhaps *all that we have* to interrogate the barbarism of power, even when these remain inadequate to fully humanize the practices of the politics of cruelty."[67]

The promise inherent in the use of rights language, therefore, is to fundamentally redefine poverty and reframe the terms of public debate surrounding poverty.[68] Human rights approaches define poverty not as misfortune, divine will, or individual failure, but as a structural deficit and a public responsibility. Thus, in working for solutions to poverty, subsistence rights direct our focus on institutional and systemic pathways and obstacles to individual well-being.

Human rights language offers activists the potential to reframe public debate on poverty by reshaping our understanding of the issue itself, and by adding value and filling in gaps that other approaches leave open. While many different discourses on poverty exist, practically all of which can be used simultaneously, I will focus on a few of the most common and noteworthy, including charity, self-interest, and religious arguments.

Perhaps the most common way that issues like poverty, hunger and disease are framed in the West is through the lens of charity. Poverty is framed as a "private trouble instead of a public issue," as politicians, aid organizations, and celebrities frequently ask for compassion, sympathy, and kindness in response.[69] Within the charity frame, solutions to poverty arise from gifts rather than obligations or institutional changes. Although private charity is obviously important, the problem with this frame is that it reinforces assumptions that "make the most outrageous injustices appear normal."[70] Framing poverty in terms of charity depoliticizes the issue, excuses the state from its obligations, and stigmatizes the poor by emphasizing their cultural and socioeconomic distance from everyone else.[71] After all, "one cannot demand charity. All one can do is plead for it."[72] Charity-based frames therefore silence the poor by failing to question the assumption—so prevalent in the U.S. culture—of individualism, that the poor are exclusively responsible for their own well-being.[73] Charity also does not question the donor-beneficiary relationship or the donors' supposed entitlement to their own wealth. In addition, charitable responses by themselves have historically proven insufficient to meet the scale of the need, either globally or domestically, and are unlikely to do so in the near future.[74]

Rights-based approaches attempt to correct these deficiencies by explicitly addressing institutions and injustice, and by turning passive victims and dependent beneficiaries into active claimants.[75] Poor people and victims of human rights violations thereby can make demands without embarrassment or shame,[76] and subsistence rights approaches provide the opportunity for people to educate themselves about what they can legitimately claim.[77] In effect, human rights approaches try to reframe what is perceived as normal as an outrageous injustice, and as such are diametrically opposed to charity-based understandings of poverty. Within a rights-based approach, private charity may play a role in the solution to poverty, but the fundamental justification for alleviating poverty and the assignment of responsibility are wholly different.

Another widely used approach is to frame solutions to poverty in terms of utilitarian costs and benefits, economic efficiency, and enlightened self-interest. This approach is not incompatible with subsistence rights, and is also a form of moral discourse, but it has significant limitations when standing alone. A common (and historically accurate) argument within this understanding is that reducing extreme poverty ultimately benefits people in wealthy countries by providing a market for their exports.[78] In that sense, it is claimed that "investment in people has high rates of return."[79] A related argument is that it is less expensive, in both economic and human terms, to deal with poverty sooner rather than later, before extreme poverty sows the seeds of violence and insecurity.[80] Before September 11, 2001, many people in the United States argued that it was possible to insulate ourselves from the negative effects of extreme poverty, but since 9/11, the self-interested elimination of extreme poverty has become the "standard fare of strategic analysis."[81] Because economic growth is often seen as simultaneously a key to long-term poverty reduction and the self-interests of the wealthy, policies that prioritize growth tend to be favored by those who employ this frame. In that sense, Jeffrey Sachs has framed global antipoverty efforts as an "investment" toward a form of "enlightened globalization" that creates new markets and reinforces peace.[82] Describing the elimination of poverty as economically efficient (i.e., supportive of economic growth) also ties it to our cultural notions of what "modernization" and "development" should entail.[83]

However, approaching poverty through a rights-based lens adds important elements to these arguments: "The human rights discourse is a powerful means to counter [the] casting of social issues like hunger as questions of mere economic efficiency and numerical cost/benefit analysis. It is profoundly different to talk about hunger in terms of human rights. When we speak in numbers we might decide that while 30 million hungry are too many, 18 million might be an acceptable policy goal. But if we say that food is a human right, that we all have the inalienable right to be able to feed ourselves and our families, then to have even one hungry family in the richest nation on Earth constitutes a human rights violation, and must be fully addressed."[84]

Indeed, framing economic and social issues in terms of cost-efficiency can threaten the realization of human rights for the most vulnerable as, for example, efficiency arguments are frequently used to deny access to medical care for the poor.[85] As Farmer notes, "A human rights approach to health economics and health policy helps to bring into relief the ill effects of the efficacy-equity trade-off: that is, only if unnecessary sickness and premature death don't matter can inegalitarian systems ever be considered efficacious." [86] By focusing attention on individual people at risk, human rights requires that certain populations cannot be overlooked in the name of economic efficiency or the greater good. Nevertheless, William Schulz has argued correctly that the human rights movement needs to incorporate more arguments based on enlightened self-interest if they hope to win public approval.[87]

Finally, rights-based approaches to dealing with poverty differ from religious appeals. For example, faith-based organizations like Bread for the World often frame their antihunger messages in Biblical terminology because it resonates with their constituency. In the United States, religious appeals can be powerful tools to bridge political divides, as witnessed by the inclusion of the televangelist Pat Robertson and other conservative Christians in the One Campaign coalition.[88] Yet arguing that ending poverty is the "highest purpose under heaven," although extremely powerful in certain contexts, is obviously limited by the particularities of the audience it targets.[89]

Challenges Inherent in a Moral Approach to Subsistence Rights

By taking a moral approach to human rights, social justice organizations are able to advance a transformative vision of poverty through highly resonant and accessible language. Even so, moral rights discourse is sufficiently ambiguous that it can often be used in a way that is counterproductive or confusing to the speaker's own strategic goals. Because they are not grounded in a specific corpus of law, moral approaches to rights open organizations up to additional ambiguity in terms of what specific policies subsistence rights require. Because social justice organizations are so ideologically diverse, the range of policies promoted is extremely large, which complicates the task of developing a unified and unifying message on subsistence rights. Two of the most common ambiguities involve how social justice organizations treat notions of "justice" and "equality."

Human Rights as "Justice"

Although human rights and social justice movements are successfully reframing poverty as an issue of justice rather than charity, in practice these activists often use the "justice" terminology ambiguously. As a result, multiple

Figure 2. Human Rights as "Social Justice"

┌------------------"Human rights / Social justice"-----------------┐

◄───►

Legal rights:	"Thick" social justice:	"Thin" social justice:	Charity:
The state is legally obligated toward the poor.	Causal link established, resulting in moral obligation toward poor.	No causal link, but the poor deserve to have their basic needs met.	No causal link, no obligation to help.

conceptions of justice arise within the rights-based approach, in part because participants approach the idea of social and economic justice from very different philosophical perspectives.[90] Activists would be well served to clarify their definitions and focus on a justice-based frame that is most effective in the particular context in which they operate (Figure 2).

Human rights and social justice frames are fundamentally incompatible with the charity-based approach to poverty that defines assistance as gifts that are subject to the individual preferences of the donor. As such, they challenge the conventional wisdom about poverty, as noted on the right end of the spectrum. Yet a rights-based approach to basic subsistence can manifest itself in at least three conceptions of social justice, each of which has different cultural and political implications. One understanding of justice is what I have labeled "thin" social justice, which is closest to the charity-based approach in that it does not attempt to establish any direct causal link between society (i.e., its structures, institutions, and actions) and the condition of the poor. The "thin" social justice approach, however, does base its policy advocacy on the argument that the poor deserve to have their basic needs met because of the dignity and equality of all people. These are the kinds of rights-based frames predominantly used by the One Campaign's member organizations, the Jubilee Network, and other politically centrist, bipartisan social justice movements. For them, poverty is an injustice because it is unfair that the poor are denied subsistence in an era when society has the technical capacity to provide for those needs, yet social institutions themselves are rarely the target of criticism as the source of poverty in the first place.

A large number of social justice organizations adopting a rights-based approach have explicitly based it on a critique of social structures and institutions as the root causes of poverty. I have labeled this approach "thick" social justice, by which an argument about the causal link between society and poverty forms the basis for an appeal to society's political and moral obligation to create solutions. The target of criticism within society can be the state, but can also include market forces, corporations, racism, classism, sexism, and other structures, practices and institutions. This kind of approach to justice is common among politically progressive organizations like the Center for Economic Justice and the Ecumenical Program on Central America. For them, an appeal to human rights means not only that poor people deserve subsistence, but also that those actors who are implicated in the root causes of poverty are obligated to create solutions. An example of particularly sharp rhetoric from this perspective comes from the Poor People's Economic Human Rights Campaign (PPEHRC), which claims that the U.S. government is "committing grave human rights violations against its own people," and that U.S. economic policies "impoverish and kill people" and are the "real weapons of mass destruction."[91]

At the far end of the spectrum are social justice organizations that argue for both moral and legal responsibility to ensure subsistence for the poor. Because the focus is on legal obligations, they tend to direct attention primarily (but not exclusively) at the state, and base the state's obligations on international human rights law. When the state fails to live up to its obligations—thus becomes implicated in the causes of extreme poverty—they argue that it has committed a violation of a particular legal standard, not simply a dereliction of its moral or political duty. These are the activities that resemble the methods of traditional human rights organizations, which view rights as primarily rooted in international legal standards. For them, poverty is an injustice when private or public actors commit a violation against legal standards that provide poor people with legal entitlements.

The political and cultural implications of these wide-ranging conceptions of justice within human rights approaches should be fairly self-evident. The further an organization moves to the left of the spectrum above, the more it directly challenges the predominant assumptions within U.S. culture about individual responsibility and the proper role for the state in the economy. This is in many ways the most powerful kind of critique, yet it inevitably invites counterattack. According to an *Economist* editorial that is fairly typical of more conservative thinking on the issue: "They are quite right, these champions of the world's poor, that poverty in an age of plenty is shameful and disgusting. But they are quite wrong to suppose, as so many of them do, that the rich enjoy their privileges at the expense of the poor—that poverty, in other words, is inseparable from a system, capitalism, that thrives on injustice. This way of thinking is not just false. It entrenches the very problem it purports to address."[92]

Thus, while a "thick" justice frame or a legal approach can appeal to and mobilize a movement's most dedicated members, it can also alienate large portions of the U.S. population so long as the predominant way of framing poverty remains oriented toward charity. This is why an organization like Bread for the World or the One Campaign, whose membership spans the ideological spectrum and whose organizing strategy deliberately attempts to appeal to the political middle, chooses to frame its approach to poverty in "thin" justice terms.

One possible outcome of this heterogeneity within the social justice and human rights movements is described by the radical flank effect, in which more extreme elements within the movement (for example, those who take a "thicker" approach to justice) make moderates' positions appear more attractive and safe, thereby allowing moderates to achieve political gains.[93] Although positive radical flank effects are the focus of much of the academic literature on this topic, there are also several possible harmful effects of this intramovement diversity, including that moderates may be disregarded or demonized because of their association with radical elements.[94] Haines's study of the U.S. civil rights movement showed that moderate groups like the NAACP took advantage of a positive radical flank effect only because they were able to clearly articulate their goals and dissociate themselves from more radical or violent groups. On the other hand, Gupta's study of Welsh and Basque nationalist movements demonstrated that when distinctions between moderate and radical groups are not clearly framed and understood, then negative effects are more likely (i.e., moderates are harmed by being associated with radicals).[95] For U.S. social justice groups advocating freedom from poverty, the risk of a negative radical flank effect looms large, due to the ease with which any claim to economic rights can be disparaged as socialist, foreign, and un-American. Because these organizations take such different approaches to justice, which involve vastly different models of political accountability, the challenge is for social justice organizations to develop a consistent message that resonates within the existing cultural environment.

Human Rights as "Equality"

Another source of ambiguity and some conceptual confusion within the human rights and social justice discourses arises from the close association between human rights and notions of equality. Equality-based themes suffuse virtually all rights-based approaches, but "equality" takes on vastly different meanings in different contexts; these meanings are often implicit rather than explicit. For example, when activists claim that "human rights are about equality," do they mean that all human beings are born equal in dignity (i.e., philosophical equality)?[96] That people should receive equal protection under the law (i.e., nondiscrimination and procedural equality)? That the state should ensure an equal provision of public goods (i.e., distributional equality)?[97] That there should be an equality of outcomes among the population on a range of social and economic indicators (i.e., substantive equality)?[98] Or some combination of the above? Participants in the movement have associated human rights with all of these notions, some of which are in conflict, and all of which have different political implications.

There is a virtual consensus within the human rights movement, and widespread support within U.S. culture, in favor of equal dignity and procedural equality. It is well accepted that people are born equal in dignity, and that the state should not be allowed to arbitrarily discriminate against anyone in implementing the law. The Universal Declaration of Human Rights explicitly recognizes the concepts of equal dignity, equality before the law, and equal protection against discrimination.[99] In that sense, equity insofar as it relates to economic subsistence could be defined as "making the rules fair for poor people and ensuring that [procedural] justice prevails."[100]

However, for those who promote notions of distributional or substantive equality, any significant inequality of outcomes (i.e., relative poverty) is itself a human rights violation.[101] There are two problems with this kind of equality frame: First, it defies common sense, since two highly unequal people can both be wealthy and have their subsistence rights met. There is an enormous amount of social and economic inequality between me and Bill Gates (at least for the moment), but I would never claim that my subsistence rights are being threatened as a result. Second, arguments about distributional and substantive equality conjure up images of utopian socialism, a frame that has little chance of success in the United States or the post–Cold War world. Thomas Sowell dismisses this perspective as a "quest for cosmic justice" and argues that even if inequities need to be corrected, "the knowledge required to sort this out intellectually, much less rectify it politically, is staggering and superhuman."[102] He argues that distributional and substantive equality remains "the hallmark of the intellectual elite that advocates an expanding agenda of government intervention, regulation, and redistributive welfare statism."[103]

Health-care professionals have admitted that "it is hard, perhaps impossible, to meet the highest standards of health care in every situation"—that is, distributional equality—as Article 12 of the International Covenant on Economic, Social and Cultural Rights seems to require.[104] As Michael Mandler has noted, if you promote human rights as distributional or substantive equality, "you will find yourself on a slippery slope. Why talk to us about equality in health care, they'll ask you, when all you really want to do is redistribute wealth?" There's a "suspicion that a sweeping agenda underlies the call for redistribution."[105] There is probably some merit in this suspicion, because a number of social justice groups have more revolutionary redistributive plans in mind when they speak of economic and social rights. For example, at the inaugural conference of the U.S. Human Rights Network, which was titled "No Retreat, No Compromise,"[106] one speaker at the opening plenary received vigorous applause when she identified herself as a "communist" (which she defined as sharing resources equally), and another called for nonviolent "revolution."[107] Although this rhetoric can be energizing for specific constituencies, these framings of social justice have little chance of resonating with wider segments of the American public or policy makers.

Because of this, it would garner greater support in the United States to disassociate human rights from notions of distributional and substantive equality, and to reconnect subsistence rights with the notion of a minimum standard, or what Henry Shue calls the "morality of the depths."[108] The notion of subsistence rights as a floor below which no one can fall is consistent with philosophical and procedural equality, and is not based on "some utopian vision of equality" but on the claim that "society must ensure universal access to some things."[109] Under this approach, even some extreme levels of inequality may be acceptable so long as everyone is living above a minimum standard.[110] Thus, the goal of promoting subsistence rights is not necessarily to end all poverty, or to close the gap between the rich and poor, but to end a very specific kind of extreme poverty that denies people their right to physical survival.[111] This is why some subsistence rights activists describe the goal of human rights as ending extreme inequality, rather than achieving substantive equality.[112] The distinction may seem slight, but it has important implications. This way of framing human rights as equality is marketable to a broad portion of the U.S. population, and politically feasible in terms of the solutions required. Economists estimate that an additional $40–70 billion in aid specifically targeted toward the fulfillment of basic needs around the world would result in drastic improvements in extreme poverty.[113] While this amount might sound daunting, it represents far less than 1 percent of developed nations' annual income, thus would cause neither significant economic dislocation nor any radical equalization of global wealth.

In sum, social justice organizations face important strategic decisions about whether to frame their campaigns in human rights terms. Even if they choose a rights-based approach, they must decide how to express notions of equality and justice in a way that most effectively resonates with their constituencies and wider audiences. Because moral approaches to subsistence rights are grounded in the heterogeneous practices and perspectives of a wide range of social justice groups, the challenge is to develop and promote a consistent message as a movement, or at least a complementary set of messages.

How Do Moral Approaches to Rights Differ from Legal Approaches in Their Strategic Effects?

As I mentioned above, the majority of social justice organizations that have adopted human rights approaches to fight extreme poverty understand human rights as primarily rooted in basic moral principles, regardless of their expression in international legal documents. Human rights lawyers often welcome moral approaches to rights but argue that it never hurts to understand the legal aspect of rights. While this is true, what human rights lawyers tend not to acknowledge is that a legal approach to rights imposes costs that may be greater than the benefits that it provides for social justice organizations. In the previous chapter, I discussed several challenges inherent in a legal approach to human rights, including the fact that courts have been unwilling to adjudicate subsistence rights; the U.S. government opposes economic and social rights; legal rights language is inaccessible to most activists; and international legal standards have failed to resolve ideological debates about the content of rights, the obligations of various actors, and the required solutions to end poverty. I now turn to a discussion of how the moral approach modifies, helps to resolve, or similarly confronts some of the same challenges inherent in the legal approach.

Making Courts More Willing and Able to Adjudicate Subsistence Rights

Legal rights are implementable when courts are willing and empowered to enforce them. Courts throughout the world have been reluctant to enforce subsistence rights not because of any inherent nonjusticiability of subsistence rights, but because of the predominant cultural assumptions about rights and the perceived role of the courts in interpreting them. In order for more progressive judicial interpretations to be perceived as acceptable and legitimate, those basic cultural assumptions must change first. This is precisely what the social justice movement is attempting to do with subsistence rights.

Constitutional scholar Jack Balkin has noted that social movements have two types of influence over judicial interpretations of the law.[114] In the first instance, social movements work through the political process to elect presidents and legislatures they believe will be sympathetic to their cause, who then appoint like-minded judges to the courts. As the 2005 battles over the nominations of Justices John Roberts and Samuel Alito to the U.S. Supreme Court illustrate, the composition of courts matter in how laws are interpreted, and the influence of social movements to affect that composition is widely recognized. Second, social movements also work in the informal arena of public opinion to have their own interpretation of the law legitimized. Because judges tend to adopt similar beliefs and assumptions as other national elites, they often unwittingly respond to changes in broad cultural ideas about what is and is not plausible legal reasoning. In other words, "by changing the background expectations of judges and lawyers," social movements "reshape constitutional common sense, moving the boundaries of what is plausible and implausible in the world of constitutional interpretation, what is thinkable legal argument and what is constitutionally 'off the wall.'"[115] Balkin explains that these two processes create a pattern in which judicial decisions generally tend to mirror public opinion over the long term.

For example, legal scholar Cass Sunstein described an interpretive change in the U.S. Supreme Court between 1923 and 1937 on minimum wage law in precisely these terms.[116] He states: "What is most striking [in the Court's interpretation of the minimum wage] is the reversal of what is considered a subsidy. In 1923 a minimum wage law was seen as forcing employers to subsidize the community; fifteen years later, the absence of a minimum wage law was forcing the community to subsidize employers." According to Sunstein and Bruce Ackerman, the text of the Constitution and the major actors on the Court remained the same, but the cultural understanding of minimum wage law was turned on its head by a "massive popular movement that did the same work as literal constitutional change."[117] Balkin cites a similar example of the Supreme Court mostly following, rather than leading, changes in national attitudes about segregation in its 1954 *Brown v. Board of Education* ruling.[118]

Although sometimes social movements' interpretive claims are couched in legal arguments, often they are broad, informal appeals to justice, liberty, equality, or even self-interest and protection.[119] As such, "when social movements successfully appeal to changes in the social world, they not only shift perceptions of facts but also reshape the values that are used to interpret and frame those facts. Social movements promote constitutional change by shaping the public's (and especially political elites') experience of salience and relevance, through tutoring their common sense about how the world has changed and what should be done about it. When a social movement is truly successful, judges will see their conception of the social world not as the forbidden imposition of personal values on an unwilling public but as the application of simple common sense.[120]

Thus "successful legal strategies, not just human rights but any legal strategies, depend upon having a degree of public support, enough standing, that will enable judges to do the right thing."[121] Public support, in turn, depends on changing the predominant cultural understandings that pervade a society; therefore culture becomes one of the main rhetorical battlegrounds on which social movements fight. In that sense, much of the work to be done for subsistence rights needs to take place outside of legal arenas, and in the often intangible realm of what Paul Wapner calls "civic politics."[122] The role of social justice organizations in this struggle, employing their moral approach to rights, is to legitimize a justice-based understanding of poverty that changes society's notion of its responsibility to end poverty.

Making Rights Language Accessible and Empowering

The kind of cultural change discussed above requires a strong and active social movement. Balkin concludes that the best strategy to protect legal rights is not only through litigation or changes in legislation, but simply to become stronger politically by gaining members and resources.[123] As Chidi Anselm Odinkalu contends, "Throughout history, the protection of human rights has been won through struggle, and struggle requires mobilization."[124] In turn, effective mobilization requires a clear, consistent message and "an accessible strategy that people can relate to their daily lives."[125] Human rights as basic moral principles provide this clear message in a way that everyone can understand. After all, the "most fundamental training that's needed is just to get people to know that these [rights] are theirs to claim. That's all."[126] The technical language of international legal standards, while based in the same fundamental principles, can be a stumbling block toward grassroots empowerment. Legal rights discourse leads to a technical discussion between experts over justiciability, customary law, legal exceptions, progressive realization, core content, maximum available resources, and transnational obligations, often stifling the empowering expression of the basic principles by grassroots activists. As David Kennedy suggests: "Increasingly, people of good will concerned about poverty are drawn into debate about a series of ultimately impossible legal quandaries—right of whom, against whom, remediable how, and so on—and into institutional projects of codification and reporting familiar from other human rights efforts, without evaluating how these might compare with other uses for this talent and these resources." [127] This is why Sarah Blackstock of the Canadian National Anti-Poverty Organization has argued: "Even for the anti-poverty movement, it is hard to see how human rights law could have a meaningful impact on our work in the foreseeable future. Indeed, until recently, human rights has largely been the domain of well-paid bureaucrats in New York City and Geneva and a few elite nongovernmental organizations." [128] It is far more empowering for a grassroots organizer to frame an argument in simple, clear terms, such as: We are all human and we deserve better from our government. Thus, according to one local rights activist, it is important that "we do our own defining of human rights" and not get trapped within an externally imposed framework. [129]

Virtually all human rights practitioners recognize that human rights can be a very mobilizing discourse, and that rights language needs to be made more accessible to nonlawyers. [130] The most effective way to accomplish this is not only by providing grassroots groups with training in international law, but also to rediscover the social and moral roots of human rights by promoting the basic principles of equal human dignity and the duty to protect the most vulnerable. Human rights trainers themselves acknowledge that grassroots activists tend to be more interested in the basic principles than in the details of international law. [131] Human rights language is particularly mobilizing when it is kept simple, when it provides grassroots groups with the rhetorical tools to claim what they deserve. As Cheri Honkala states, "People have been going hungry all along, [but] without a way to describe what was happening to them. We now have a movement where poor people have taken ownership of the language and their lives." [132]

Likewise, practitioners agree that human rights hold the power to unite disparate groups to work toward a common goal, thereby broadening the influence of the movement. Human rights transcend distinctions based in geography, ideology, gender, race, or other categories because there is an "underlying commonality of simply being human." [133] Human rights lawyers and experts tend to think that national and international law is the common thread that diverse groups can build toward, and that grassroots groups need to refer to the legal standards in order to build toward a common goal. [134] This book argues, however, that the uniting power of human rights rests much more in the basic principles that ensue from "simply being human." Clear and unifying messages can be built around equality, justice, and empowerment as much as legal documents; these concepts are more easily accessible to the majority of the population.

Confronting U.S. Exceptionalism on Human Rights

In the previous chapter, I discussed the well-known fact that the U.S. government has been openly hostile to legal understandings of economic and social rights for decades. Certainly one reason for this hostility is because the U.S. government does not want to be held legally accountable for deficiencies in its own economic and social policy. Although it is certainly useful to try to make the state accept and implement legal obligations, most practitioners acknowledge that the United States is not ready to accept legal obligations anytime soon.

Conceptualizing rights as basic moral principles can help subsistence rights activists confront the U.S. government while circumventing the debate over legal rights, by encouraging other kinds of commitments to which the state can be held politically accountable. As Hans-Otto Sano has argued, "the real problem is a political one," that of persuading the state to accept its duty to protect its weakest members. [135] Human rights packaged as basic principles can encourage a variety of commitments from the state, such as funding targets (e.g., foreign aid at 0.7 percent of GDP) or commitments to certain outcomes (e.g., the Millennium Development Goals). [136] Or it can create a culture in which poverty is understood as a social responsibility rather than an individual problem, which would lead to social guarantees for the poor in policy making, laws, and institutions. While it is difficult to extract any commitment from the U.S. government, much less hold the state accountable to its obligations, commitments that are not legally binding are typically an easier accomplishment to achieve politically. [137] Yet they can still serve as the basis for holding the state accountable, and there are various forms of social action that can promote public accountability outside of the legal realm.[138] For example, Peter Uvin argues that "there exist many non-judiciary, non-legal, and yet effective enforcement mechanisms to ensure that claims can be met, accountability exercised, and violations addressed. Accountability is not only a matter of being able to litigate in courts of law. After all, the impact of human rights on the behavior of states was never exclusively a matter of judicial enforcement; rather, it has always taken place through a variety of mechanisms, including dissemination and internalization of norms, redefinitions of the interests and legitimacy of actors, collective learning about strategies and policies, and the like."[139] In the end, political and moral accountability can be just as effective in ensuring remedies for victims of poverty and other policy changes as legal accountability might be.[140]

The moral approach can also speak to the U.S. population who, on the whole, believe that the state has certain economic and social obligations to its poorest citizens, but who are mostly unaware of international human rights law. In a 1997 Hart Research poll, only 8 percent of American respondents could name the Universal Declaration of Human Rights as an "official document that sets forth human rights for everyone worldwide."[141] Yet in similar polling data, most Americans continue to believe that their government has a basic moral responsibility to help end poverty.[142] Social justice organizations note that there is an unprecedented focus in the West on global poverty, as illustrated by the massive Live 8 concerts organized at the time of the G8 summit in Gleneagles, Scotland, in July 2005. Interestingly, these concerts revolved around the theme of justice and systemic change, which was a major departure from the charity-based approach of the Live Aid concerts twenty years earlier.[143] A broader acceptance of the basic moral responsibility for subsistence rights is perhaps more important than any particular policy, institution, or legal commitment.

Because of the culture of U.S. exceptionalism and the lack of knowledge about human rights law within the United States, it is probably more effective to frame human rights in such a way as to dissociate it from ideas of socialism, intrusive government, legal obligations, and external influence on U.S. policy. A moral approach to subsistence rights, packaged in savvy ways, can confront the United States on its economic and social policies without falling into some of these rhetorical traps. Subsistence rights conceptualized as international legal standards, as "thick" social justice, or as substantive and distributional equality will engender heavy opposition within the United

States. It is far better to frame subsistence rights within the United States as an essentially American concept (rather than based in "foreign" or "international" law), as Cass Sunstein argues in *The Second Bill of Rights*. Sunstein traces the historical roots of economic and social rights in the United States back to Franklin Delano Roosevelt, who viewed these rights as consistent with regulated capitalism, rugged individualism, and American notions of freedom. Roosevelt "saw the second bill not as a legal document but as a set of public commitments" or foundational principles that become embedded in our public culture; and "while he sought a decent floor for those at the bottom, he did not seek anything like economic equality." [144]

Similarly, in the Oprah Winfrey program cited earlier, her guests framed the right to health care as an inherently American, even Christian idea, and directly countered the idea that health rights are "socialist" or "foreign." As health-care economist Uwe Reinhardt stated, "We should take a pledge not to talk about socialized medicine anymore. It's a stupid term and it's a mindless term. We have socialized insurance for hurricanes. When Katrina came, it was the Republican governors of Mississippi asking for the federal government for help. That's social insurance. And what I'm asking is, well, it was a natural disaster, and I would say if a lady in Mississippi has breast cancer, isn't that a natural disaster too? And if it is, should I not also care?" [145] Documentary filmmaker Michael Moore continued, "We have socialized medicine in the army. Thank god, right? I mean, what if we forced the soldiers to pay for their own health insurance? We would never do that. We believe in socialized medicine so much, we believe the army should have it first." [146] This kind of framing strategy—based on traditional American principles but devoid of any specific legal entitlement—has a reasonable chance of success in moving U.S. culture toward an acceptance of subsistence rights.

It appears that this kind of rights-based understanding of health care is accepted by President Obama. In an October 7, 2008, presidential debate with John McCain, in response to a question about whether health care is a privilege, right, or responsibility, then-Senator Obama stated, "I think it should be a right for every American. In a country as wealthy as ours, for us to have people who are going bankrupt because they can't pay their medical bills; for my mother to die of cancer at the age of 53, and have to spend the last months of her life in the hospital room arguing with insurance companies because they're saying that this may be a preexisting condition and they don't have to pay her treatment; there's something fundamentally wrong about that." [147] Notably, as the moral approach would stress, there would be multiple pathways to achieving this right in practice, and the Obama Administration has thus far chosen the path of public policy reform rather than a constitutional entitlement.

Confronting Ideological Debates over the State
and Market in Addressing Poverty

As discussed in the previous chapter, because of the lack of precision in legal texts and the ideological controversies involved in economic debates over welfare policy, human rights law does not sufficiently restrict the state's options in choosing what economic policies to pursue. Those who promote economic neoliberalism as a solution to extreme poverty often advance contradictory policies to those who promote a version of the welfare state. As a result, the state can adopt rights-violating policies and justify them in rights-promoting terms, all while claiming to comply with international law on subsistence rights.

Social justice groups face the same ideological challenges, because anyone working to eradicate extreme poverty must confront these polarizing issues. The question is, on what rhetorical grounds should social justice organizations enter these debates? By attempting to elaborate the content of legal texts, as many human rights organizations have undertaken? Or by directly confronting a set of policies, and the beliefs that underlie them, on the basis that these policies are wrong and harmful to the poor? The latter approach is more explicitly political than the former, and cannot rely on the supposed objectivity, authority, and institutional mechanisms of the law. Yet social justice groups have tended to take this latter approach, which may prove equally effective.

Many human rights practitioners try to stay above the fray by claiming that human rights law sets standards, then surrender the details of implementation to the state's discretion. Other human rights advocates try to circumvent the larger debates by targeting only the most obvious or egregious violations of legal rights. Social justice advocates, however, stand at the center of these debates, and provide some of the strongest critiques of the neoliberal economic model of development. These so-called antiglobalization activists (an unfortunate and inaccurate label) have taken their struggle to the streets, the media, and to international negotiations and national legislatures to argue that the expansion of the free market is not an adequate response to poverty. They claim that it is the moral responsibility of governments to implement certain redistributive and regulative policies that protect the poor, and to create an international economic system that does not exclude or disadvantage its poorest participants. Some human rights organizations are joining them, grounding their critiques of the international economic system in the basic principles of the law. These new coalitions are increasingly challenging governments, international institutions, and private corporations on issues such as making HIV treatments available to all, ensuring that extractive industries are not socially and environmentally destructive, preventing infrastructure projects from displacing large populations, and protecting poor people's access to clean water.[148]

While there is certainly no guarantee that these efforts will be successful, the debates cannot be won by either side through avoidance. A moral approach refocuses attention on clarifying economic policy positions and basic assumptions, rather than allowing technical debates over the interpretation of legal texts to obscure these issues.

Conclusions

The prevailing practice of social justice movements and their predominantly moral approach to human rights leads to the conclusion that practitioners and theorists should not be afraid to have more expansive notions of what human rights includes. Subsistence rights are powerful not only as legal standards, but also as rhetorical tools to empower the poor as legitimate claimants, to address debates over economic policy, and to redefine poverty as a social responsibility based on our common vision of human equality and dignity. While international law is important and influential, it also comes with its own set of costs, and grassroots activists and the poor do not necessarily need to reference it to claim their rights effectively. Local groups involved in political struggles are "adapting and expanding" the human rights framework to make claims for social justice.[149] They often reinterpret human rights away from its traditional focus on legal instruments and processes, in part because the poor have so little access to formal institutions in the first place.[150] Yet moral approaches also come with their own set of costs related to developing a clear and unifying message among ideologically diverse groups.

Human rights have always been understood as both legal and moral instruments. Early in the U.S. human rights movement's history, practitioners were primarily church members, community workers, and other laypersons. Mary Ann Glendon notes that "for most of our history, political discourse was not so liberally salted with rights talk as it is today, nor was rights discourse so legalistic." [151] Gradually, as the human rights movement became more professionalized in the West, organizations such as Amnesty International and Human Rights Watch became dominated by lawyers, and research on human rights became located in law schools. By the early 1990s, activists came to emphasize the legal aspects of human rights to the neglect of the moral. As Larry Cox explains:

> In my experience, the increasingly legalistic approach to human rights has overshadowed a moral approach, which for me is what resonated early on. In the 1970s, when I had the good fortune to be a part of Amnesty International before it was a very wide network, questions of right and wrong formed the dominant discourse. I was not a lawyer. It was not a question of whether something violated Article X of this covenant or that covenant. It was that torture is wrong. Starvation is wrong. It was a language of morality, and it captured people's imagination and made the human rights movement grow. Once human rights started to become a specialist language that only certain people who had been to school could access and only the experts could interpret correctly, it lost the ability to mobilize the vast majority of people. [152]

Thanks to the emerging practice of social justice groups on subsistence rights, the legal and moral aspects of human rights are beginning to come back into balance. It is time for our understanding of human rights to be brought back into balance as well, by accepting moral rights back within the mainstream. A social theory of human rights provides the justification for that balance, by subsuming both legal and moral approaches to rights within a broader social context. Legal and moral approaches are both important tools, but the effectiveness of each tool depends on how well it resonates within particular social contexts.

5

Humanitarian Organizations

While social justice groups have adopted economic and social rights rather quietly, the incorporation of human rights into the work of Western humanitarian NGOs[1] over the past decade has arrived with much fanfare. The diverse and multifaceted trend among humanitarian NGOs has coalesced into a single label: the use of a "rights-based approach" to development work. This chapter will describe and investigate that trend by asking: Why are humanitarian organizations adopting or resisting rights-based approaches in their work? Does this trend signal significant changes in humanitarian organizations' programming? How do these groups approach subsistence rights, and what are the strategic implications of their approach for the human rights field?

In this chapter, I argue that humanitarian organizations have responded to the growing definitional linkage between human rights and development by increasingly adopting rights-based approaches in their project work. For these groups, human rights has been interpreted as an umbrella term that encapsulates many of the recent trends emerging in the international development industry, such as becoming more politically engaged, focusing on systemic causes and solutions to poverty, and empowering the poor. In so doing, organizations such as CARE and Oxfam International have adopted a moral approach to subsistence rights (similar to social justice organizations) that translates international law into basic principles to guide organizational programming. While some organizations have used human rights primarily to legitimize their existing practices, the rights-based approach is beginning to result in some important changes in how humanitarian organizations view their mission, analyze local contexts, and relate with their stakeholders.

Human rights require humanitarian organizations to fundamentally redefine development not as a technical process of delivering aid but as a political negotiation that they must enter on behalf of the poor. As such, humanitarian organizations are demonstrating that a moral approach to subsistence rights can be effective in changing widespread behavior even outside of legal processes and institutions. Yet adopting a rights-based approach also imposes significant challenges for humanitarian NGOs to overcome.

My focus in this chapter is on humanitarian NGOs (often called private voluntary organizations) with an international mission to provide goods and services to the poor. I will briefly discuss state-based and multilateral development agencies, however, as well as international financial institutions, which act both as sources of funding for NGOs and as implementing agencies. I discuss state-based actors primarily to compare their perspectives on rights-based approaches to those of humanitarian NGOs.

Although there are various definitions of rights-based approaches with slightly different emphases, one of the most widely used among humanitarian agencies comes from CARE's Andrew Jones: "A rights-based approach deliberately and explicitly focuses on people realizing their human rights. It does so by exposing the root causes of vulnerability and marginalization and expanding the range of responses. It empowers people to claim and exercise their rights and fulfill their responsibilities. A rights-based approach recognizes poor, displaced and war-affected people as having inherent rights essential to livelihood security—rights that are validated by international standards and law."[2] In other words, rights-based approaches include working with the most vulnerable people in society to make claims on resources that would allow them to live in basic dignity. By allowing human rights to guide the implementation of their project work among the extreme poor, humanitarian organizations are increasingly promoting freedom from poverty.

The earliest efforts to link development and human rights were at the conceptual level. Throughout the 1990s, economists, academics and human rights theorists worked through the UN and other arenas to provide a conceptual and theoretical basis for rights-based approaches and began to integrate them into organizational programming. For example, thanks in large part to the work of Amartya Sen and Martha Nussbaum in the 1990s, development and human rights became increasingly integrated by definition. The 2000 Human Development Report in particular, which was based largely on Sen's *Development as Freedom*,[3] argued that: "The promotion of human development and the fulfillment of human rights share, in many ways, a common motivation, and reflect a fundamental commitment to promoting the freedom, well-being and dignity of individuals in all societies. . . . If human development focuses on the enhancement of the capabilities and freedoms that the members of a community enjoy, human rights represent the claims that individuals have on the conduct of individual and collective agents and on the design of social arrangements to facilitate or secure these capabilities and freedoms."[4] Thus, by redefining development as enhancing people's basic capabilities and freedoms, Sen ensured that "one can define development and human rights with a sufficient degree of abstraction as to be virtually identical and essentially unimpeachable."[5] As a result, there is a considerable amount of consensus within the international development industry that the two theoretical concepts are mutually compatible. There is also widespread agreement about the value that rights-based approaches should add to development work: enhanced accountability by framing development in terms of obligations, greater empowerment and participation by beneficiaries in the development process, a universal normative framework to legitimate development work, a more thorough analysis of the causes of poverty, and an authoritative basis for policy advocacy.[6]

While Sen and others laid out the theoretical groundwork for rights-based approaches, putting it into practice has been a different challenge. As the UN Development Program states, "Despite the compatibility of the two approaches, their strategic form and focus are rather different."[7] Thus, there is still a practical difference between the work of human rights and humanitarian organizations[8] and a lack of clarity about how humanitarian agencies should actually implement rights-based approaches.

Humanitarian agencies are in the process of discovering how implementing a rights-based approach will change internal organizational practices; affect their relations with donors, host states, and other stakeholders; and translate into effective results. Because the practical changes implied by rights-based approaches are potentially enormous for an organization, it is easier to discuss the theoretical linkages between human rights and development than to learn how to apply them in the field.

The proliferation of theoretical writing on rights-based approaches, as well as the long history of rhetorical trends in the development industry, has led many critics to be skeptical of whether they represent anything really new in international development practice. The dominant discourses of international development have evolved through the decades without much significant change in development practice.[9] Rights-based approaches have thus been described as the "flavor of the month." [10] Given the history of other development trends, it is certainly valid to ask in what sense the current trend is meaningful. The point of this chapter is not to assess the effectiveness of these new approaches, nor to determine conclusively if humanitarian agencies are really serious about human rights. The trend is very recent, and even if humanitarian agencies take rights-based approaches seriously, it will likely take decades to make a measurable difference in social structures and in the lives of the poor. Rather, the purpose of this chapter is to explain how humanitarian agencies came to adopt human rights, how their moral approach to rights has facilitated changes in organizational practice, and what this implies for the politics of development and human rights.

Describing the Increasing Use of Human Rights by Humanitarian Organizations

The increasing incorporation of rights-based approaches by international humanitarian groups has proceeded parallel to, but in many ways separate from, the trend among human rights and social justice groups. Humanitarian NGOs are only one set of international development actors who have attempted to integrate human rights and development. Chris Jochnick and Paulina Garzon have delineated three categories of international development actors who have incorporated human rights into their work: UN agencies, private humanitarian NGOs, and state-based bilateral aid agencies.[11] According to Jochnick and Garzon, the UN "provided much of the theoretical, legal and political impetus for rights-based approaches" in the 1990s. Building on global conferences relating to economic and social development at Rio de Janeiro, Vienna, Cairo, Copenhagen, Istanbul, Rome, Beijing, and elsewhere, UN agencies provided the space in the 1990s to redefine development around individual needs and rights rather than national economic growth.[12] This process culminated in Kofi Annan calling upon all UN agencies to "mainstream" human rights into their work in 1997; that call was taken up to its greatest extent by the UN Development Program and the UN Children's Fund.[13] All UN agencies now have a common understanding of the rights-based approach,[14] at least at the conceptual level.

Although there is significant overlap between the two concepts, the "right to development" movement within the UN predated and followed a distinct path from the movement toward rights-based approaches to development. At a conceptual level, the 1986 Declaration on the Right to Development places individual well-being at the center of development and frames development in terms of rights explicitly laid out in international treaties. As such, it is entirely compatible with rights-based approaches. However, the right to development movement emerged from demands by developing countries for a New International Economic Order in the 1970s, in the political context of the Cold War, which set this movement on a different pathway than rights-based approaches. In effect, the call for a right to development became associated with developing countries' demand for state sovereignty over natural resources within their territory[15] as well as the redistribution of wealth and power on a global scale, thus has been largely resisted by Western states and large donors.[16] On the other hand, rights-based approaches have emerged after the Cold War and have not incorporated explicit demands for massive global redistribution of wealth or economic sovereignty for nations of the global South. As such, rights-based approaches have gained a much more supportive audience in the West and within the UN.

Provided with a supportive arena at the UN in which to link development with human rights, the major relief and development NGOs began around the end of the 1990s to adopt human rights officially and incorporate them into their programming. One of the first NGOs to advocate a closer relationship between human rights and development was the Human Rights Council of Australia, which published *The Rights Way to Development* in 1995 urging a more consistent incorporation of human rights standards, especially economic and social rights, into the planning of development aid.[17] Although *The Rights Way* received a mixed reaction from other humanitarian organizations,[18] the idea of adopting rights-based approaches to development eventually "succeeded beyond their wildest dreams."[19] Most of the major international humanitarian NGOs have now adopted these principles, including CARE, Oxfam, Save the Children, ActionAid, World Vision, and dozens of others. Oxfam is one of the NGOs that has taken subsistence rights the furthest, as all twelve of its autonomous national offices signed onto Oxfam International's strategic plan (2001–2004), which defined Oxfam's focus as the "realization of economic and social rights within the wider human rights continuum."[20] Oxfam began using human rights language as early as the mid-1990s, but has only begun to implement the rights-based approach programmatically within the past decade.[21] Oxfam International named former UN High Commissioner for Human Rights Mary Robinson as honorary president, and as Oxfam America's president Ray Offenheiser states, "The conscious choice to center all programming on a rights-based approach and to focus more particularly on economic and social rights has represented a major organizational shift for all Oxfam affiliates." [22]

The adoption of rights-based approaches by humanitarian NGOs has also been facilitated by their participation in horizontal networks that promote information sharing. For example, Dochas, an Irish association of thirty-five humanitarian organizations, initiated a working group led by Christian Aid in 2000 to study how rights-based approaches can be implemented in the field. [23] In the United States, the largest network of humanitarian NGOs is InterAction, which began a similar working group in 2004. These networks have served as arenas for disseminating the idea and advantages of a rights-based approach among all of the major agencies.

In terms of state-based bilateral aid agencies, almost all of the major European state donors have made explicit commitments to incorporating human rights considerations into their aid, led by Britain's Department for International Development, the Swedish Agency for International Development Cooperation, the Norwegian Agency for Development Cooperation, and Danish International Development Assistance. [24] This "has greatly increased the resources available for rights-based development work and has led to a number of conferences and publications." [25] However, the U.S. counterpart, the U.S. Agency for International Development, has rejected a rights-based approach.

Why Are Western NGOs Adopting or Resisting Rights-based Approaches?

As the above discussion indicates, the trend toward human rights among humanitarian NGOs is strongly related to broader trends taking place within the UN and other international development actors. UN agencies, international financial institutions, and bilateral aid agencies act as rhetorical and practical models to emulate in part because they serve as funders to the NGOs themselves. [26] As such, it is more accurate to describe rights-based approaches not as a sea change by individual NGOs making exclusively principled decisions, but rather as a new way to express larger trends already occurring in how development is defined, how the causes of poverty are analyzed, and how solutions are conceptualized. Once again, principled ideas and strategic interests merge to form the basis of humanitarian organizations' decisions to adopt rights-based approaches. But what specifically led to these decisions?

The concept of neutrality has been important in international relief work ever since the inception of a global aid industry in the mid-twentieth century. Since humanitarian organizations tended to provide aid to everyone who needed it without taking partisan positions, the normative concept of "humanitarian space" has taken root, meaning that even in the midst of war, aid should be delivered free from interference.[27] For many organizations, then, embracing the principle of neutrality has reduced the risk that the delivery of aid would be manipulated or obstructed.[28] However, in the past two decades humanitarian organizations have become increasingly attuned to the inevitable political effects of their aid, often noting that aid exacerbated local conflict or was not used for its intended purpose. Virtually all of the major humanitarian organizations, with the notable exception of the International Red Cross and Médecins Sans Frontières, loosened their grip on the supposed neutrality of development work, and began to acknowledge the political implications of their aid and the role that NGOs played in ensuring that states fulfilled their development obligations. The shift toward human rights represents one aspect of NGOs' more open embrace of political engagement.

Because humanitarian NGOs are often put into the position of being the first responders to humanitarian emergencies and extreme poverty worldwide, they have also tended to be particularly disturbed by the persistence of poverty in the latter part of the twentieth century. For example, Oxfam's Ray Offenheiser describes many practitioners' response to the worsening economic conditions of the poor as "disillusionment," not only with the meager results of decades of humanitarian aid but more specifically with the "welfare model" of assistance, whereby it was "assumed that if the means can be provided to deliver the public goods or services more affordably" then development would automatically ensue.[29] As a result, in the 1980s and 1990s the international development industry paid increasing attention to more overtly social, political, and structural issues involved in development. They increasingly committed themselves to analyzing the root causes of poverty, addressing poverty through systemic approaches, doing no harm in their interventions, building local capacities and empowering local communities, increasing individuals' ability to gain sustainable livelihoods, and ensuring local participation in development projects.[30] All of these phrases—root causes, systemic approaches, do no harm, local capacities, empowerment, participation, sustainable livelihoods, participation—became rhetorical signposts for humanitarian organizations both in their public relations and internal operational guidelines.

These are all laudable goals; one source of value in the rights-based approach is that it encapsulates all of the concepts above into a single term. Therefore it makes sense that humanitarian organizations are now thinking of and expressing their work in terms of justice and human rights. In one sense, "human rights" is an umbrella term for many of the rhetorical and practical trends that humanitarian organizations have adopted over the past two decades.[31] As a result, the rights-based approach has now become one of the main signposts of the international development industry.

And yet not all humanitarian NGOs or projects have explicitly adopted human rights language, for a variety of reasons that are largely related to the organizations' own identity or history. Faith-based humanitarian organizations such as Catholic Relief Services, Mercy Corps, Lutheran World Relief, and World Vision have been less eager to adopt a human rights approach than secular organizations.[32] Although these faith-based organizations have adopted policies and principles that are entirely consistent with a rights-based approach, they have tended to frame their approach in terms that resonate with their core constituencies who have a religious worldview. Each organization's guiding principles are "closely tied to the core values and beliefs that drive each one."[33] Thus, for example, Catholic Relief Services uses a "justice lens" to approach their development work, based on the principles of Catholic social teachings, that is often called a rights-based approach by outsiders. Mercy Corps employs human rights language regularly but subsumes it within a "civil society" approach, in part because of the concern that human rights language "might make people uncomfortable."[34] Some faith-based NGOs that have adopted a rights-based approach, such as World Vision, openly acknowledge that human rights language should be used when—and only when—it fits into superordinate religious principles. As a World Vision representative has stated: "Christians may use the language of human rights in a development context but they will use it where it is in agreement with a Christian worldview. There will be times when it is not appropriate. There will be times when something is being claimed as a right which is in direct conflict with Christian principles or where the consequences of a human rights approach is not felt to be Christian. It may also be the case that Christian agencies believe that a rights-based approach is not as appropriate as another [approach]."[35] An example of conflict between rights claims and Christian principles (insofar as some people interpret them) is in the area of reproductive rights, where many Christian agencies oppose contraceptive methods advanced by rights claimants, and thereby restrict funding for development work in that area.

Other humanitarian NGOs—religious or secular—may be reluctant to adopt a rights-based approach because they have no experience with policy advocacy, they are tied to institutional donors that oppose them, they can't afford to be confrontational with host governments, or they fear a complete change in mission and organizational structure.[36] For example, because the U.S. Agency for International Development (USAID) does not fund rights-based approaches, organizations such as Catholic Relief Services—who receive a large proportion of their funds from USAID—are not likely to promote their work via rights language. Some NGOs, such as the International Committee of the Red Cross, depend on a strict interpretation of neutrality in order to fulfill their mission in extremely sensitive political situations, such as visiting prisoners of war on both sides of a conflict. While the mission of the Red Cross is not inconsistent with human rights principles, the perception that rights-based approaches involve more open political advocacy could become a hindrance to their work and is arguably contrary to its identity. Other NGOs have expressed a fear that rights-based approaches require a fundamental shift in an organization's mission toward political and legal advocacy, and a shift in staff competencies toward legal expertise, thus have dismissed them as outside of their core mission.[37]

Even within organizations that have explicitly adopted a rights-based approach, some internal variation in how they are implemented across country programs and individual projects is inevitable. In part this is because many international humanitarian NGOs are decentralized structures composed of autonomous or semi-autonomous national offices, and some national groups are more eager or capable of adopting rights-based approaches than others. For example, Save the Children is an international network of twenty-seven autonomous national offices; their United Kingdom and Sweden programs have been the most active in orienting their work toward human rights.[38] Some variation in how consistently these approaches are implemented on the ground is also likely due to the fact that some communities may be subject to severe repression by their government if they engage in confrontational politics.[39] Some projects may not explicitly refer to human rights because they find that "tapping into the values, beliefs, and principles of the [local] culture" is more effective.[40] Thus, several organizations have been testing the effectiveness of a rights-based approach through a series of pilot projects rather than committing their entire organization to the concept.[41]

A social theory of human rights would view this variation as potentially positive rather than as a disturbing sign. If human rights are shaped in different ways in different social contexts, it would be sensible to test rights-based approaches in those specific contexts. Conversely, if human rights derive from a unitary set of texts and institutions, as most analysts believe, then gradual and diverse approaches to rights would be more worrisome.

In spite of this variation, it is clear that human rights have become embedded in the mindset and the public discourse of the majority of international humanitarian NGOs. In that sense, rights-based approaches have become the most recent expression of legitimate organizational form within the humanitarian aid industry. The industry has evolved to a point that "any serious player must at least have a position with respect to rights-based approaches."[42] But how do humanitarian organizations actually approach rights and use them in their work?

The Moral Approach to Rights in Humanitarian Work

International humanitarian organizations take a predominantly moral approach to rights, interpreting human rights in similar ways to social justice groups, but for different ends. For most humanitarian organizations, the moral understanding of human rights defines rights in terms of basic principles that can justify, strengthen, or modify development work. Human rights—i.e., these basic principles—act as a lens to reevaluate the organization's own policies and practices and the context in which it works.

For a handful of development practitioners, the rights-based approach is inseparable from its source in international law. For those taking a legal approach, the moral principles underlying human rights are not unimportant; but these principles are entitlements entirely derived from international law. Under this interpretation of human rights, development work therefore must include a focus on the establishment of a functioning judicial system that can provide effective remedies for those whose rights are violated.[43] The goal of humanitarian aid is to assist the recipient state in meeting its treaty obligations,[44] thus humanitarian NGOs implementing economic and social rights should be able to use UN treaty bodies, refer to General Comments, and take other action related to the international legal system of human rights.[45] Approaching human rights through the lens of international law leads to specific pathways of action for humanitarian NGOs: advocating for new legislation and state institutions, using international mechanisms to hold the state accountable to its obligations, identifying specific violations and finding means of legal redress, monitoring standard benchmarks to determine whether a state is realizing rights progressively, and so on.[46] Grassroots educational efforts typically take the form of "disseminating information about laws and legal procedures."[47]

However, it is clear from emerging practice that the majority of international humanitarian NGOs interpret human rights differently.[48] In order to make development practice adaptive to local articulations of rights and needs, and to make rights relevant to the service delivery functions that NGOs have historically engaged in, most humanitarian organizations interpret human rights as basic moral principles that guide operational practice. These basic principles are essentially the same lens through which most social justice groups perceive human rights, but adapted to the context of the relationship between the humanitarian NGO and its stakeholders—donors, beneficiaries, states, and others. Thus, humanitarian organizations tend to translate international law into "key normative principles" such as "human freedom; universalism and equality; the multi-dimensional character of well-being; participation; transparency and empowerment; responsibility and accountability; and sustainability."[49] Given the complexities and ethical trade-offs of development work, humanitarian NGOs are aware that they cannot approach their work in a legalistic way,[50] thus they seek to dig beneath the complexity of the international legal structure to elaborate the "very simple first principles regarding human rights," such as giving priority to the most vulnerable people they encounter.[51] One of the basic principles underlying a rights-based approach to development is that an improvement in macro-economic statistics is not sufficient to realize rights. Human rights are claims that structural, cultural and systemic changes be enacted that would establish long-term, social guarantees for the poorest people in achieving a basic livelihood.[52]

The kind of rights-based approaches adopted by CARE and Oxfam serve as typical illustrations of this approach. Oxfam understands human rights to be a "general foundation of human dignity" that is broader than international law indicates.[53] Thus Oxfam began with UN human rights instruments, but extrapolated from them to generate five general principles that are designed to serve as a "simple planning tool" for field staff.[54] The five rights-based principles include the right to a sustainable livelihood, access to basic social services, life and security, social and political citizenship, and identity. Similarly, CARE has boiled down the corpus of international law into six basic principles or operational objectives: to promote empowerment, work with partners, ensure accountability and promote responsibility, address discrimination, promote nonviolent resolution of conflicts, and seek sustainable results.[55] Katarina Tomasevski has further condensed these human rights principles into two central concepts: empowerment of the most vulnerable populations, and accountability to those same populations.[56]

For most humanitarian organizations, human rights therefore are understood as basic principles that guide relationships among NGOs and various stakeholders, thus the explicit reference to international law or even to rights language itself is much less important than taking the basic principles seriously. This is why many development practitioners consider NGOs like Catholic Relief Services to be implementing rights-based approaches even though it does not explicitly refer to rights. In an evaluation of sixteen CARE country-level projects implementing rights-based approaches, Mary Picard and Jay Goulden found that: "In [some] projects, the reference to rights lent legitimacy to community groups to engage in public advocacy around a common cause. Other examples spanned a wide spectrum of rights, both legal and moral, but without an explicit reference to any rights framework. Many fell within the broad category of economic, social and cultural or simply human rights. [But it was] not always perceptible whether the cases deliberately used rights language. Similarly it was not always clear when projects deliberately refrained from the use of rights language in their relationship with partners and clients, while still maintaining human rights as a conceptual framework for their work."[57] They concluded that "all of the case study projects took as their starting point the need to give voice to the most marginalized groups, whether or not the projects chose to invoke the language of rights."[58] In other words, because the moral approach is used to guide internal practice, following the basic principles is far more important than evoking the precise language of international law or human rights rhetoric itself.

How a Moral Approach to Subsistence Rights
Changes Development Work

The above sections describe a process whereby in the past decade humanitarian organizations have adopted rights-based approaches increasingly as basic moral principles to guide their internal operations and relations with stakeholders. These principles encapsulate many of the recent trends in the jargon the international development industry uses to describe its own work: participation, empowerment, root cause analysis, systemic change, and building local capacities. However, many observers, both within the humanitarian field and in the human rights movement, are skeptical of whether the new rights rhetoric will translate into any meaningful change in development practice. For example, Jochnick and Garzon argue that adopting a rights-based approach "may involve a significant change in an organization's programming or a more superficial overlay of rights rhetoric with little substance."[59] There are four reasons why skepticism about the meaningfulness of human rights rhetoric might be warranted.

First, many of the traditional human rights practitioners who are skeptical of the human rights shift in humanitarian organizations come from the legal perspective on human rights, in which the power of human rights ostensibly derives from direct application of the international standards. According to these advocates, practicing human rights by definition means taking the legal approach to rights described above. This is why some private grant-making foundations have required organizations to refer explicitly to international legal standards in order to successfully qualify for human rights funding.[60] However, many of the humanitarian NGOs adopting rights-based approaches have found the legal approach to rights limiting and inappropriate as a guide to their practical operations in the field. Because, as I will argue, rights-based approaches can still translate into meaningful development practice outside of legalistic interpretations of rights, this criticism falls short. Nevertheless, these skeptics raise a legitimate point that for many humanitarian organizations, it remains to be seen how human rights rhetoric will be made meaningful in practice.[61]

Second, the way that several humanitarian NGOs justify their own adoption of rights-based approaches leads some to question whether the new rhetoric adds any real value. In order to allay concerns about massive changes in organizational structures, humanitarian NGOs often claim that they have really been doing human rights all along.[62] As Oxfam states, "The empowerment of poor and excluded people has underpinned much of Oxfam's work for many years."[63] Oxfam itself recognizes the marketing function that human rights serve, calling its approach a "brand" in addition to a fundamental change.[64] Concern Worldwide "believes the [rights-based approach] will be compatible with their present work, which focuses on participation, empowerment, capacity building, partnership, accountability and mobilization of local capacities."[65] Clearly, one of the uses for human rights rhetoric is to legitimize humanitarian organizations' existing work before donors and other supporters. However, the point is that if the new rhetoric is entirely compatible with an organization's existing work, it is fair to question whether anything substantive is added to development practice by using human rights rhetoric.

Third, it appears that humanitarian organizations do have a financial incentive to overstate the degree of organizational change when communicating with potential donors. The international development industry has survived for decades based on appeals for billions of dollars each year with the promise of implementing effective and lasting solutions to extreme global poverty. Yet after the disappointing results of the past two decades, during which global poverty worsened in many parts of the world, there is an incentive to assert that now humanitarian organizations are trying a brand new approach, and that this time it will work. Thus many practitioners have a tendency to create a straw man from previous development practice to tear it down with the new rights-based approaches.[66] In this context, the "development of attractive visions is the primary recipe for survival and growth."[67] Claims that rights-based approaches represent fundamental shifts or entirely new practices are therefore justifiably received with some skepticism until organizational practice demonstrates it in the field.

Fourth, there is well-grounded suspicion that international financial institutions and bilateral donors have "appropriated rights language without changing underlying beliefs" about development.[68] For example, Former World Bank president James Wolfenson has stated that "creating the conditions for the attainment of human rights is a central and irreducible goal of development."[69] Although the World Bank has initiated an internal review process that recognizes a very limited range of human rights complaints,[70] it essentially equates human rights with macro-level indicators of economic growth, and thus argues that its existing practice is automatically in compliance with any human rights claims that may be placed on it.[71] Thus, by redefining human rights in terms of growth-centered poverty reduction, it ensures that human rights does not transform its practices. The increased rhetoric from the World Bank on human rights has served to legitimize its current practices, but has not yet resulted in any significant change in programming. Its social lending portfolio has never exceeded 6 percent of total lending, and its structural adjustment policies have proceeded despite widespread criticism from antipoverty activists.[72] Katarina Tomasevski similarly argues that the main providers of bilateral aid, especially the United States, use human rights language and conditionalities primarily as an excuse to limit development assistance to certain unfavored countries based on a narrow range of civil and political rights and market policies.[73] Thus there is a fear "that rights will be used selectively by powerful development actors to foster a favourable environment for marketisation,"[74] or that the rights-based approach "facilitates the neoliberal agenda of development by cloaking it in the current language of legitimacy, namely, that of human rights."[75] This is why Peter Uvin has described the rhetorical adoption of human rights by many official donors and lending institutions as "thinly disguised repackaging of old wine in new bottles."[76] Making human rights rhetoric meaningful for these actors would require the equal application of rights-based analyses to official donors' and financial institutions' own practices, something that has never been attempted and is unlikely to be in the near future.[77] It would require imposing development obligations on both donor and recipient countries, redefining the relationship between the two and serving as the basis for people of the global South to gain greater control over the aid and economic policies that affect them.[78]

Given these grounds for skepticism, we need to be clear about what changes we would expect to see from the rhetorical invocation of rights by humanitarian organizations. As I argued in the previous chapter, even "mere" rhetoric can serve important strategic functions for organizations, such as legitimizing their work and connecting them to like-minded donors. Rhetorical change may also "constitute the first steps toward a true change of vision," by redefining appropriate action and changing expectations about what humanitarian organizations are supposed to do.[79] However, because the moral approach to rights is supposed to guide organizational programming, most observers would agree that rights-based approaches will be ultimately disappointing if they do not make a noticeable difference in humanitarian organizations' operations and in the lives of people in extreme poverty.

Has such a change begun to take place within humanitarian NGOs? Indeed it has. Over the past decade, rights-based approaches have begun to result in some important innovations in organizational practice. Because the movement is relatively recent, and if taken seriously would require many years to make a meaningful difference in organizational practice and people's lives, it is far too early to make a conclusive judgment about the "effectiveness" of the new approach or the embeddedness of new practices. However, I will discuss how humanitarian practice is beginning to change based on NGOs' predominantly moral understanding of rights, and some of the implications for development work if NGOs continue to pursue this path.

We should not expect the implementation of rights-based approaches to translate into a single kind of organizational practice, even for those NGOs that interpret them similarly, simply because humanitarian NGOs carry out so many different functions in many different arenas. Caroline Moser and

How a Rights-based Approach Affects Humanitarian Work

Level of impact	*How humanitarian work changes*
Normative	Redefines the NGO's mandate and the goal of development itself
Analytical	Provides a lens to analyze the social context of humanitarian work
Operational	Guides the actual implementation of programs

her colleagues identified twenty-one "arenas for action" in which humanitarian NGOs can implement rights-based approaches, depending on the level at which they work (local, national, global, etc.) and the kind of work that they do.[80] Some humanitarian NGOs implement a rights-based approach through a separate legal advocacy project.[81] But most NGOs claim that the rights-based approach should infuse all of the organization's work and inform all of its relations with stakeholders. A meaningful rights-based approach should require a "fundamental rethinking of the entire development practice: its ideology, its partners, its aims, its processes, its systems and procedures."[82]

In that vein, Piron and Watkins devised a three-fold typology for understanding the impact of rights-based approaches on organizational practice at the normative, analytical, and operational levels (see table).[83] At the normative level, rights serve as the "scaffolding of development policy,"[84] the principled framework through which an organization perceives its central mission and all of its work. In that sense, the fulfillment of rights is seen as the goal of development itself,[85] which affects how an organization perceives its identity, organizational culture, role, and approach to development. For example, the Association for Women in Development, which began as simply a forum for professional networking, changed its name when it adopted a rights-based approach (to the Association for Women's Rights in Development) and reconceptualized its mission to involve more advocacy and political engagement.[86] Oxfam and CARE understand the basic normative principles of the rights-based approach to require a change of focus toward supporting vulnerable groups' ability to advocate for their own needs, a more egalitarian organizational culture, and a commitment to move beyond the model of individual projects to broader participation in civil society.[87] Again, these normative changes are based on a moral approach to rights rather than a detailed investigation of the legal instruments or any specific legal obligations they would entail.

While principles like accountability and empowerment affect an organization's overall identity and orientation, they must still be translated into practice at the analytical and operational levels.[88] Implementing a rights-based approach at the analytical level "requires rigorous analysis of social and political processes that determine the likelihood of poor people's claims being reflected in the definition, interpretation or implementation of rights. It also calls for the identification of social characteristics (gender, citizenship, social status, ethnicity etc.) that empower, or disempower, people in different arenas of negotiation. . . . [It should lead to] a better understanding of the way that power impacts on the production and reproduction of poverty and insecurity."[89] In other words, adopting a rights-based approach has led humanitarian NGOs to direct more money and staff time to researching human rights conditions in the field and analyzing the root causes of poverty during the planning stages of development.[90] For example, CARE has sought "to differentiate its client population more systematically and analyse inequities. This extends to disaggregating within marginalised or excluded groups by gender and other relevant categories."[91]

At the operational level, human rights have affected organizational practice in the field in a number of ways, including the redefinition of what the "field" constitutes. One of the most significant practical effects within NGOs has been a shift in resources toward policy advocacy on global economic issues.[92] Oxfam, CARE, World Vision, Christian Aid, Concern, ActionAid, and dozens of other humanitarian NGOs are now committed to pursuing enormous structural goals, including debt relief for the poorest countries, reform of the rules that govern global trade and intellectual property, encouraging ethical consumption and investment, increasing official development aid, and strengthening the international human rights system.[93] While humanitarian NGOs have always been dedicated to idealistic goals such as ending poverty, it is a significant shift from focusing on one individual at a time, to pursuing systemic change. In that sense, NGOs are recognizing that places like Washington, D.C., New York, and Geneva are sites of fieldwork comparable in importance to the developing world. This shift in focus has also necessitated devoting more organizational resources to human rights training and other forms of education, both for the NGOs' own staff, their local partners, and the vulnerable communities in which they work.[94] In some cases, this has resulted in hiring new staff members and a reduction in the amount of funds allocated for traditional service delivery.[95]

Rights-based approaches have also led humanitarian NGOs to select different partners and collaborate in different ways in the various contexts in which they work. This has meant that they frequently team up with human rights and social justice groups on transnational advocacy campaigns such as Make Trade Fair and Make Poverty History, as well as on country-specific human rights appeals. In the global South, this has translated into increasing collaboration with local groups that mobilize poor people, provide legal aid, monitor national budgets, and lobby all levels of government.[96] It has also resulted in humanitarian NGOs moving beyond their relationship with local partners, reaching out both horizontally and vertically to serve as an advocate, networker, facilitator, and broker among all stakeholders in the development process.[97] The role of international humanitarian NGOs "will become increasingly that of a mediating and capacity building agent at all levels in facilitating the ability of excluded communities and groups to strengthen their voice in negotiations over the prioritization and means of gaining access to goods and services necessary to secure their livelihoods."[98] This involves not only empowering vulnerable groups to exercise their voice, but also working with those in power (culturally, economically and politically) at all levels to recognize their obligations to the poor and create new solutions.

In the best cases, therefore, articulating their mission through moral rights–based rhetoric reinforces and extends humanitarian NGOs' commitment to the set of principles they have invoked over the past decade: empowerment, accountability, participation, and systemic change. Human rights approaches take notions of empowerment and participation a step further than previous approaches, by trying to improve vulnerable groups' ability not only to shape a particular development project, but also to influence broader development policy and social relations.[99] International development analysts have noted that "participation is often framed narrowly as a methodology to improve project performance, rather than a process of fostering critical consciousness and decision-making as the basis for active citizenship. Rarely is participation implemented as a mutual decision-making process, where different actors share power and set agendas jointly. Participation, in this sense, involves conflict, and demands a capacity to analyse, negotiate and alter unequal relations at all levels."[100] To summarize, in an evaluation of ActionAid International's implementation of rights-based approaches in four country programs, Jennifer Chapman and her colleagues found that in successful cases a rights-based approach encouraged an overall shift in focus from discrete projects to broader structural change (the normative level); more detailed investigation of the systemic causes of poverty and barriers to development (the analytical level); and a greater commitment to engage a range of actors to improve the ability of the poor to gain access to their own rights (the operational level).[101]

These "best practices" are laudable. If development practitioners take human rights principles seriously and continue to deepen and spread the implementation of rights-based approaches within their organizations, it will have a profound effect not only on these organizations' roles within development processes, but also on how development itself is conceptualized. For decades, development has been predominantly understood through the modernization paradigm, which frames development as a *technical* enterprise managed by economists and other experts. Within this paradigm, development is seen as an inevitable, universal, linear process whereby societies are transformed economically and culturally as they are infused with capital and other resources.[102] The role of humanitarian organizations within this approach is to serve as "neutral" actors that oversee and speed up the logistics of this process by facilitating the free flow of resources and ensuring that the rising economic tide lifts all boats. Development is unqualifiedly good for everyone, and faster, more stable, and more broadly distributed economic growth is equated with better development.

In contrast, a rights-based approach understands development as an inherently conflict-inducing, political power struggle. Development does not and cannot benefit everyone equally, and it is often inequitable or exploitative of the poor precisely because of the embedded power relations within and between societies.[103] Pro-poor development policies will occur only as a result of power being diffused within society—that is, when poor people are able to effectively make claims on political authorities.[104] A rights-based approach "is inherently a political approach—one that takes into consideration power, struggle and a vision of a better society as key factors in development. It opposes a depoliticized interpretation of development which portrays problems as purely technical matters that can be resolved outside the political arena without conflict when in fact, they are rooted in differences of power, income and assets. Rights cannot be truly realized without changes in the structure and relationships of power in all their forms."[105] For humanitarian organizations, human rights principles indicate that development processes begin with an understanding of discrimination, social exclusion, inequalities in power and wealth, and systematic obstacles to self-sufficiency.[106] Rather than a technical challenge of getting resources to the right places, development is framed as a negotiation among competing stakeholders—between private groups with opposing interests, between private groups and the state, and between states of the global South and North.[107] In this context, the role of humanitarian organizations is to understand the terms of the negotiation and engage it on behalf of the most vulnerable members of society.

When development is viewed in this way, it becomes clear why donor states and international financial institutions are unlikely to employ human rights as anything more than a device to justify a neoliberal economic agenda. State donors have thus far used the language of rights largely as an instrument of power to impose new conditionalities on recipient states, or as an excuse to selectively restrict aid to regimes that fall out of favor.[108] Western states have deliberately avoided the use of rights language that examines global inequalities of wealth and power, or imposes duties on their own aid practice.[109]

Humanitarian NGOs, on the other hand, are in a uniquely advantageous position to give deeper meaning to rights-based approaches because of their long histories of working on the ground in areas of poverty and their explicit mandates to work on behalf of the most vulnerable. If NGOs view themselves merely as logisticians in the modernizing project, all of the rhetoric about participation and empowerment is likely to fall short. But if they do take human rights seriously, they will continue to deepen the organizational reforms mentioned above. As humanitarian organizations have adopted predominantly moral approaches to subsistence rights, they have found them to be advantageous in guiding their programming and changing their conceptions of development.

Challenges Inherent in a Moral Approach to Rights in Humanitarian Work

The moral approach to rights is also resulting in a new set of challenges that humanitarian NGOs will have to overcome in order to implement rights-based approaches successfully—challenges both within the organizations themselves and in their relations with various stakeholders.

Changing Course Amid Scarce Resources

The first set of challenges involves the difficulties associated with any major transition in a well-established bureaucracy. Many forces within the bureaucracy resist change, both because of their own vested interests and because of uncertainty about the effectiveness of moving in a new direction. In humanitarian NGOs, the lack of a clear understanding about what rights-based approaches entail in practice has led to resistance among some staff members who think that it is just another development trend, adopted by top administrators to please their donors, with no practical guidance for staff about how to implement them.[110] There remains much skepticism within humanitarian organizations that the "whole human rights issue is a diversion, a complication, and unnecessary fluff."[111] Some staff members may be reluctant to implement change because they are comfortable with the traditional service delivery approach, they think they are already doing rights-related work, or they fear that they will lose their jobs or influence within the organization.[112] This challenge is exacerbated by humanitarian organizations' moral approach to rights, because it is not grounded in any set of positive law or easily identifiable methodologies. Because of these internal barriers, organizations are faced with the task not only of demystifying rights-based approaches by clearly explaining how they should translate into practice for their particular organizations,[113] but also of commiting sufficient resources to build organizational capacity and staff skills to implement their rights-based approaches effectively.

NGOs have acknowledged that they need to develop new skills in "facilitation, mediation, advocacy, relationship-building, community organizing, cultural sensitivity and analysis" as well as hire staff with a broad "social science orientation rather than purely technical skills."[114] However, this is tremendously difficult, because historically humanitarian organizations' comparative advantage has not been in conducting analyses of social inequalities, monitoring economic policies, fostering social movements, and other typical rights-based practices.[115] Some observers might argue that humanitarian NGOs have no business advocating on global economic issues when they have little expertise in international trade or economic policy.[116] Can humanitarian NGOs, that are already starved for funds in comparison with the scale of their mission, afford to spend their time and financial resources building these capacities?[117]

This challenge is further complicated by the fact that rights-based approaches can involve shifting organizational budgets away from direct services, even though providing those basic goods and services remains a central mission of the organization.[118] NGOs are often called in to provide immediate material assistance in short-term emergencies; in these situations they lack the time to conduct rigorous analyses or pursue slow structural change. In addition, most of the funds provided by large donors are earmarked for specific projects, making it more difficult to free up resources for research, analysis, advocacy, internal capacity building, and other organizational needs.[119]

Donors tend to want NGOs to produce tangible, measurable evidence of their accomplishments, which does not fit well with the rights-based goal of long-term, more intangible, structural change.[120] State-based donors are increasingly keeping humanitarian NGOs on a short leash through short-term contracts, competitive bidding processes, and rigorous reporting rules.[121] Rights-based approaches necessitate a greater financial and staff commitment from NGOs, even as individual organizations would have less direct influence on deep structural issues and the root causes of poverty than they would on individual recipients.[122] Because "human rights can't deliver in the short run,"[123] humanitarian NGOs will have to persuade donors that their methods are effective according to a new set of criteria that prizes long-term efforts. If donors expect rights-based approaches to achieve immediate results, then it will be exceedingly difficult for humanitarian NGOs to justify their rights-based work to funders, particularly when NGOs historically have raised funds based on the short-term urgency of the need. Humanitarian NGOs seeking funds often find that "pressing the apolitical, victim-oriented philanthropic button is easier than 'enlightening' people on rights issues."[124] Peter Uvin argues that international development evolved into a $50 billion global industry (dwarfing the resources devoted to human rights work) precisely because the development enterprise has been presented as the technical pursuit of a widely shared goal rather than a process of political contestation.[125] These challenges, however, are not insurmountable.

Because of the challenge inherent in scarce resources, development practitioners are implementing two mutually compatible strategies to make rights-based approaches possible. First, as mentioned earlier, many NGOs are attempting to integrate rights-based principles into their existing work as much as possible rather than create a separate set of human rights projects.[126] Although some rights-based work will inevitably involve new projects—including legal work and policy advocacy at the international level—the point is that organizations should still provide basic goods and services in such a way that it contributes to the empowerment of vulnerable communities, the building of horizontal networks, and long-term structural change.[127] Public health expert Paul Farmer argues that "the spirit in which the services are delivered makes all the difference. Service delivery can be just that—or it can be pragmatic solidarity, linked to the broader goals of equality and justice for the poor."[128]

Second, in order to provide services in a spirit of "pragmatic solidarity," humanitarian NGOs are increasingly collaborating with and relying on other organizations to provide the expertise in particular areas where they lack it. John Ambler of CARE calls this "strategic partnering" with other organizations.[129] To the extent that this is carried out, the three kinds of actors studied in this book—human rights, social justice, and humanitarian groups—begin to coalesce into a single movement fighting for freedom from poverty, and the boundaries of identity between the three groups begin to blur.

Overcoming Barriers to Participation

Doing development work in a spirit of pragmatic solidarity must also overcome significant barriers to political participation and claim making by the poor. As Craig Johnson and Daniel Start explain, "For the poor, the costs of engaging in sustained political action (including and beyond the act of voting) are often disproportionately high." This is not only because they lack the resources to get involved, but also because "formal and informal institutions may be structured in a way that prevents poor people from engaging in direct political action." [130] Poor communities are stuck in a vicious cycle—they need resources to make claims on other actors, but they need to make claims effectively if they hope to secure adequate resources.[131] Taking a rights-based approach to poverty, if it involves confrontation with political authorities, can therefore subject poor communities to greater risk of violence, or prove empty if it is not accompanied by resources to make political participation effective and sustained.[132]

This is why the principle of "downward accountability" and a long-term commitment to vulnerable communities is central to implementing a rights-based approach.[133] Downward accountability requires that NGOs be accountable primarily to local stakeholders rather than overseas donors,[134] particularly to the marginalized communities in which they work. "Stakeholders and beneficiaries should be given the opportunity, for example, to express their opinions about the quality, relevance and effectiveness of [the NGO's] work and partnership." [135] The problem is that accountability to donors is often in tension with accountability to clients, because donors use very different reporting mechanisms and criteria to judge an NGO's effectiveness.[136] Donors often expect results in terms of measurable short-term goals, such as the quantity of goods delivered or a specific change in government policy. Because NGOs cannot exist without funding, this provides a strong incentive to pursue high-profile advocacy campaigns that are geared toward Western donors rather than the expressed needs of vulnerable populations. The focus on global policy and advocacy work can lead to a disconnect between relatively powerful global actors and powerless local ones.[137] If humanitarian NGOs intend to take rights-based approaches seriously, they cannot assume that rights-based work is equated with global policy advocacy; rather, they must put the principles of local participation, empowerment, and downward accountability at the forefront. Thus, to evaluate whether an NGO is "really" taking rights-based approaches seriously, instead of asking what proportion of its budget is directed toward policy advocacy, whether it explicitly refers to international human rights standards, or whether it has instituted legal aid projects, the following questions may be more helpful: Is the organization working toward the creation of social guarantees for the poor? Has the organization implemented specific processes and mechanisms whereby its poor stakeholders can contribute to the design, implementation, and monitoring of projects? Does the NGO determine in isolation what rights are threatened and what strategies to pursue, or does it collaborate with local partners in identifying needs and strategies? Are the poor empowered to pursue long-term change and take control of their own lives even after a project's life span ends? The implementation of any rights-based approach "must be interrogated for the extent to which it enables those whose lives are affected the most to articulate their priorities and claim genuine accountability from development agencies, and also, the extent to which the agencies become critically self-aware and address inherent power inequalities in their interaction with those people."[138] As humanitarian organizations are demonstrating through their adoption of moral approaches to subsistence rights, they are beginning to take accountability, empowerment, and structural change seriously. There is a long distance to travel before they can claim effectiveness, but the path ahead is gradually becoming clearer. *but that was before*

Conclusions

Because of the centrality of local participation and empowerment described above, a legalistic understanding of rights is insufficient to describe NGOs' work in the field. For most organizations, an exclusively legal approach to rights in development would impose costs that outweigh its benefits. Legal approaches assume that for human rights to be meaningful, humanitarian NGOs must be able to understand international law, identify states' obligations, measure specific violations, and propose solutions. Advocates of a legal approach recommend a "systematic educational effort" for NGO staff to train them in international law, and a dissemination of international law into local communities.[139] The problem is that devoting energy to identifying legal rights violations "may unduly focus on minimal requirements and negative aspects of development" rather than collaborating with stakeholders at all levels to design creative solutions to poverty.[140] Human rights conceived as legal violations narrows the discourse of development in potentially unhelpful ways. Legal remedies are formal by definition and tend to be "exclusively individualistic . . . which is obviously unsuitable to challenge structural issues."[141] In contrast, local solutions to poverty in the global South often involve informal arrangements achieved through collaboration and negotiation with local authorities, which requires engagement and collaboration to develop mutual interests, rather than condemning violations.[142] As discussed in previous chapters, training NGO staff in international law and "bringing" rights to poor communities tends to lead to an elite/grassroots split due to the inaccessibility of legal language and institutions.

Although international law can be an important normative foundation, and legal strategies can play a role in their work, the imperative that humanitarian NGOs work directly to empower local communities inherently assumes that "local concepts of rights are also very important. Local interpretations of statutory law, religious law, and customary law are enormously influential in determining what is considered right and just in a local context. . . . [In other words], 'all rights are local,' no matter what higher-level legal instruments might have to say."[143] Humanitarian organizations' understanding of human rights necessarily must be based on moral principles that are locally adaptable and socially actionable, more than international standards of legal accountability. In other words, humanitarian NGOs are implementing rights-based approaches "by 'rooting rights' in the expressed social and economic needs of marginalized and excluded sectors" of the local population, which are "emerging and articulating demands without necessarily making use of formal rights language or legal procedures."[144] Human rights are not a legal magic bullet for the poor, because "the agent that safeguards their interest is their own collective capacity, rather than professional legal structures and systems."[145] In the context of realizing subsistence rights on the ground, which is the central task of humanitarian NGOs,

> Rights do not come in neat packages, but rather are part of dynamic, sometimes messy, processes of resistance and change that work to engage and transform relations of power. Despite the existence of the international human rights system, the terrain of rights remains an

ever-changing, political arena where some groups' rights compete and conflict with others. . . . Rights are not a cold legalistic formula to be arbitrated by well meaning, well educated and sophisticated experts on behalf of the majority. Rather they are a manifestation of what the human spirit aspires to and can achieve through collective and positive struggle. As such they can only be made real by the involvement and empowerment of the community at large, particularly those whose rights are most violated, thereby challenging and eventually overturning the exploitative power relationships that deny rights.[146]

By implementing subsistence rights primarily outside of legal arenas, humanitarian NGOs are demonstrating that human rights understood as basic moral principles are equal in importance to legal standards. As Mary Robinson has stated, "Lawyers should not be the only voice in human rights, and equally, economists should not be the only voice in development."[147] The main strength of the rights-based approach thus is not the diffusion of international legal standards into local contexts, but in humanitarian organizations taking rights-based principles seriously and increasing the capacity of the poor to participate in political and social struggles—as well as transferring the technical capacities—inherent in development. Poor people throughout the world regularly engage in political and social struggle for their basic subsistence. A rights-based approach provides a basis for humanitarian organizations to begin supporting these local struggles, which they have failed to do in the past.[148] As Lisa VeneKlasen and her colleagues argue: "In the absence of this grounding [in local struggles for social change], rights-based approaches are merely a new form of technical fix that combines expert-driven social and economic interventions with legal change that may not be relevant to people and communities or engage them as citizens."[149] In that sense, rights-based approaches in humanitarian work are not so much about changing the mindset of the poor (to know their rights or conceive of themselves as agents) but about changing the mindset of humanitarian organizations themselves. Most of the poor and marginalized people in the world already know that they are suffering an injustice and that they should have a right to an adequate livelihood, even if they do not phrase their claims in terms of universal human rights.[150] A basic conceptualization of livelihood rights has always been a central focus within the historical struggles by the poor to secure their basic economic and social necessities. When these Southern struggles got reframed as "development" by wealthy states and NGOs in the twentieth century, it resulted in the depoliticization of poverty.[151] By increasingly adopting rights-based approaches, the challenge for Western humanitarian organizations is to reverse the previous shift and return to the historical sources of antipoverty work that were rooted in political struggle.

When poor people are able to define human rights for themselves, it "rarely turns over the fine soil of international legislation" or results in any "waving of the UN Charter."[152] Rather than legal terminology, they need effective support from powerful actors who will help them demand resources.[153] Humanitarian NGOs will build this movement not by trying to deliver rights from above, but by learning from "advocacy movements and groups that work to promote the process of socio-political empowerment among the marginalised [which] requires mobilising people to challenge and change unequal and unjust power relationships and enabling them to advocate for themselves."[154] These advocacy movements, like the social justice groups mentioned earlier, require a rights framework that is accessible and empowering in order to mobilize marginalized populations. By framing rights in terms of basic moral principles, humanitarian NGOs are seeking to make rights accessible to the most vulnerable and marginalized populations on the planet. By entering into ideological and political debates about the role of the state and market in economic policy (as evidenced by global campaigns on debt, trade, intellectual property, and other issues), humanitarian NGOs are illustrating the futility of taking a purely technical approach to rights and development, and reinforcing the notion that gaining freedom from poverty is inherently a political struggle. A social theory of human rights recognizes this contribution to subsistence rights as valid, and suggests that each approach to rights will have costs and benefits that depend on the particular social context.

6

Using a Social Theory to Interpret NGO Efforts

This book seeks to explain the recent increase in Western NGOs' work to achieve freedom from poverty, and to understand its meaning for human rights politics more broadly. Subsistence rights, as a subset of economic and social rights, had been delegitimized, opposed, or ignored within the West for decades, in large part due to a particular understanding of human rights that defined them as legal instruments protecting individuals against government interference. Within this framework, civil and political rights were perceived as valid legal rights outlining negative duties on the state, while economic and social rights were regarded as positive entitlements and thus—for geopolitical and ideological reasons—were deemed to be an inappropriate object for human rights activity. The recent emergence of subsistence rights work, and the range of strategic approaches to this work, has important implications for how we understand human rights and how we use them as tools for social transformation. In this chapter, I review what led to the rise of subsistence rights, and argue that a social theory of human rights helps us understand its meaning for human rights politics.

The Mutual Interplay of Interests and Principles

An increasing number of human rights, social justice, and humanitarian NGOs in the past decade have used the human rights framework to work for solutions to extreme poverty. Traditional human rights organizations are adding subsistence rights, along with other economic and social rights, to their portfolio. New human rights organizations devoted specifically to the realization of economic and social rights are appearing. Social justice groups are using human rights language to frame their arguments about extreme poverty in a way that resonates with their constituencies and wider audiences. Humanitarian organizations are adopting rights-based approaches to analyze the environments in which they work and guide the implementation of their projects among the poor. Although these organizations approach rights in different ways, they all have one thing in common: they are advocating for freedom from poverty—the claim that nutrition, housing, health care, and other basic necessities be socially guaranteed.

All of these NGOs have adopted subsistence rights for both principled and strategic reasons, which have been largely harmonious rather than conflicting. Normative entrepreneurs within these organizations responded to what they perceived as opportunities within their strategic environments—for example, the end of the Cold War, the intractability of global poverty, and the legitimacy of rights language—by promoting subsistence rights as a way to respond effectively to these demands. Human rights organizations such as Amnesty International, many of whose members had always believed in the importance and validity of subsistence rights, began to perceive that their future effectiveness required an expansion into economic and social rights. They understood that their relevance, legitimacy, and survival as human rights organizations increasingly depended on promoting these rights, which were being taken up throughout the global South and by young activists in wealthy countries. Yet human rights organizations' expansion into subsistence rights has been limited by ongoing principled and strategic concerns that they do not have the internal capacity or appropriate methodology to advance these rights effectively.

Likewise, most social justice organizations believe in the principled ideas flowing from the human rights framework about the inherent dignity and equality of all people. They have responded to the prevalent rights psychology in the West, the increasing willingness of donors to fund work that bridges human rights and social justice, and increasing support from human rights organizations, by framing some of their organizing and advocacy efforts in terms of human rights. Their use of human rights rhetoric is variable, depending on their organizational identity and the strategic contexts in which they work.

Humanitarian organizations have always been mandated to lift people out of extreme poverty through delivering goods and services. In the 1990s, however, the goals of development and human rights became increasingly linked conceptually; both were defined as improving disadvantaged people's basic capabilities and freedoms. This conceptual linkage was enhanced by the growing belief among humanitarian organizations that they needed to become more engaged politically, more concerned with the structural causes of poverty, and more focused on empowering local communities to meet their own needs—all of which comfortably fit within the rubric of human rights language. With this ideational grounding, and support from UN development agencies and donors, humanitarian NGOs perceived that their strategic interests lay in adopting rights-based approaches to their work. While some institutions, most notably the World Bank, have used rights language primarily to improve their public image and justify existing development practices, most humanitarian NGOs are making a real (but difficult) attempt to use a rights-based approach to reform their programs on the ground.

Principled and strategic (or ideational and rational) factors therefore are not mutually exclusive or even in conflict; principled motives must always be mediated by strategic and organizational concerns. Those who dismiss subsistence rights as invalid are not likely to find rights-based approaches to poverty particularly effective or conducive to organizational survival and growth. Those who believe philosophically in subsistence rights must still find a way to promote them strategically; otherwise the organization will not survive to carry out its work. Organizational interests are primarily generated from and expressed through ideas, and ideas are built on a foundation of interests and promoted through strategic, often calculated, practice.

But why do they all move that way? vomorphism?

NGOs Interpret Human Rights Through Both Legal and Moral Lenses

All of these organizations operate in particular arenas with specific mandates. It should be no surprise, then, that they maintain varying interpretations of human rights and varying uses for the rights framework. I have labeled these approaches to rights *legal* and *moral*. Legal and moral approaches to rights are not mutually exclusive, and sometimes occur within the same organization, but they have generally been used by different groups of actors, with different strategic implications. Although scholars have long identified both legal and moral aspects of rights, they have largely failed to describe how moral rights translate into tangible strategic practice. This study has sought to fill that gap by showing how subsistence rights find expression in NGO practice through a diversity of approaches to rights. An approach to rights is more than a set of decisions about strategies and tactics; it is a fundamental way of interpreting, conceptualizing, and framing what human rights are and what they require from the actors involved.

Human rights organizations have taken a predominantly legal approach to rights. These organizations historically developed methodologies based in their work on civil and political rights that were compatible with a legal understanding of rights, such as publicly shaming governments for violating their legal obligations, and enforcing rights in courts and quasi-judicial arenas. They have largely carried over this approach into their work on poverty. The legal approach to subsistence rights closely identifies these rights with the international legal system, and privileges efforts that are focused on the ultimate establishment of legal rights. When these practitioners talk about using the human rights framework, they tend to refer to a specific corpus of positive international law that can be used as a model to guide a state's domestic legislation, or as a set of legal obligations to which an actor can be held accountable. By adopting a legal approach to subsistence rights, these organizations are helping to break new ground in holding states legally accountable to their destitute populations, through public education campaigns, naming and shaming strategies, elaborating international law, and litigating cases before national courts and quasi-judicial bodies. As such, they are demonstrating that subsistence rights are indeed valid legal rights—powerful legal tools that are justiciable in the appropriate contexts.

Social justice and humanitarian organizations have largely adopted a moral approach to rights that is consistent with their historical mandates and social contexts. The moral approach to rights separates human rights from their international legal sources, and interprets rights as basic moral principles synonymous with equality, justice, participation, empowerment, and dignity. Social justice and humanitarian organizations tend to be more concerned with how human rights speaks to questions of right and wrong, rather than whether an act is legal or illegal. Human rights are therefore claims that lead to social and political action, which may include but is not limited to legal accountability.

The moral approach to rights leads social justice and humanitarian organizations to employ the human rights framework in somewhat unconventional ways. Social justice groups use human rights language to mobilize their constituencies or to lobby directly for policy and institutional reform. In its more simplistic form, human rights language resonates with a range of actors, including donors, policy makers, broad segments of society, and the poor and disadvantaged themselves. By framing poverty in terms of rights and justice, these organizations are working to radically transform basic cultural assumptions about poverty that are prevalent in liberal societies like the United States. Their potential lies in redefining poverty as an issue of systemic failure subject to social responsibility, rather than individual failure subject to charity. Humanitarian organizations use human rights to provide a set of basic principles that guide their efforts to reform their on-the-ground programming. For them, human rights is an umbrella term that describes humanitarian organizations' efforts to take the politics of development seriously, analyze the root causes of poverty, address structural constraints on development, become more accountable to their beneficiaries, and empower disadvantaged people to claim their own resources. Human rights principles operate on three levels: as a normative basis to reconsider humanitarian organizations' overall mandates, as an analytical guide to understanding their operational environments, and as an operational guide to reform on-the-ground practices. Adopting rights-based approaches is therefore leading humanitarian organizations to reframe development as a political negotiation, and to commit themselves to take a principled stand on behalf of the weakest participants in the negotiation.

Particular Approaches to Subsistence Rights Entail Their Own Unique Challenges

Legal and moral approaches envision different strategic pathways to the realization of human rights. Human rights organizations are primarily concerned with creating and implementing a specific legal framework that holds states and other social actors accountable to their legal obligations. Decades of work on civil and political rights has demonstrated that legal accountability is a tremendously powerful mechanism to shape states' calculations of interests and enforce compliance with their basic obligations. Social justice organizations are concerned with reshaping basic cultural assumptions and building constituencies that can put political pressure on social actors. This political pressure and cultural transformation can serve to reinforce legal progress, or it could bypass the legal realm entirely. Humanitarian organizations are concerned with implementing the most effective programs and advocating for economic policies and systems that allow destitute people to lift themselves out of poverty. Therefore, both legal and moral approaches should view human rights as providing different but important strategic tools to establish social guarantees against extreme poverty.

Just as legal and moral tools provide unique advantages in the promotion of human rights, they also entail specific costs. A legal approach to rights tends to orient discourse around the technical details of existing positive law, and thereby encourages criticism of the relative weakness of subsistence rights law and their validity as legal rights. A legal approach to subsistence rights must overcome an entrenched unwillingness among most national courts to delve into social and economic policy, and deal with the U.S. government, which is openly hostile to the notion of legal subsistence rights. A legal approach has the potential danger of being elitist and inaccessible to nonlawyers, thereby alienating the very people in their implementation that subsistence rights are designed to protect. A legal approach must confront the difficult challenge of clarifying and elaborating legal texts so that states' obligations to uphold sub-sistence rights are understood more precisely. In so doing, a legal approach cannot hope to avoid the political and ideological controversies involved in promoting subsistence rights, such as debates over economic policy and the culture of individualism, by claiming to inhabit the legal high ground.

By simplifying and delegalizing human rights language, moral approaches can avoid some of the costs inherent in a legal approach, and they can build the cultural and political support that makes a legal approach more effective. Yet moral approaches also entail specific costs because they are not anchored in the international legal system and thus are unable to take direct advantage of the benefits of legal accountability and enforcement. For example, there is considerable ideological heterogeneity within the social justice movement, so that a moral approach to human rights can involve very different understand-ings of the extent to which certain economic policies and institutions are to blame for poverty, or of whether the goal of social justice is the massive redis-tribution of wealth or more minimalist goals. Although there is also debate within the human rights movement about these issues, the legal approach attempts to narrow the ideological range by eliciting consensus on a specific set of legal standards. In a similar way, humanitarian organizations, lacking an explicit grounding in international law, are tasked with the difficult chal-lenge of translating generic rights principles into fundamental organizational reforms amid a critical scarcity of resources.

NGOs Are Redefining Human Rights Politics

The emergence of subsistence rights advocacy has resulted in two kinds of changes in human rights politics in the West. The most obvious change is that economic and social rights are now understood by NGOs to fall within the purview of legitimate human rights work; as such, human rights politics is no longer confined to the realm of civil and political rights. As the global human rights framework has always included the right of everyone to live in conditions that respect their inherent dignity, this new activity is a welcome and necessary shift in human rights politics. The less obvious but equally important change that has accompanied the rise of subsistence rights is that moral approaches to rights, which were prevalent early in the history of human rights politics but later overshadowed by the legalization of rights practice, have re-emerged through the work of social justice and humanitarian organizations. The realm of human rights politics is now increasingly populated by organizations and networks such as Oxfam, CARE, Public Citizen, and the Jubilee Network, all of whom take a predominantly moral approach to subsistence rights. Due to the nonlegal ways in which these organizations are promoting subsistence rights, the legal and moral are starting to be brought back into balance in human rights politics. Legal approaches will remain tremendously valuable tools, but they are increasingly supplemented and supported by a variety of alternative approaches that are equally valuable. In summarizing this trend, Chris Jochnick predicts that future efforts to promote subsistence rights are likely to be characterized by "greater emphasis on education to address the pervasive biases and ignorance about [economic and social] rights; less focus on courts and judicial remedies . . . ; more leadership from grass-roots organizations, representing the natural advocates of these rights; less concern with the appearance of neutrality, or nonpartisanship; less focus on state actors and more on transnational corporations, international financial institutions, and intergovernmental organizations; and more South-North and coalition-based advocacy, which takes into account the international roots of violations and the need for multidisciplinary monitoring." [1]

The extent to which human rights politics continues to be reconstructed in this way will depend on how much traditional human rights organizations begin to readopt moral approaches, even in their work on civil and political rights. There is some evidence that this is beginning to occur. Smaller human rights organizations, including many new groups created specifically to advance economic and social rights, are broadening their grounds of inquiry and action beyond the law. For example, Joanna Wheeler and Jethro Pettit found that many human rights organizations in Nigeria, Zimbabwe, and Kenya traditionally focused their work on legal education and defense campaigns grounded in international law to protect civil and political rights. But as the scope of their work expanded into subsistence rights, these organizations found the legal approach limited, and have begun to reconceptualize their work by defining rights in terms of the needs of marginalized populations.[2] Similarly, as Amnesty International has moved into campaigns in the past decade on conflict diamonds, the arms trade, violence against women, transnational corporate responsibility, child soldiers, and refugees, it appears to be increasingly welcoming strategic approaches to rights that are only loosely connected to international law at the same time as it is breaking down the artificial barrier between generations of rights. The National Economic and Social Rights Initiative also appears to be moving in this direction in an exemplary way, by getting more involved in public policy debates and grassroots mobilization in its campaigns on the right housing and health in the United States.[3]

Thus, the expansion of work on subsistence rights and the diversity of approaches contained within it has served as an opportunity for traditional human rights organizations to reconsider their approach to all of their work.[4] Emerging work on subsistence rights, as well as other economic and social rights, is resensitizing the human rights community to the social embeddedness of all law and to the utility of human rights as more than legal instruments. Subsistence rights are controversial and politically contested because they are embedded within economic systems, cultural assumptions, and practices in the private sphere; yet human rights organizations have accepted their contestability and still recognized their validity as tools of action. Since the attacks of September 11, 2001, and the resulting war on terror, issues of torture, illegal detention, personal privacy, and other civil rights have become just as controversial and politically contested as the freedom from poverty has been. It seems increasingly clear that human rights organizations cannot hide behind the veil of political neutrality and objective expertise, even with civil and political rights, because the validity of international law itself, not to mention its interpretation, has become a politically charged and partisan topic in the United States. In recent polling data, roughly half of all Americans support the use of torture to thwart a terrorist attack, and President Obama has signaled his opposition to torture not through an appeal to international law, but with arguments about moral identity and political effectiveness.

In sum, the rise of economic and social rights

> may make it clearer that, as Vieira and Dupree argue, "the realization of rights springs from deep, gradual and ongoing processes of social negotiation," requiring changing not only patterns of interaction but

a more subtle process of shifting people's consciousness as well. But, as constitutional and public debates over the death penalty and what constitutes cruel, inhuman and degrading treatment attest, the same is true of civil and political rights. Lasting social change demands active social participation toward the entrenchment of a culture of human rights; promoting such participation, in turn, demands re-assessing the boundaries of what constitutes human rights work and by whom it can be done.[5]

This book argues for just such an expansion of the boundaries of what we understand as human rights work. Social justice and humanitarian organizations were not previously viewed as central human rights actors, and moral approaches were not previously viewed as central human rights strategies. Now they are.

A Social Theory on the Emergence of Subsistence Rights

This book's arguments have been grounded in a social theory of human rights, which merges a constructivist understanding of rights (as strategically constructed ideas subject to ongoing interpretive practices) with a post-positivist understanding of the law (as deeply embedded in cultural and social practices). Regardless of how rights are philosophically justified and grounded, a social theory argues that human rights are socially constructed ideas that are subject to ongoing processes of interpretation and legitimation. The power of these ideas depends on how they are interpreted and how well they are strategically framed and promoted. A social theory argues that ideas and interests are inextricably intertwined in producing outcomes that matter: how people define and validate some human rights and not others, and how people use them to promote visions of a better society. Using the rhetoric of human rights is important because rhetoric provides an arena in which this process of legitimation plays out. Thus, the best question to ask about the use of human rights language is not whether it is "mere" rhetoric, but what social practices and interests the rhetoric is used to legitimize.

Throughout the Cold War, subsistence rights—as part of a package of economic and social rights—were delegitimized in the West because they were defined as nonjusticiable or inappropriate to human rights methodologies. As the Cold War ended, Western NGOs began to change their ideas about the validity of subsistence rights, and made strategic calculations that their survival, legitimacy, and effectiveness would be enhanced by incorporating subsistence rights into their work. These two "steps" were really one process: ideas about the validity of subsistence rights depended on calculations of their strategic value, and their strategic value depended on ideas about their validity. For human rights organizations, for example, understandings of subsistence rights as valid legal rights depended on strategic assessments of their potential effectiveness in litigation, treaty elaboration, incorporation into national legislation, and naming and shaming campaigns. Although constructivists acknowledge that ideas and interests can conflict in certain situations, in this case they appeared to be mutually harmonious in producing both the increasing acceptance of subsistence rights and the ongoing resistance to them.

A social theory of human rights also asserts the importance of a broader social context encompassing both legal and moral approaches to rights. If human rights are constructed ideas, then a social theory of rights explains that the effectiveness of these ideas depends as much on processes of legitimation—which occur primarily in nonlegal arenas—as on processes of legalization. A social theory argues that these two realms are inseparable in practice because they are subsumed by a broader social context.[6] Even operating within the legal realm, it is therefore impossible to eliminate the impact of political pressure, cultural assumptions, and prevailing social practices on the creation, interpretation, and implementation of the law.

A social theory of human rights thus defines subsistence rights in terms of claims for social guarantees against extreme poverty. Under this definition, not all service delivery projects among the poor would count as human rights work, but any efforts to establish social guarantees against extreme poverty—through legal, cultural, policy, or institutional reforms—are included. Social guarantees are conceptually distinct from legal guarantees, and the two are not always congruent. In some cases, a norm is both socially and legally guaranteed: for example, the freedom of expression in the U.S. Constitution, which has enjoyed both broad public legitimacy and legal protection. However, some practices are socially guaranteed through cultural norms and prevailing social practices absent any legal protection; any deviance from this kind of guarantee elicits social condemnation. One example of a socially guaranteed practice is the social security system for the elderly in the United States, which Cass Sunstein has described as a "constitutive commitment" outlined by legislation but not required by law.[7] Social security is guaranteed because the overwhelming majority of people have come to think of themselves as entitled to it, because it is an accepted cultural practice, and because large institutions have become established to protect it. The legitimation of social security therefore makes it very resistant to change, as illustrated by the failure of George W. Bush's attempts to alter the system through privatization. Similarly, the right to a basic education is an effective foundational principle, even while not being a constitutional right in the United States.[8] Another example of a social guarantee absent any formal or legal process is the widespread change in behavior resulting from the diffusion of an "ecological sensibility" over the past few decades.[9] Paul Wapner notes that NGOs such as Greenpeace have operated primarily in the "global cultural realm" to foster this sensibility, which has encouraged people around the world to adopt more environmentally sound practices.

On the other hand, many practices are legally guaranteed, but still lacking in social legitimation and practical implementation. One example of a toothless law is an unfunded legal mandate, such as the U.S. No Child Left Behind Act in 2002. Several states have resisted the implementation of this federal legislation because it assigns the legal responsibility to states to improve student achievement without providing the required funds. Another example is a law that attempts to override embedded cultural assumptions, such as the legal prohibition against female genital mutilation in countries such as Benin, Ghana, and Ethiopia that is often not enforced.

Therefore, the most important question to ask of human rights is not "Are they valid legal instruments?"—a question that kept economic and social rights in the shadows for decades—but "Are they effective in changing widespread behavior?" Legal practitioners argue that the law provides a text, a process, a sense of authority, and mechanisms of accountability that make it a central tool in the fight for human rights.[10] As such, they claim that it is more effective to criticize a policy or behavior as illegal than as simply wrong, because only through a legal claim can one take advantage of the powerful resources of the law. This is true in many cases, but not all. When legal texts are vague or controversial, when the social legitimacy of legal rights is undermined, or when legal mechanisms of accountability are not sufficient to elicit compliance, it may be more effective to focus on the moral aspects or anticipated social effects of behavior, rather than its legality.[11] The formalism of legal processes and discourse can blind us to contextual aspects of a problem while allowing for technical legal exceptions and defenses.[12] This is why the realization of subsistence rights will require attention not only to legal efforts but also to efforts in nonlegal arenas, such as economic policy, cultural norms, family relations, and political mobilization. As many practitioners have stated, perhaps the largest obstacle to realizing subsistence rights is the lack of a basic understanding that they are *rights*, that poverty is an issue of systemic failure rather than an unfortunate tragedy or individual failure.[13] A social theory of subsistence rights recognizes and validates both moral and legal approaches to subsistence rights as equally valuable tools for effective social change.

Ultimately the question of effectiveness leads us to ask whether the collective efforts of NGOs will help to end extreme global poverty and establish social guarantees against severe deprivation. At this point, it is impossible to predict. Extreme poverty may never be effectively eliminated, or it may be ended due to factors entirely unrelated to NGO activity. Yet previous research into the impact of NGOs on security policy, environmental policy, democratization, and a host of other issues has demonstrated that NGOs can and do play an important role in defining interests, setting agendas, and applying political pressure on other actors to conform to normative expectations. In the realm of extreme poverty, NGOs are using human rights as the moral and legal bases to encourage the state—and themselves—to change how they understand their basic responsibilities in dealing with poverty. The legalization of subsistence rights is an important, but not the only, strategic pathway to achieve this goal. Legal and moral approaches both provide tools for the realization of human rights, but each tool contains its own set of costs and benefits.

In sum, recent NGO activity has demonstrated that the conventional argument about subsistence rights—that they are not valid rights because they are positive, expensive, programmatic, and nonjusticiable—is misguided in two respects. First, human rights organizations are demonstrating that subsistence rights are valid legal rights by making them justiciable within certain contexts, and by using the legal instruments as tools of public accountability. Second, by adopting moral approaches to rights, social justice and humanitarian organizations are demonstrating that human rights can be effective tools to mobilize the public, generate accountability, transform cultural assumptions, and guide organizational practices even when they are not conceived as legal rights.

According to Mary Robinson, the former UN High Commissioner for Human Rights, "Economic and social rights can become both a powerful moral call to action and a powerful legal tool for addressing today's most urgent global problems."[14] Thanks to the diversity of approaches taken by human rights, social justice, and humanitarian organizations, these groups have already begun to demonstrate both the legal and moral power inherent in the claim to the right to be free from poverty.

Appendix

NGOs Working for Freedom from Poverty

Included here is a brief description of just a few of the hundreds of organizations worldwide that are using the human rights framework to combat extreme poverty. Because this book focuses primarily on NGOs located in the West, where economic and social rights were historically ignored, this list centers around those NGOs. I have categorized the NGOs according to the typology laid out in the book: human rights, social justice, and humanitarian organizations. The "human rights" category is further divided between traditional NGOs (whose mission originally included only civil and political rights) and NGOs that were more recently established to focus exclusively on economic and social rights. Social justice organizations, because they are so numerous, are limited to a narrow selection of those operating in the United States. As with any typology in the social sciences, the categories often overlap; as a result, some of the NGOs listed below may fall into more than one category. I have also included a list several networks of NGOs that have been established to work in coalition to advance freedom from poverty.

Traditional Human Rights NGOs

Amnesty International

Originally formed to support political prisoners, Amnesty expanded its mandate in 2001 to include the "full spectrum" of rights, and remains one of the traditional human rights NGOs that has gone the furthest in integrating issues of poverty into its work. It is currently operating a Global Campaign for Human Dignity, which focuses on the relationship between poverty and human rights. Amnesty is one of the largest human rights organizations in

the world, with headquarters in London and dozens of national offices worldwide. See http://www.amnesty.org/en/economic-and-social-cultural-rights/
ai-action-escr.

Asociacion pro Derechos Humanos (APRODEH)

APRODEH was founded in Lima, Peru in 1983 to protect civil and political
rights during its civil war. In the 1990s, APRODEH expanded its mission to
include economic and social rights, operating programs on trade agreements,
transnational corporations, the right to health, and discrimination. See (in
Spanish) http://www.aprodeh.org.pe/desc/index.htm.

Center for Constitutional Rights (CCR)

Based in New York, the CCR focuses on legal advocacy and operates a program on racial, social, and economic justice. It has helped to litigate major
economic rights cases such as *Doe v. Unocal* and *Wiwa v. Royal Dutch Shell*,
and uses its expertise to allow vulnerable populations access to the legal system. See http://ccrjustice.org/.

Centro de Derechos Humanos (Centro Prodh)

Established in 1988 in Mexico City to promote civil and political rights, Centro Prodh expanded its work to include economic and social rights in 2002
in response to the effects of NAFTA and structural adjustment policies in
Mexico. See http://centroprodh.org.mx/english/.

Centro de Estudios Legales y Sociales (CELS)

Founded in Argentina in 1979 to expose the human rights violations of the
"dirty war," CELS began advocating for economic and social rights in 1997. It
primarily undertakes litigation in accordance with the economic and social
rights provisions of Argentina's constitution, but also conducts research, public education, and advocacy within regional systems and the UN. See http://
www.cels.org.ar.

Global Rights

Although it does not operate a program targeted to economic and social
rights, Global Rights (formerly the International Human Rights Law Group)
has incorporated these rights into its programs on racial discrimination and
the training of young activists worldwide. See http://www.globalrights.org.

Human Rights Council of Australia (HRCA)

Founded in 1978, the HRCA's mission is to promote all human rights. It published *The Rights Way to Development* in 1995, which called for humanitarian organizations to adopt rights-based approaches. The HRCA now operates a program on business and human rights. See http://hrca.org.au/.

Human Rights First (HRF)

Formerly the Lawyers' Committee for Human Rights, HRF focuses on legally defending people at risk for human rights violations. It has incorporated poverty issues in its programs on refugees and transnational corporations. HRF is based in New York and Washington, D.C. See http://www.humanrights first.org/index.aspx.

Human Rights Watch (HRW)

Founded in 1978 in New York, HRW uses field investigations, media campaigns, and direct lobbying of governments to monitor and enforce civil and political rights. In the late 1990s, HRW began to incorporate economic and social rights into its reporting and advocacy strategies, in cases in which these rights interacted with civil and political rights violations. See http://www.hrw .org/en/category/topic/economic-social-and-cultural-rights.

Institute for International Education, International Human Rights Internship Program (IHRIP)

Based in Washington, D.C., the IHRIP brings together experts from around the world to conduct professional exchanges, training, and research. The IHRIP started an economic and social rights project in 1994 that has led to significant publications on these rights, including *Ripple in Still Water* and *Circle of Rights*. See http://www.iie.org//Website/WPreview.cfm?CWID= 658&WID=189.

International Centre for the Legal Protection of Human Rights (Interights)

Based in London, Interights focuses on litigating important human rights cases, primarily in the European system. It operates a program on economic and social rights that advocates for the right to health and education under the European Social Charter. See http://www.interights.org/esr-programme/ index.htm.

International Commission of Jurists (ICJ)

Located in Geneva, Switzerland, the ICJ is comprised of legal experts who consult with local organizations on international law. It was one of the first human rights NGOs to incorporate economic and social rights into its work in the early 1980s. The ICJ convened a set of meetings in 1986 that led to the Limburg Principles, which try to clarify state obligations to realize economic and social rights. See http://www.icj.org/.

International Council on Human Rights Policy (ICHRP)

The ICHRP was founded in 1994 by human rights experts in order to conduct research and publish forward-thinking reports on all human rights. It has produced research on several aspects of economic and social rights, including analyzing the impact of corruption, foreign aid, poverty reduction programs, and transnational corporations on the poor. See http://www.ichrp.org/.

People's Movement for Human Rights Learning (PDHRE)

Founded in 1988, PDHRE is located in New York, and works with a network of social justice organizations to build a culture of human rights around the world through education and training seminars. It is mandated to address all human rights, but now has a significant economic and social rights component. See http://www.pdhre.org/.

Physicians for Human Rights (PHR)

Located in Cambridge, Massachusetts, PHR is a network of health professionals dedicated to protecting human rights since 1986. In 2009, PHR launched a Global Health Action Campaign, advocating for policies around the world that protect the right to health. See http://physiciansforhuman rights.org/.

World Organization against Torture (OMCT)

Founded in Geneva, Switzerland in 1986, the OMCT's core mission is to fight against torture and forced disappearances. The OMCT created a program on economic, social, and cultural rights in 1988 that seeks to identify how poverty leads to increased vulnerability to torture. See http://www.omct.org.

NGOs Created Specifically to Advance Economic and Social Rights

Center for Economic and Social Rights (CESR)

CESR was established in 1993 in New York to use international human rights law to fight against economic injustice. It is now located in Spain, and is working to develop monitoring tools to hold states accountable to their legal obligations on economic and social rights. See http://cesr.org/.

Center for Human Rights and the Environment (CEDHA)

CEDHA is based in Argentina. Its mission is to help victims of environmental degradation—who live primarily in poverty—gain access to legal remedies. It operates a program called Poverty, Human Rights, and the Environment. See http://www.cedha.org.ar/en/.

Centre for Development and Human Rights (CDHR)

Founded in New Delhi in 2002, CDHR is a think tank dedicated to clarifying the notion of the right to development by breaking down the concept into individual economic and social rights. See http://www.cdhr.org.in/.

Centre for Equality Rights in Accommodations (CERA)

Established in 1987 in Ontario, CERA promotes the right to housing primarily in Canada. It seeks to apply national and international law to issues of homelessness and poverty through litigation, public education, and the prevention of evictions. See http://www.equalityrights.org/cera/.

Centre on Housing Rights and Evictions (COHRE)

COHRE is located in Geneva, with several regional offices worldwide. It focuses on realizing the right to housing through a broad range of activities, including litigation, UN advocacy, investigations, public education and training. See http://www.cohre.org/.

Centro de Derechos Económicos y Sociales (CDES)

CDES was founded in 1997 in Ecuador, with support from CESR, in order to combat violations of economic and social rights in Ecuador. Its programming has targeted the issues of foreign debt, the activities of transnational corporations, and the evaluation of national budgets. See (in Spanish) http://www.cdes.org.ec/.

Dignity International

Though tasked with defending all human rights, Dignity devotes special attention to training and capacity building programs to realize economic and social rights. Dignity is located in The Netherlands, and primarily works by supporting the struggles of local communities to achieve their rights. See http://www.dignityinternational.org.

FoodFirst Information and Action Network (FIAN)

FIAN was established in 1986, with a Secretariat in Heidelberg, Germany and over 60 national affiliates. Through legal advocacy, lobbying, grassroots campaigns, and public education, FIAN works to realize the right to food around the world. See http://www.fian.org/.

International Centre on Economic, Social and Cultural Rights (CIDESC)

Founded in Portugal in 2004, CIDESC promotes freedom from poverty through research, lobbying, and collaboration with community organizations. See http://www.esc-rights.org.

Jerusalem Center for Social and Economic Rights (JCSER)

JCSER was established in 1997 to provide legal assistance to Palestinians whose economic and social rights were violated by the Israeli government. It targets discriminatory practices on a range of issues that include social security, taxation, citizenship, housing, and land. See http://www.jcser.org/english.

National Economic and Social Rights Initiative (NESRI)

NESRI was founded in New York in 2004 to help social justice organizations use international law to advocate for economic and social rights. It combines research, training, community organizing, and other methods to support existing movements for change. See http://www.nesri.org/.

Observatori DESC

The Observatori is a Spanish organization created in 1998 from seventeen peace, social justice, and development groups devoted to protecting economic and social rights within a framework of human rights indivisibility. It operates programs on women, migration, external debt, and subsistence rights. http://www.descweb.org.

Realizing Rights, The Ethical Globalization Initiative

Founded in 2002 by former UN High Commissioner for Human Rights Mary Robinson, Realizing Rights seeks to advance the rights of the poor on a global stage. Its work centers around five program areas: trade policies, the right to health, migration, women's leadership, and corporate responsibility. See http://www.realizingrights.org.

Rights and Humanity

Located in the United Kingdom, Rights and Humanity was founded in 1986 to promote a rights-based approach to development among UN agencies, governments, NGOs, and poor communities. It pursues its mission through research, training workshops, and community empowerment initiatives. See http://www.rightsandhumanity.org.

Social and Economic Rights Action Centre (SERAC)

This Nigerian NGO was founded in 1995 to promote economic and social rights through litigation, community organizing, policy advocacy, and monitoring strategies. See http://www.serac.org.

Social Rights Advocacy Centre (SRAC)

SRAC was founded in 2002 in Toronto, Canada to fight poverty through research, education, and legal advocacy. In a variety of arenas, SRAC works to realize economic and social rights such as food, housing, education and health. See http://www.socialrights.ca/.

Trade, Human Rights, and Equitable Economy (3D)

Based in Geneva, 3D brings human rights, social justice, and humanitarian NGOs together to apply human rights principles to international trade policy. Although their work includes national and regional trade policy, 3D is primarily focused on the activities of the WTO. See http://www.3dthree.org.

Social Justice NGOs

American Association for the Advancement of Science (AAAS), Washington, D.C.

AAAS operates a Science and Human Rights program that enlists scientists in the support of human rights, including economic and social rights. For example, one project analyzes government budgets to measure their commitment to economic rights standards. See http://shr.aaas.org/.

Bank Information Center (BIC), Washington, D.C.

Although not explicitly citing international law, BIC emphasizes principles of participation, accountability, transparency, and the protection of human rights as it analyzes the impact of World Bank activities on populations living in poverty. See http://www.bicusa.org.

Border Network for Human Rights (BNHR), El Paso

The BNHR organizes immigrant communities on both sides of the U.S./ Mexico border to defend their rights, including economic and social rights. Though rooted in the principles of the Universal Declaration and the U.S. Constitution, the BNHR has constructed a list of thirteen basic human rights that emerged from community-based discussions about their own priorities. See http://www.bnhr.org/.

Bread for the World, Washington, D.C.

Bread for the World is a Christian organization dedicated to ending hunger in the United States and around the world. It briefly advocated for the Right to Food Resolution in the U.S. Congress in 1975, but has since largely abandoned human rights language in favor of religious or other moral appeals. See http://www.bread.org/.

Carnegie Council on Ethics and International Affairs (CCEIA), New York

The CCEIA is a research institute operating a program on Global Social Justice that analyzes the link between poverty and economic globalization. It produces lectures and publications linking poverty, health, foreign debt, trade practices, and human rights. See http://www.cceia.org/themes/global/index. html.

Center for Human Rights and Global Justice (CHR&GJ), New York

The CHR&GJ is an academic institute, affiliated with the NYU School of Law, which has provided research and teaching on human rights issues since 2002. It maintains a program on economic, social, and cultural rights that tries to clarify the obligations held by a range of actors. See http://www.chrgj.org/projects/escr.html.

Center of Concern (COC), Washington, D.C.

The COC is a faith-based organization advocating on a range of social and economic justice issues through research, networking, and lobbying. In its campaigns on food security, women's rights, and economic development, the COC intersperses language of justice, human rights, and Catholic social teaching. See http://www.coc.org/.

Chicago Coalition for the Homeless, Chicago

The Chicago Coalition brought public housing residents from poor communities together with local NGOs to fight for the right to housing. It led a successful campaign to impose a $10 tax on all real estate transactions in Illinois to be paid into an affordable housing fund, and it conducts a range of other public policy and community organizing initiatives. See http://www.chicago-homeless.org/.

Coalition of Immokalee Workers (CIW), Florida

Established in 1993, the CIW is a group of agricultural workers in Immokalee who have organized for better wages on the basis of claims to human rights. They have mobilized protests against major fast-food brands such as Taco Bell, McDonald's, Subway, and Burger King to ensure that the farmworkers who grow the food for these corporations are paid a fair wage. See http://www.ciw-online.org/.

François-Xavier Bagnoud Center for Health and Human Rights (FXB Center), Boston

The FXB Center, affiliated with the Harvard School of Public Health, was created in 1993 as a research institute to support the global right to health through education and policy advocacy. See http://www.harvardfxbcenter.org/.

Green America (formerly Co-op America), Washington, D.C.

Green America's antisweatshop program uses human rights language in its attempts to end child labor and poor working conditions. Through shareholder activism, they also pressure corporations to implement human rights-specific policies. See http://www.coopamerica.org/programs/sweatshops/.

Heartland Alliance for Human Needs and Human Rights, Chicago

The Heartland Alliance is engaged in both service provision and policy advocacy, and grounds its work in a nonlegalistic human rights framework. Although the founding of the organization dates back over 100 years, it changed its name in 1995 to reflect its growing involvement in housing, subsistence, and health care. See http://www.heartlandalliance.org/.

Human Rights Tech, Philadelphia

Human Rights Tech trains grassroots antipoverty organizations to use the Internet and gain other technical skills to amplify their message. Founded in 1999, it works directly with poor communities across the country, and supports many of the other organizations on this list. See http://www.humanrightstech.org/.

International Rivers Network, Berkeley

International Rivers supports local communities around the world whose sources of fresh water are threatened by dams, overuse, or discriminatory policies. They helped create the Movement for Rivers and Rights in 1997, a global network of social justice organizations working to protect the rights of dam-affected communities. See http://www.internationalrivers.org/.

Kensington Welfare Rights Union (KWRU), Philadelphia

KWRU is a grassroots organization led by homeless and poor individuals mobilizing to claim their economic and social rights. It organizes legal and political campaigns at the local, national, and international levels. In 1997, KWRU helped to establish the Poor People's Economic Human Rights Campaign (PPEHRC), a national network of groups claiming their economic and social rights in the United States. See http://www.kwru.org/.

National Law Center on Homelessness and Poverty (NLCHP), Washington, D.C.

NLCHP provides legal support to the national movement to end homelessness, assisting in the litigation of housing and social services cases. It operates a human rights program, and collaborated in 2005 with COHRE to develop training materials on housing as a human right. See http://www.nlchp.org.

ONE Campaign, Washington, D.C.

ONE was established in 2004 by a coalition of social justice and humanitarian organizations to advocate for policies that would eliminate extreme global poverty and preventable diseases. Within a year, ONE had enlisted over two million members to participate in grassroots organizing efforts. From ONE's perspective, poverty is an issue of economic justice and human rights rather than charity. See http://www.one.org.

Public Citizen, Washington, D.C.

This organization lobbies on a range of public policy issues, including auto safety, energy, global trade, and health. It has adopted a nonlegal rights framework in its programs on water privatization and food sovereignty, arguing that water and food are fundamental rights rather than commodities. See http://www.citizen.org/cmep/Water/.

Urban Justice Center, New York

The Urban Justice Center provides legal services and community education for poor and homeless populations in New York, and engages in policy advocacy to achieve economic justice. Its human rights project attempts to hold U.S. economic policy up to international human rights standards by documenting and reporting on economic rights violations. See http://www.urbanjustice.org/.

Washington Office on Latin America (WOLA), Washington, D.C.

WOLA's mission is to promote U.S. foreign policies that advance human rights, democracy, and social justice in Latin America. Its Rights and Development program works to incorporate human rights concerns into U.S. development and trade policy. See http://www.wola.org.

Women's Economic Agenda Project (WEAP), Oakland

WEAP's mission is to organize low-income communities in the Oakland area, particularly women in poverty, to claim their economic rights. WEAP has organized bus tours, marches, teach-ins, and a human rights documentation project that has collected nearly two thousand stories of economic rights violations in the United States. See http://weap.org/.

Global Humanitarian NGOs

ActionAid

Originally founded in the United Kingdom, ActionAid is now located in South Africa, with a mission to fight poverty and injustice in fifty countries. It adopted a rights-based approach that is centered around working with local organizations in developing countries to empower poor people to claim their rights. Its program on Food Rights advocates on issues regarding corporate accountability, trade policies, foreign aid, and debt. See http://www.actionaid.org/.

Association of Women's Rights in Development (AWID)

AWID is a global network of humanitarian professionals dedicated to gender equity in development. Originally called the Association of Women in Development, AWID changed its name to focus on human rights in 2001. It carries out its work through policy advocacy and capacity building for local organizations. See http://www.awid.org/.

CARE International

CARE provides relief for poor and hungry populations in sixty-six countries throughout the world. It adopted a rights-based approach to development in 1999, which has increased its resources devoted to policy advocacy and its strategic focus on dignity and empowerment. See http://www.care.org/.

Christian Aid

Based in the United Kingdom, Christian Aid is a relief and development organization that adopted a rights-based approach in 2000. This approach is manifested in Christian Aid's Rights and Justice program, which works to empower local communities and engages in policy advocacy among the governments of the United Kingdom. See http://www.christianaid.org.uk/.

Church World Service (CWS)

CWS fights hunger and poverty throughout the world, with projects focusing on emergency relief, agricultural development, refugees, access to water, and economic policy. It is an ecumenical Christian organization that has intermittently used human rights language to guide its work. See http://www.churchworldservice.org/.

Concern Worldwide

Concern is an Irish NGO providing relief in 28 developing countries throughout the world. It adopted a rights-based approach to programming in 2002, and has incorporated this perspective into its projects on education, emergency response, health, and livelihoods. See http://www.concern.net/.

Lutheran World Relief (LWR)

Based in Baltimore, LWR focuses on emergency relief and rural development in nineteen poor countries. LWR adopted a rights-based approach that was consistent with its Christian values and carried out within its Peace and Justice program. It conducts training, advocates for global economic policies, and builds the capacity of local organizations. See http://www.lwr.org/.

Mercy Corps

Mercy Corps is a Christian-based organization that fights poverty in thirty-six countries in a variety of sectors. In the past decade, Mercy Corps began orienting its projects around strengthening civil society in the places where it works. Although not explicitly a rights-based approach, Mercy Corps views its civil society focus as consistent with support for human rights. See http://www.mercycorps.org/.

Oxfam International

Oxfam provides emergency relief and development assistance to people throughout the world. In the late 1990s, Oxfam began adopting a rights-based approach to development, which has led it to reorient its work in local communities and increase its involvement in policy advocacy. In conjunction with its relief work, Oxfam now lobbies for policies related to agriculture, climate change, health and education, and global trade. See http://www.oxfam.org/.

Plan International

Plan fights against child poverty in 48 developing countries. Plan incorporated human rights language into its core mission, and works in the areas of education, health, water and sanitation, domestic violence, economic security, and political participation. See http://plan-international.org/.

Save the Children

Like many global humanitarian organizations, Save the Children consists of several autonomous national offices linked in a confederation. It operates programs in child nutrition and education in forty-two countries. Its affiliates in the United Kingdom and Sweden have adopted the strongest rights-based orientation within the Save the Children network. See http://www.save thechildren.org.uk/.

Water Aid

Based in London, Water Aid works in seventeen countries to provide clean water and basic sanitation to the world's poorest people. In 2003, together with several other NGOs on this list, it launched the Right to Water campaign, which highlights legal and policy issues related to realizing this basic right for all. See http://www.righttowater.info/.

Networks of NGOs

Asian Forum for Human Rights and Development
(Forum-Asia)

Founded in 1991, Forum-Asia is a regional coalition of 42 organizations throughout Asia dedicated to protecting all human rights, but particularly economic and social rights. See http://www.forum-asia.org/. For a list of member organizations, see http://www.forum-asia.org/index.php?option=com_content&task=view&id=186&Itemid=85.

Habitat International Coalition (HIC)

Organized around the UN Conference on Human Settlements in 1976, HIC has grown into a global network of 72 NGOs dedicated to protecting the right to housing. Based in Geneva. See http://www.hic-net.org. For a list of members, see http://hic-net.org/media/reports/annual_report_hic_bw.pdf, p. 39.

International Federation for Human Rights (FIDH)

Based in Paris, FIDH is a network of 155 NGOs worldwide with a mission to defend all human rights. FIDH officially adopted a platform to advocate for economic and social rights in 1997, which now revolves around globalization and corporate accountability, making economic and social rights justiciable, and analyzing trade agreements through a rights lens. See http://www.fidh.

org/-Globalization-ESC-Rights-. For a list of members, see http://www.fidh.
org/-FIDH-network-.

International Network for Economic, Social and Cultural Rights (ESCR-Net)

This is the largest global network of NGOs and individuals struggling to defend economic and social rights, launched in 2003. It links grassroots social justice, humanitarian, human rights, and academic institutions together through working groups and common actions. Headquartered in New York. See http://www.escr-net.org/. For a list of members, see http://www.escr-net.org/members/.

Poor People's Economic Human Rights Campaign (PPEHRC)

The PPEHRC is a network of poor people's organizations across the United States, created in 1998 to mobilize support for economic human rights such as food, housing, and health care. It has organized a range of nonviolent actions, including a nationwide bus tour, a truth commission, a march on Washington, and a training center for young activists. See http://old.economichumanrights.org/. For a list of members, see http://old.economichumanrights.org/members.html.

U.S. Human Rights Network (USHRN)

Established in 2003, the USHRN is dedicated to ending U.S. exceptionalism on a range of human rights issues including freedom from poverty. The network includes a broad array of over one hundred member organizations, from traditional human rights NGOs to small, local grassroots advocacy groups. It includes a working group on economic and social rights. See http://www.ushrnetwork.org/. For a list of USHRN members, see http://www.ushrnetwork.org/about_us/members.

Notes

Chapter 1. NGOs and Freedom from Poverty

1. In June 2003, hundreds of human rights organizations and other NGOs came together to launch the International Network for Economic, Social and Cultural Rights. The world conferences in Vienna, Copenhagen, Johannesburg, and elsewhere also provided opportunities to discuss and support economic and social rights.

2. Within the UN, major development agencies such as the United Nations Development Program, the United Nations Children's Fund, and the World Health Organization have agreed to a common understanding in adopting a human rights framework. This common understanding was outlined in a 2003 statement entitled, "The Human Rights Based Approach to Development Cooperation: Toward a Common Understanding among UN Agencies," available at http://www.unescobkk.org/fileadmin/user_upload/appeal/human_rights/UN_Common_understanding_RBA.pdf (accessed June 4, 2009). It called for all UN agencies to ground their programming in the principles outlined in the Universal Declaration of Human Rights.

3. Private foundations in the United States that are now funding economic and social rights work include the Ford Foundation, the Samuel Rubin Foundation, the Otto Bremer Foundation, and the Mertz-Gilmore Foundation.

4. For a brief description of a few of these organizations, see the Appendix.

5. Mary Ann Glendon, *Rights Talk: The Impoverishment of Political Discourse* (New York: Free Press, 1991), 3.

6. I distinguish three categories of organizational actors based on how they identify themselves and are labeled by other researchers and actors in the field. See, for example, Paul Nelson and Ellen Dorsey, *New Rights Advocacy: Changing Strategies of Development and Human Rights NGOs* (Washington, D.C.: Georgetown University Press, 2008). Similar analytical distinctions between categories of actors are apparent in networks such as the ESCR-Net and the U.S. Human Rights Network. While these categories are useful analytically, we should remember that the boundaries between categories are often blurry, and a single organization can often comfortably fit within more than one category. Indeed, this study shows that as human rights groups increasingly address extreme poverty, and as social justice and humanitarian groups increasingly adopt human rights approaches, the boundaries between them are becoming even more empirically blurred. For a list of organizational members of ESCR-Net,

see http://www.escr-net.org/members/members_list.htm (accessed June 2009). For a list of members in the U.S. Human Rights Network, see http://www.ushrnetwork.org/about_us/members (accessed June 2009).

7. Many social justice groups also provide goods and services to the poor, but this typically occurs in a local context, in contrast with humanitarian organizations' more global reach. For me, by definition a social justice organization must go beyond providing services to incorporate lobbying, education, or other public advocacy strategies designed to foster social change. One coalition in the United States that has gathered these organizations together is the Poor People's Economic Human Rights Campaign (PPEHRC). For a list of PPEHRC's members, see http://www.ppehrc.org (accessed June 2009).

8. As Peter Uvin notes, human rights work is "promoting human dignity through the development of claims that seek to empower excluded groups and that seek to create socially guaranteed improvements in policy." See Uvin, *Human Rights and Development* (Bloomfield, Conn.: Kumarian Press, 2004), 63.

9. This definition is extrapolated from Henry Shue, *Basic Rights: Subsistence, Affluence and U.S. Foreign Policy*, 2nd ed. (Princeton, N.J.: Princeton University Press, 1996), 13.

10. United Nations General Assembly, "Universal Declaration of Human Rights," *adopted* 10 Dec. 1948, GA Res. 217A (III), UN GAOR, 3d Sess. (Resolutions, pt. 1), at 71, art. 25(1), UN Doc. A/810 (1948).

11. United Nations General Assembly, "International Covenant on Economic, Social and Cultural Rights," *adopted* 16 Dec. 1966, GA Res. 2200 (XXI), UN GAOR, 21st Sess., Supp. No. 16, UN Doc. A/6316 (1966), 993 UNTS 3 (entered into force 3 Jan. 1976).

12. For subsistence social rights, see Ran Hirschl, " 'Negative' Rights vs. 'Positive' Entitlements: A Comparative Study of Judicial Interpretations of Rights in an Emerging Neo-Liberal Economic Order," *Human Rights Quarterly* 22, no. 4 (2000): 1083. For the right to an adequate standard of living, see Asbjorn Eide, "Economic, Social and Cultural Rights as Human Rights," in *Economic, Social and Cultural Rights: A Textbook*, ed. Asbjorn Eide, Catarina Krause, and Allan Rosas (London: Martinus Nijhoff, 1995), 31. For the right to be saved from preventable death, see William Aiken, "The Right to be Saved from Starvation," in *World Hunger and Moral Obligation*, ed. William Aiken and Hugh La Follette (Englewood Cliffs, N.J.: Prentice-Hall, 1977), 86.

13. Shue, *Basic Rights*, 5, 19.

14. Isaiah Berlin, *Four Essays on Liberty* (New York: Oxford University Press, 1970), 122ff.

15. The converse is often argued as well, and is true: One cannot meaningfully demand a social response to extreme poverty without being able to exercise free speech or influence the political process. See Amartya Sen, *Development as Freedom* (New York: Alfred A. Knopf, 1999). Thus, I am not arguing that subsistence rights are *more* important than other human rights, but that they serve an essential role in the interlinked web of human rights.

16. For a discussion of the capabilities approach to poverty, which conceives of development as people's ability to "lead the kind of lives they value," as opposed to a focus

on measures of income and wealth, see Sen, *Development as Freedom*, 18. I use the term "extreme poverty" to distinguish it from moderate poverty and relative poverty—situations in which people can still be considered "poor" but able to meet their basic needs. See Jeffrey Sachs, *The End of Poverty: Economic Possibilities for Our Time* (New York: The Penguin Press, 2005), 20.

17. United Nations Development Program, "Human Development Report 2000: Human Rights and Human Development" (2000), 73.

18. United Nations High Commissioner for Human Rights, "Human Rights Dimension of Poverty," *UNHCHR Online*; available at http://www.ohchr.org/english/issues/poverty/index.htm (accessed December 1, 2005).

19. See Katarina Tomasevski, *Development Aid and Human Rights* (New York: St. Martin's Press, 1989), 155.

20. Nanak Kakwani and Hyun H. Son, "New Global Poverty Counts," Working paper no. 29 (Brasilia, Brazil: UNDP International Poverty Centre, September 2006). This study sets the international poverty threshold based on a minimum caloric intake equivalent to $1.22 per day in 1993 PPP exchange rates.

21. For example, according to Bread for the World's 2002 Hunger Report, in the past 30 years hunger has been reduced from one-third of the world's population to one-fifth. See also Kakwani and Son, "New Global Poverty Counts."

22. Cited in Leonard S. Rubenstein, "How International Human Rights Organizations Can Advance Economic, Social, and Cultural Rights: A Response to Kenneth Roth," *Human Rights Quarterly* 26, no. 4 (2004): 846. According to the 2003 Human Development Report, 54 states experienced economic decline in the previous decade, and 21 states experienced an absolute decline in their Human Development Index statistics. The rate of extreme global poverty is declining slightly in terms of the proportion of the world's population, but with population growth, the absolute number of people living in extreme poverty remains stagnant or increases.

23. See, for example, Sachs, *The End of Poverty*, 266ff. Of course, any estimate of additional resources required to reduce extreme poverty assumes that the aid is well directed toward countries and programs that effectively address poverty. Many have argued that this is achievable, but it is certainly not a given. The majority of current official development aid is not directed to the poorest countries, much less to the poorest people within those countries. And even progressive aid policies are often counterbalanced by destructive trade, investment, security, migration, and environmental policies. For a summary of wealthy nations' commitment to poverty reduction, see the Center for Global Development's "Commitment to Development Index," available at http://www.cgdev.org/section/initiatives/_active/cdi (accessed July 22, 2008).

24. Jack Donnelly disputes the conventional wisdom in this regard, arguing that the labeling of economic and social rights in the late 1940s as directive principles rather than justiciable rights was neither a denigration of these rights, nor a particularly Western phenomenon. See Donnelly, "The West and Economic Rights," in *Economic Rights: Conceptual, Measurement, and Policy Issues*, ed. Shareen Hertel and Lanse Minkler

(Cambridge, U.K.: Cambridge University Press, 2007), 37. Even if Donnelly is correct, the underlying fact remains that these rights, originally equivalent to civil and political rights in the Universal Declaration, evolved to assume a lower legal status. This lower legal status was due to their perceived nonjusticiability, as well as the perceived central-ity of justiciability to the notion of rights. These perceptions were strongest in the West, and this book challenges both of them.

25. Quoted in Shue, *Basic Rights,* 221, note 5. Italics are mine.

26. For example, Secretary of State Cyrus Vance noted that "there is a right to the fulfillment of such vital needs as food, shelter, health care, and education." Quoted in Shue, *Basic Rights,* 5. Yet the U.S. government did not incorporate subsistence rights into its policy concerns even during the Carter administration.

27. Philip Alston, quoted in Paul Hunt, *Reclaiming Social Rights: International and Comparative Perspectives* (Brookfield, Vt.: Dartmouth, 1996), xv.

28. Scott Leckie, "Another Step Towards Indivisibility: Identifying the Key Features of Violations of Economic, Social and Cultural Rights," *Human Rights Quarterly* 20, no. 1 (1998): 82.

29. Based on the author's interview with a human rights donor/practitioner, August 2005.

30. See, for example, Philip Alston, "U.S. Ratification of the Covenant on Economic, Social and Cultural Rights: The Need for an Entirely New Strategy," *American Journal of International Law* 84 (1990): 372–78.

31. Anthony Woodiwiss, "The Law Cannot Be Enough: Human Rights and the Limits of Legalism," in *The Legalization of Human Rights*, ed. Basak Çali and Saladin Meckled-Garcia (London: Routledge, 2006), 33.

32. Shue devised a typology of duties that apply to all rights that has gained almost universal acceptance. The duty to respect involves the traditionally "negative" obliga-tion to avoid violating a right oneself. The duty to protect involves the government's obligation to ensure that other private parties do not violate a right, and to implement a remedy in case of a violation. The duty to fulfill involves the obligation to create the positive economic, social and political conditions whereby the right will be realized. See Shue, *Basic Rights,* 52; Tomasevski, *Development Aid and Human Rights,* 106; Charles Jones, *Global Justice: Defending Cosmopolitanism* (Oxford, U.K.: Oxford University Press, 1999), 64.

33. For example, Henry Shue describes subsistence rights as the "morality of the depths"—that is, a minimum standard that a person needs to achieve to survive. See Shue, *Basic Rights,* 18.

34. See, for example, the comments by Philip Alston, Henry Steiner, and Keith Han-sen in "Economic and Social Rights and the Right to Health" (Boston: Harvard Law School Human Rights Program, 1995). Available at http://www.law/harvard.edu/pro-grams/hrp/Publications/economic1.html (accessed February 2005), Session 3.

35. Indeed, even civil and political rights are probably less "taken for granted" than

most human rights activists in the United States would like to admit. For example, the post-9/11 public debates surrounding torture and the increasing willingness of the U.S. public to endorse harsh interrogation techniques show that torture is neither as settled nor as simple an issue as we might think.

36. See, for example, Donnelly, "The West and Economic Rights," 48.

37. See, for example, Ishafan Merali and Valerie Oosterveld, eds., *Giving Meaning to Economic, Social and Cultural Rights* (Philadelphia: University of Pennsylvania Press, 2001), 1; Barbara Von Tigerstrom, "Implementing Economic, Social and Cultural Rights: The Role of National Human Rights Institutions," in *Giving Meaning to Economic, Social and Cultural Rights*, 139.

38. Social constructivists acknowledge the fact that human rights claims are often grounded in appeals to natural law or universal, transcendental values. Rather than challenging these philosophical groundings, I use constructivism to focus on the social *effects* of these claims—that is, how they are legitimized or resisted based on contingent historical processes.

39. Hunt, *Reclaiming Social Rights*, 2.

40. United Nations General Assembly, "International Covenant on Economic, Social and Cultural Rights."

41. Dilys M. Hill, "Rights and Their Realization," in *Economic, Social and Cultural Rights: Progress and Achievement*, ed. Ralph Beddard and Dilys M. Hill (New York: St. Martin's Press, 1992), 17.

42. Hunt, *Reclaiming Social Rights*, 26.

43. Martin Scheinin, "Economic and Social Rights as Legal Rights," in *Economic, Social and Cultural Rights: A Textbook*, ed. Asbjorn Eide, Catarina Krause, and Allan Rosas (London: Martinus Nijhoff, 1995), 42. See also Donnelly, "The West and Economic Rights."

44. Ann Blyberg and Dana Buhl, *Ripple in Still Water: Reflections by Activists on Local- and National-level Work on Economic, Social and Cultural Rights* (Washington, D.C.: Institute for International Education, International Human Rights Internship Program, 1997), Ch. 1.

45. Scheinin, "Economic and Social Rights," 53.

46. Jack Donnelly, "The Virtues of Legalization," in *The Legalization of Human Rights*, ed. Basak Çali and Saladin Meckled-Garcia (London: Routledge, 2006), 69.

47. Kenneth Roth, "Defending Economic, Social and Cultural Rights: Practical Issues Faced by an International Human Rights Organization," *Human Rights Quarterly* 26, no. 1 (2004): 68.

48. Michael Ignatieff, *Human Rights as Politics and Idolatry* (Princeton, N.J.: Princeton University Press, 2001), 89; Emilio Garcia Mendez, "Origin, Concept, and Future of Human Rights: Reflections for a New Agenda," *Sur: International Journal on Human Rights* 1, no. 1 (2004): 7–19.

49. Aryeh Neier, "Perspectives on Economic, Social and Cultural Rights," Lecture

given at the Washington College of Law, American University, Washington, D.C., January 19, 2006. Available at http://www.wcl.american.edu/podcast/audio/20060119_WCL_Neier.mp3?rd=1 (accessed March 1, 2006).

Chapter 2. A Social Theory of Human Rights

1. Kenneth W. Abbott, "International Relations Theory, International Law, and the Regime Governing Atrocities in Internal Conflicts," *American Journal of International Law* 93, no. 2 (1999): 362. This gap in the academic literature between international relations and international law has begun to narrow in the past decade, as evident in a 1996 book on international rules (see Robert J. Beck, Anthony Clark Arend, and Robert D. Vander Lugt, eds. *International Rules: Approaches from International Law and International Relations* [Oxford, U.K.: Oxford University Press, 1996]), an April 1999 symposium in the *American Journal of International Law* (see Steven R. Ratner and Anne-Marie Slaughter, "Appraising the Methods of International Law: A Prospectus for Readers," *American Journal of International Law* 93, no. 2 [1999)]); and a Summer 2000 issue of *International Organization* devoted to the concept of legalization in world politics (see Judith Goldstein and others, eds., *Legalization and World Politics* 54, no. [3]).

2. Neoliberal institutionalists explain the durability of international norms by arguing that they provide decision makers with common information and reduce transaction costs, thereby making it easier for all involved to pursue their self-interests. Thus neoliberalists are somewhat more attuned to studying international law, attributing some influence to norms, but still argue that calculations of interests underlie all behavior.

3. Beck, Arend, and Vander Lugt, *International Rules*, 97.

4. Quoted in ibid., 96.

5. Bruno Simma and Andreas L. Paulus, "The Responsibility of Individuals for Human Rights Abuses in Internal Conflicts: A Positivist View," *American Journal of International Law* 93, no. 2 (1999): 304.

6. Ibid.

7. See, for example, Paul Wapner, *Environmental Activism and World Civic Politics* (Albany, N.Y.: SUNY Press, 1996); Jackie Smith, Charles Chatfield, and Ron Pagnucco, eds., *Transnational Social Movements and Global Politics: Solidarity Beyond the State* (Syracuse, N.Y.: Syracuse University Press, 1997).

8. See, for example, Margaret E. Keck and Kathryn Sikkink, *Activists Beyond Borders: Advocacy Networks in International Politics* (Ithaca, N.Y.: Cornell University Press, 1998).

9. See, for example, Martha Finnemore, *National Interests in International Society* (Ithaca, N.Y.: Cornell University Press, 1996); Peter J. Katzenstein, ed., *The Culture of National Security: Norms and Identity in World Politics* (New York: Columbia University Press, 1996).

10. I borrow this term from Nicholas Onuf, "International Legal Theory: Where We Stand," *International Legal Theory* 1, no. 1 (1995), available at http://law.ubalt.edu/cicl/ilt/1_1_1995.doc (accessed May 10, 2006).

11. Martha Finnemore and Stephen J. Toope, "Alternatives to 'Legalization': Richer Views of Law and Politics," *International Organization* 55, no. 3 (2001): 750.

12. See, for example, Nicholas Onuf, *World of Our Making: Rules and Rule in Social Theory and International Relations* (Columbia: University of South Carolina Press, 1989); and Friedrich Kratochwil, *Rules, Norms and Decisions: On the Conditions of Practical and Legal Reasoning in International Relations and Domestic Society* (Cambridge, U.K.: Cambridge University Press, 1989).

13. See, for example, Alexander Wendt, *Social Theory of International Politics* (Cambridge, U.K.: Cambridge University Press, 1999), 3; and John Gerard Ruggie, *Constructing the World Polity: Essays on International Institutionalization* (London: Routledge, 1998), 35.

14. See Wendt, *Social Theory,* 131.

15. In that sense, then, I find myself in agreement with much of Wendt's ontology in *Social Theory.* Yet while I believe in some "brute material forces" that preclude "ideas all the way down" (96), I believe that these essential interests are individual rather than social. Thus I reject Wendt's adaptation of Bhaskarian scientific realism, which assigns essential characteristics to social entities such as the state (197).

16. Ibid, 113.

17. Keck and Sikkink, *Activists Beyond Borders.*

18. Thomas Risse, Steven C. Popp, and Kathryn Sikkink, eds., *The Power of Human Rights: International Norms and Domestic Change* (Cambridge, U.K.: Cambridge University Press, 1999).

19. Power can be manifested in different ways, as rump material force (the power to physically coerce), or as the perceived legitimacy to act (authority). The second form of power is obviously dependent on the ideational construction of interests and actorhood. See Wendt, *Social Theory,* 41.

20. Abram Chayes and Antonia Handler Chayes, "On Compliance," *International Organization* 47 (1993); Jeffery W. Legro, "Which Norms Matter? Revisiting the Failure of Internationalism," *International Organization* 51 (1997); Friedrich Kratochwil, "Contract and Regimes: Do Issue Specificity and Variations of Formality Matter?" in *Regime Theory and International Relations,* ed. Volker Rittberger (Oxford, U.K.: Clarendon Press, 1993); and Thomas M. Franck, *The Power of Legitimacy Among Nations* (New York: Oxford University Press, 1990).

21. Ethan A. Nadelmann, "Global Prohibition Regimes: The Evolution of Norms in International Society," *International Organization* 44, no. 4 (1990): 479–526; Clifford Bob, "Merchants of Morality," *Foreign Policy* (March–April 2002): 38.

22. Keck and Sikkink, *Activists Beyond Borders.*

23. Kathryn Sikkink, "Codes of Conduct for Transnational Corporations: The Case of the WHO/UNICEF Code," *International Organization* 40, no. 4 (1986): 815–40.

24. See David A. Snow and Robert D. Benford, "Alternative Types of Cross-national Diffusion in the Social Movement Arena," in *Social Movements in a Globalizing World,*

ed. Donatella della Porta, Hanspeter Kriesi, and Dieter Rucht (New York: St. Martin's Press, 1999), 38.

25. Patrick T. Jackson. "Relational Constructivism: A War of Words," in *Making Sense of International Relations Theory*, ed. Jennifer Sterling-Folker (Boulder, Colo.: Lynne Rienner Publishers, 2006), 139.

26. See, for example, Franck, *The Power of Legitimacy*.

27. Finnemore and Toope, "Alternatives to Legalization," 744.

28. Snow and Benford, drawing on the work of Erving Goffman, define framing as "conscious strategic efforts by groups of people to fashion shared understandings of the world and of themselves that legitimate and motivate collective action." Quoted in Doug McAdam, John D. McCarthy, and Mayer N. Zald, eds., *Comparative Perspectives on Social Movements: Political Opportunities, Mobilizing Structures, and Cultural Framings* (Cambridge, U.K.: Cambridge University Press, 1996), 6. See other contributions in this edited volume for further discussion on framing strategies.

29. Martha Finnemore and Kathryn Sikkink, "International Norm Dynamics and Political Change," *International Organization* 52, no. 4 (1998): 897.

30. See Holly McCammon and others, "How Movements Win: Gendered Opportunity Structures and U.S. Women's Suffrage Movements, 1866 to 1919," *American Sociological Review* 66, no. (February 2001): 49–70.

31. Bert Klandermans and Sjoerd Goslinga, "Media Discourse, Movement Publicity, and the Generation of Collective Action Frames: Theoretical and Empirical Exercises in Meaning Construction," in *Comparative Perspectives on Social Movements: Political Opportunities, Mobilizing Structures, and Cultural Framings*, ed. Doug McAdam, John D. McCarthy, and Mayer N. Zald (Cambridge, U.K.: Cambridge University Press, 1996), 336.

32. David E. Snow and Robert Benford, "Master Frames and Cycles of Protest," in *Frontiers in Social Movement Theory*, ed. Aldon Morris and Carol McClurg Mueller (New Haven, Conn.: Yale University Press, 1992), 137.

33. For a discussion on the "food security" frame see, for example, FIAN International, "Spearheading the Right to Food: FIAN Is 15," *Hungry for What Is Right* (December 2001), 19. For "moral obligation," see Onora O'Neill, *Bounds of Justice* (Cambridge, U.K.: Cambridge University Press, 2000). For "basic needs," see FIAN International, "Spearheading the Right to Food," 11.

34. Dieter Rucht combines the cultural, political, and material environment into a single term, "context structure," which attempts to encapsulate the structural aspects of all three classical social movement factors—political opportunity structure, resource mobilization, and cultural framing. In other words, the context structure provides certain political opportunities, cultural themes, and material resources that a movement or organization can draw on in its strategic efforts to promote an issue. See Dieter Rucht, "The Impact of National Contexts on Social Movement Structures: A Cross-movement and Cross-national Comparison," in *Comparative Perspectives on Social Movements: Political Opportunities, Mobilizing Structures, and Cultural Framings*, ed. Doug McAdam,

John D. McCarthy, and Mayer N. Zald (Cambridge, U.K.: Cambridge University Press, 1996), 188.

35. Ann Florini, "The Evolution of International Norms," *International Studies Quarterly* 40 (1996).

36. Clifford Bob, *The Marketing of Rebellion* (Cambridge, U.K.: Cambridge University Press, 2005), 18.

37. Ibid., abstract.

38. Ibid., 22.

39. See, for example, Donnelly, "The Virtues of Legalization," 67; Saladin Meckled-Garcia and Basak Çali. "Lost in Translation: The Human Rights Ideal and International Human Rights Law," in *The Legalization of Human Rights*, ed. Basak Çali and Saladin Meckled-Garcia (London: Routledge, 2006), 12; Michael Freeman, "Putting Law in Its Place: An Interdisciplinary Evaluation of National Amnesty Laws," in *The Legalization of Human Rights*, ed. Basak Çali and Saladin Meckled-Garcia (London: Routledge, 2006), 52.

40. Basak Çali and Saladin Meckled-Garcia. "Human Rights *Legalized*—Defining, Interpreting, and Implementing an Ideal," in *The Legalization of Human Rights*, ed. Basak Çali and Saladin Meckled-Garcia (London: Routledge, 2006), 1.

41. Meckled-Garcia and Çali, "Lost in Translation," 11.

42. Woodiwiss, "The Law Cannot Be Enough," 32.

43. Judith Goldstein and others, "Introduction: Legalization and World Politics," *International Organization* 54, no. 3 (2000): 387.

44. Ibid., 388.

45. Ibid., 386.

46. Ibid., 388. See also Kenneth W. Abbott and Duncan Snidal, "Hard and Soft Law in International Governance," *International Organization* 54, no. (3) (2000): 447. They note that it may be easier to reach agreement on soft law, and that soft law can provide some necessary flexibility in the interpretation and application of rules.

47. Miles Kahler, "Conclusion: The Causes and Consequences of Legalization," *International Organization* 54, no. 3 (2000): 679; Donnelly, "The Virtues of Legalization," 69.

48. Kenneth W. Abbott and others, "The Concept of Legalization," *International Organization* 54, no. 3 (2000): 413, footnote 26.

49. Çali and Meckled-Garcia. "Human Rights Legalized," 3.

50. Beck, Arend, and Vander Lugt, *International Rules*, 56. Classical versions of legal positivism assert that there are no grounds for human rights other than the positive texts voluntarily consented to by sovereign states, that legal texts themselves should determine their own interpretation, that there is no necessary connection between legal texts and moral discourses, and that the law is entirely independent of its social context. Extreme versions of positivism have been roundly criticized and discredited, thus legal positivists have adapted these positions somewhat by allowing some sources of law beyond written texts, some subjects of law beyond states, and some ways in which formal political institutions affect the law. Yet their basic suppositions about the centrality of legal texts

and uniquely legal processes and institutions remain the same. See Onuf, "International Legal Theory"; Simma and Paulus, "The Responsibility of Individuals," 302.

51. Simma and Paulus, "The Responsibility of Individuals," 304.

52. Anne-Marie Slaughter and Steven R. Ratner, "The Method Is the Message," *American Journal of International Law* 93, no. 2 (1999): 422.

53. Abbott and others, "The Concept of Legalization," 409.

54. Ibid.

55. Glendon, *Rights Talk,* x.

56. Donnelly, "The Virtues of Legalization," 67.

57. Çali and Meckled-Garcia. "Human Rights Legalized," 1.

58. Siegfried Wiessner and Andrew R. Willard, "Policy-Oriented Jurisprudence and Human Rights Abuses in Internal Conflict: Toward a World Public Order of Human Dignity," *American Journal of International Law* 93, no. 2 (1999): 319.

59. Slaughter and Ratner, "The Method Is the Message," 411; Wiessner and Willard, "Policy-Oriented Jurisprudence," 323.

60. Donnelly, "The Virtues of Legalization," 75, citing Harold Koh.

61. Beck, Arend, and Vander Lugt, *International Rules*, 110. The eight values that legal processes are supposed to realize, according to New Haven founders Harold Lasswell and Myres McDougal, are "power, enlightenment, wealth, well-being, skill, affection, respect and rectitude." Quoted in Wiessner and Willard, "Policy-Oriented Jurisprudence," 318.

62. See Kahler, "Conclusion," 673.

63. See Finnemore and Toope, "Alternatives to Legalization," 744.

64. Çali and Meckled-Garcia. "Human Rights Legalized," 6.

65. Ellen L. Lutz and Kathryn Sikkink, "International Human Rights Law and Practice in Latin America," *International Organization* 54, no. 3 (2000): 633–59.

66. See David Kennedy, "A New Stream of International Law Scholarship," in *International Rules: Approaches from International Law and International Relations*, ed. Robert J. Beck, Anthony Clark Arend, and Robert D. Vander Lugt (Oxford, U.K.: Oxford University Press, 1996), 236.

67. Critical legal scholars borrow this understanding of the law from the legal realists of the 1920s. See Steven Vago, *Law and Society* (Upper Saddle River, N.J.: Prentice Hall, 2000), 62.

68. Martti Koskenniemi, "Letter to the Editors of the Symposium," *American Journal of International Law* 93, no. 2 (1999): 354.

69. Ibid.

70. See Onuf, "International Legal Theory."

71. Çali and Meckled-Garcia. "Human Rights Legalized," 5.

Chapter 3. Human Rights Organizations

1. I look primarily, but not exclusively, at NGOs based in the United States and Europe because these are the organizations that historically have ignored economic and

social rights the most in their daily work. See Hunt, *Reclaiming Social Rights*, 147; Raymond C. Offenheiser and Susan Holcombe, "Challenges and Opportunities of Implementing a Rights-based Approach to Development: An Oxfam America Perspective" (Oxford, U.K.: Oxfam America, 2001).

2. Philip Alston, quoted in Hunt, *Reclaiming Social Rights*, xv.

3. Leonard Rubenstein, "How International Human Rights Organizations Can Advance," 846.

4. For more information on the International Commission of Jurists, see http://www.icj.org. For the World Organization against Torture, see http://www.omct.org. For the International Federation for Human Rights, see http://www.fidh.org. All websites accessed June 2009.

5. For general information on Food First, see http://www.fian.org. For the Centre on Housing Rights and Evictions, see http://www.cohre.org. For the Center on Economic and Social Rights, see http://www.cesr.org. For the National Economic and Social Rights Initiative, see http://www.nesri.org. For the Observatori DESC, see http://www.descweb.org. All websites accessed June 2009.

6. Based on the author's interview with the director of a small human rights organization, July 2005.

7. Michael K. Addo, "Justiciability Re-examined," in *Economic, Social and Cultural Rights: Progress and Achievement*, ed. Ralph Beddard and Dilys M. Hill (New York: St. Martin's Press, 1992), 107. For example, the number of NGOs with consultative status in the UN Economic and Social Council has grown from 700 in 1992 to more than 3,000 today. See http://www.un.org/esa/coordination/ngo/ (accessed June 4, 2009).

8. This history was collected from internal Amnesty International documents as well as the author's interviews with three former Amnesty senior staff and board members between 2003 and 2005. For an excellent description of the history of other organizations' adoption of subsistence rights, see Nelson and Dorsey, *New Rights Advocacy*.

9. Bob, "Merchants of Morality," 38.

10. Anuradha Mittal and Peter Rosset, eds., *America Needs Human Rights* (Oakland, Calif.: Food First Books, 1999), 172.

11. Curt Goering, "Amnesty International and Economic, Social and Cultural Rights," in *Ethics in Action: The Ethical Challenges of International Human Rights Nongovernmental Organizations*, ed. Daniel A. Bell and Jean-Marc Coicaud (Cambridge, U.K.: Cambridge University Press, 2007), 205.

12. Jonathan Power, *Like Water on Stone: The Story of Amnesty International* (Boston: Northeastern University Press, 2001), xiv.

13. Amnesty International USA, "Reframing Globalization: The Challenge for Human Rights;" available at http://www.amnestyusa.org/events/agm/agm2002/panels.html (accessed February 1, 2006).

14. Cited from the author's interview with a former Amnesty International senior staff member in June 2003.

15. Goering, "Amnesty International," 215.

16. Nelson and Dorsey, *New Rights Advocacy*, 64.

17. Amnesty International, "Q&A: Economic, Social and Cultural Rights are Human Rights," (London: Amnesty International, 2007). Available at http://web.amnesty.org/pages/economist-response-faq-eng; accessed September 24, 2007.

18. Amnesty International, "Amnesty International's Global Campaign for Human Dignity" (London: Amnesty International, 2007). Available at http://web.amnesty.org/library/pdf/ACT350032007ENGLISH/$File/ACT3500307.pdf (accessed June 2007).

19. Ibid.

20. Nelson and Dorsey, *New Rights Advocacy*, 35, 69.

21. See, for example, Roth, "Defending Economic, Social and Cultural Rights"; Neier, "Perspectives."

22. Ibid.

23. Neera Chandhoke, "How Global Is Global Civil Society?" *Journal of World-Systems Research* 11, no. 2 (2005): 365.

24. Kenneth Roth, "Response to the Critique of Neera Chandhoke," in Bell and Coicaud, *Ethics in Action*, 198.

25. Based on the author's interviews with several human rights practitioners in 2005.

26. Chandhoke, "How Global Is Global Civil Society?" 363.

27. Based on the author's interviews with several human rights practitioners in 2005.

28. Based on the author's interview with a human rights donor, July 2005.

29. See Alston in "Economic and Social Rights and the Right to Health," Session 3.

30. Neier, "Perspectives."

31. Ignatieff, *Human Rights as Politics*, 55, 90.

32. Based on the author's interview with a human rights donor/practitioner, August 2005.

33. Katarina Tomasevski, "Unasked Questions about Economic, Social, and Cultural Rights from the Experience of the Special Rapporteur on the Right to Education (1998–2004): A Response to Kenneth Roth, Leonard S. Rubenstein, and Mary Robinson," *Human Rights Quarterly* 27, no. 2 (2005): 714.

34. Power, *Like Water on Stone*, 119.

35. Ibid., xv.

36. Ibid., xv, 148. During the Cold War, Amnesty was particularly careful in maintaining its impartiality by requiring local groups to adopt at least two political prisoners simultaneously from different religious, political, or ideological backgrounds.

37. Joanne Bauer, "The Challenges to International Human Rights," in *Constructing Human Rights in an Age of Globalization*, ed. Mahmood Monshipouri, Neil Englehart, Andrew J. Nathan, and Kavita Philip (London: M. E. Sharpe, 2003), 249; Blyberg and Buhl, "Ripple in Still Water," Ch. 1. See also Leilani Farha, "Bringing Economic, Social and Cultural Rights Home: Palestinians in Occupied East Jerusalem and Israel," in *Giving Meaning to Economic, Social and Cultural Rights*, ed. Ishafan Merali and Valerie Oosterveld, (Philadelphia: University of Pennsylvania Press, 2001), 160.

38. Cited from the author's interview with a human rights donor/practitioner in August 2005.

39. Dianne Otto, "Defending Women's Economic and Social Rights: Some Thoughts on Indivisibility and a New Standard of Equality," in *Giving Meaning to Economic, Social and Cultural Rights*, 52.

40. In different terminology, these factors could be viewed as "permissive," structural causes of the rise of subsistence rights advocacy. For more "immediate" causes, one must look to the actions of human rights organizations themselves and agents within those organizations.

41. David Beetham, "What Future for Economic and Social Rights?" in *Politics and Human Rights*, ed. David Beetham (Oxford, U.K.: Blackwell Publishers, 1995), 43. This reinforcement of neoliberalism figured prominently in Francis Fukuyama's famous "end of history" argument.

42. Roger Normand, "Facing the Human Rights Abyss," *Nation*, 10 December 2003 [web-only edition]. Available at http://www.thenation.com/doc.mhtml?i= 20031222&s=normand (accessed August 5, 2005).

43. Cited from the author's interview with an international human rights lawyer, June 2003.

44. Based on the author's interview with human rights practitioners, June 2003. See also Farha, "Bringing Economic, Social and Cultural Rights Home," 160; Jim Shultz, "Promises to Keep: Using Public Budgets as a Tool to Advance Economic, Social and Cultural Rights" (Cuernavaca, Mexico: Ford Foundation and FUNDAR, January 2002), 22.

45. Power, *Like Water on Stone*, xiv.

46. Chris Jochnick and Paulina Garzon, "Rights-Based Approaches to Development: An Overview of the Field" (CARE and Oxfam America, October 2002), 2.

47. Tomasevski, *Development Aid and Human Rights*, 146.

48. Katarina Tomasevski, "Indicators," in *Economic, Social and Cultural Rights: A Textbook*, ed. Asbjorn Eide, Catarina Krause, and Allan Rosas (London: Martinus Nijhoff, 1995a), 398.

49. Lisa VeneKlasen and others, "Rights-based Approaches and Beyond: Challenges of Linking Rights and Participation" (Sussex, U.K.: Institute of Development Studies, 2004), 28; Amnesty International USA, "Reframing Globalization."

50. Offenheiser and Holcombe," Challenges and Opportunities of Implementing a Rights-based Approach to Development: An Oxfam America Perspective" (Oxford, U.K.: Oxfam America, 2001), 7. See also Blyberg and Buhl, "Ripple in Still Water," Ch. 1; and Roth, "Defending Economic, Social and Cultural Rights," 72.

51. Bauer, "The Challenges to International Human Rights."

52. Power, *Like Water on Stone*, xv.

53. See the discussion by Jim Loughran at Dochas, "Application of Rights Based Approaches—Experiences and Challenges" (Dublin: Dochas, 2003). Report from a Dochas Seminar on Rights Based Approaches to Development, 12 February 2003. Available

at http://www.dochas.ie/Working_Groups/RBA/RBA_Seminar.pdf (accessed November 2005).

54. Based on the author's interviews with two former Amnesty staff and board members in June 2003 and April 2004.

55. VeneKlasen and others, "Rights-based Approaches," 17.

56. Based on the author's interview with a human rights donor, July 2005.

57. Based on the author's interview with a human rights donor/practitioner, August 2005.

58. For further information, see http://www.internationalbudget.org/themes/ESC/index.htm (accessed June 2009).

59. See, for example, Jones, *Global Justice,* 64; and Shue, *Basic Rights,* 37.

60. See, for example, Henry J. Steiner and Philip Alston, eds., *International Human Rights in Context: Law, Politics, Morals* (Oxford, U.K.: Oxford University Press, 2000). This well-known textbook on human rights, which contains a reference to morality in its title, discusses morality very rarely in its nearly 1,500 pages of text. In my reading of the text, I could not find a single example of a specifically moral approach to rights on the ground. Morality, when mentioned at all, typically serves as a philosophical basis for rights (e.g., natural law), or as a source of debate over cultural relativism and the universality of human rights.

61. FIAN International, "Spearheading the Right to Food," 23.

62. Aiken, "The Right to be Saved," 87.

63. Carnegie Council on Ethics and International Affairs, "Litigating Human Rights: Promise v. Perils," *Human Rights Dialogue* 2, no. 2 (2000) [e-journal]. Available at http://cceia.org/media/608_hrd2-2.pdf?PHPSESSID=3931f36f3d393927197aea61facc5443 (accessed May 9, 2006).

64. Blyberg and Buhl, "Ripple in Still Water," Ch. 1; Shultz, "Promises to Keep," 7. Italics added.

65. William Schulz, *In Our Own Best Interest: How Defending Human Rights Benefits Us All* (Boston: Beacon Press, 2001), 34.

66. Based on the author's interview with a human rights lawyer, July 2005.

67. Based on the author's interview with a human rights practitioner, June 2003.

68. Alicia Ely Yamin, "The Future in the Mirror: Incorporating Strategies for the Defense and Promotion of Economic, Social, and Cultural Rights into the Mainstream Human Rights Agenda," *Human Rights Quarterly* 97, no. 4 (2005): 1213.

69. Based on the author's interview with a human rights donor, July 2005.

70. United Nations High Commissioner for Human Rights, "Rights-based Approaches: What is a Rights-based Approach to Development?" *UNHCHR Online;* available at http://www.unhchr.ch/development/approaches-04.html (accessed June 29, 2005.

71. A legal approach to rights should not be confused with *legal positivism*, which marginalizes morality entirely by asserting that "one's rights are no more or less than what the law says they are." See Glendon, *Rights Talk,* 38. Although legal positivists would tend to adopt legal approaches to rights, the converse is not necessarily true.

Adopting a legal approach to human rights—i.e., grounding rights in international law—is also not *legalistic* unless it overemphasizes the law to the detriment of other aspects of rights. Because historically the majority of human rights practice has been legally focused, however, it is accurate to say that human rights politics more generally has been legalistic.

72. Abbott and others, "The Concept of Legalization," 409.

73. Tony Evans, "International Human Rights Law as Power/Knowledge," *Human Rights Quarterly* 27, no. 3 (2005): 1051.

74. Diana Mitlin and Sheela Patel, "Re-interpreting the Rights-based Approach: A Grassroots Perspective on Rights and Development" (paper delivered at The Winners and Losers from Rights-Based Approaches to Development Conference, Manchester, U.K., February 21–22, 2005), 25.

75. Blyberg and Buhl, "Ripple in Still Water," Ch. 1.

76. Ibid., Ch. 6; Flavia Piovesan, "Social, Economic and Cultural Rights and Civil and Political Rights," *Sur: International Journal on Human Rights* 1, no. 1 (2004): 26.

77. Blyberg and Buhl, "Ripple in Still Water," Ch. 1; Piovesan, "Social, Economic and Cultural Rights," 31.

78. Power, *Like Water on Stone*, 139.

79. Leckie, "Another Step Towards Indivisibility," 96.

80. Meckled-Garcia and Çali, "Lost in Translation," 12.

81. Evans, "International Human Rights Law," 1046.

82. I attended the inaugural conference of the U.S. Human Rights Network in Atlanta in November 2005. In a meeting of the Scholarship Caucus at that conference, neither of the prominent academics I spoke with could name a single other human rights academic who was not a lawyer.

83. Based on the author's interview in June 2003.

84. Çali and Meckled-Garcia, "Human Rights Legalized," 2.

85. Based on the author's interview with a former Amnesty USA board member, April 2004.

86. United Nations Commission on Human Rights, "Question on the Realization in All Countries of the Economic, Social and Cultural Rights Contained in the Universal Declaration of Human Rights and in the ICESCR, and Study of Special Problems which the Developing Countries Face in their Efforts to Achieve these Human Rights" (Draft resolution within the 60th session, E/CN.4/2004/L.38, 2004), paragraph 3(d).

87. Rubenstein, "How International Human Rights Organizations Can Advance," 848; Mary Robinson "Advancing Economic, Social, and Cultural Rights: The Way Forward," *Human Rights Quarterly* 26, no. 4 (2004): 870.

88. Blyberg and Buhl, "Ripple in Still Water," Ch. 6; Hunt, *Reclaiming Social Rights,* 29–30.

89. Based on a workshop given by a human rights lawyer in June 2003 at the inaugural ESCR-Net Conference in Chiang Mai, Thailand.

90. Donnelly, "The West and Economic Rights," 44.

91. See http://www.borini.info/ (accessed June 2009).

92. Quoted from the author's interview with a human rights practitioner, in June 2003.

93. Hagen Schulz-Forberg and Aoife Nolan, "Legislation: The Homelessness (Scotland) Act 2003—An Analysis," *Housing and ESC Rights Law Quarterly* 1, no. 1 (2004): 9.

94. COHRE, "50 Leading Cases on Economic, Social and Cultural Rights: Summaries" (Geneva, Switzerland: Centre on Housing Rights and Evictions, ESC Rights Litigation Programme, Working Paper No. 1, 2003), 5.

95. ESCR-Net, "Case Law Database," available from http://www.escr-net.org/caselaw; accessed May 19, 2008.

96. Ibid.

97. Ibid., 24. See also FIAN International, "From Legislative Framework to Framework Legislation: A Strategy for Implementing the Right to Food," *Right to Food Journal* 1 (July 2003): 10.

98. COHRE, "50 Leading Cases," 27.

99. Justice Albie Sachs, quoted in Vinodh Jaichand, "Public Interest Litigation Strategies for Advancing Human Rights in Domestic Systems of Law," *Sur: International Journal on Human Rights* 1, no. 1 (2004): 131.

100. Cited from the author's interview with an international human rights lawyer, June 2003.

101. Jaichand, "Public Interest Litigation," 130.

102. Malcolm Langford, "The Question of Resources," *Housing and ESC Rights Law Quarterly* 1, no. 3 (2004): 4.

103. The reasonableness standard has actually been criticized as "little more than an amorphous obligation on the state to devise a reasonable plan to counter social hardship generally," rather than a real commitment to create solutions in specific instances of extreme poverty. See Marius Pieterse, "Possibilities and Pitfalls in the Domestic Enforcement of Social Rights: Contemplating the South African Experience," *Human Rights Quarterly* 26 (2004): 896.

104. COHRE, "50 Leading Cases," 5.

105. See http://www.law-lib.utoronto.ca/Diana/TAC_case_study/HCjudgment.html (accessed June 2009). While there is still controversy over the most effective medication to use and the breadth of coverage, this case certainly compelled an otherwise obstinate government to implement significant policy changes.

106. Mark Heywood, "South Africa's Treatment Action Campaign: Combining Law and Social Mobilization to Realize the Right to Health," *Journal of Human Rights Practice* 1, no. 1 (2009).

107. Jaichand, "Public Interest Litigation," 137.

108. Roth, "Defending Economic, Social and Cultural Rights," 72.

109. Jaichand, "Public Interest Litigation," 127.

110. Based on the author's interview with an international human rights lawyer, June 2003.

111. Flavia Piovesan, "The Implementation of Economic, Social and Cultural Rights: Practices and Experiences," in *Dignity and Human Rights: The Implementation of Economic, Social and Cultural Rights*, ed. Berma Klein Goldewijk, Adalid Contreras Baspineiro, and Paulo Cesar Carbonari (New York: Intersentia, 2002), 113.

112. Based on the author's interview with an international human rights practitioner, June 2003.

113. As will be discussed elsewhere, some observers criticize the attention directed to strengthening and developing international norms and mechanisms because states can so easily ignore or discard it anyway. Upendra Baxi refers satirically to this process as the "endless normativity of human rights standards," in which it becomes necessary to regularly publish and update, through the unique discursive instrumentality of the UN system, in ever-exploding volumes of fine print, the various texts of instruments relating to human rights." See Upendra Baxi, *The Future of Human Rights* (Oxford, U.K.: Oxford University Press, 2002), 1.

114. For a sample list, see Kenneth Roth, "Response to Leonard S. Rubenstein," *Human Rights Quarterly* 26, no. 4 (2004): 876.

115. Chisanga Puta-Chekwe and Nora Flood, "From Division to Integration: Economic, Social, and Cultural Rights as Basic Human Rights," in *Giving Meaning to Economic, Social and Cultural Rights*, ed. Ishafan Merali and Valerie Oosterveld (Philadelphia: University of Pennsylvania Press, 2001), 44.

116. Piovesan, "The Implementation," 120.

117. Hirschl, "Negative Rights."

118. Woodiwiss, "The Law Cannot Be Enough," 37.

119. Sebastian Tedeschi and Julieta Rossi. "The Villa La Dulce Case: Including the Excluded in Social Housing Plans," *Housing and ESC Rights Law Quarterly* 1, no. 1 (2004): 4.

120. Elisabeth Wickeri, "Grootboom's Legacy: Securing the Right of Access to Adequate Housing in South Africa?," NYU School of Law, Center for Human Rights and Global Justice Working Paper No. 5, 2004.

121. Mitlin and Patel, "Re-interpreting the Rights-based Approach," 10.

122. Mendez, "Origin, Concept," 16.

123. William Felice, *The Global New Deal: Economic and Social Human Rights in World Politics* (Oxford, U.K.: Rowman and Littlefield, 2003), 28; Baxi, *The Future of Human Rights*, 8; Yamin, "The Future in the Mirror," 1220.

124. Mittal and Rosset, *America Needs Human Rights*, 173.

125. Roth, "Defending Economic, Social and Cultural Rights," 66.

126. Von Tigerstrom, "Implementing Economic, Social and Cultural Rights," 153.

127. Sarah Blackstock, "Using International Human Rights Law for Anti-Poverty Organizing" (Ottawa, Canada: National Anti-Poverty Organization, 2002); available at http://www.napo-onap.ca/en/issues/using human rights.htm (accessed May 5, 2006).

128. See, for example, Ford Foundation, *Close to Home: Case Studies of Human Rights Work in the United States* (New York: Ford Foundation, 2004), 30.

129. Based on the author's interview with a human rights donor/practitioner, September 2005.

130. Romina Picolotti, "The Right to Safe Drinking Water as a Human Right," *Housing and ESC Rights Law Quarterly* 2, no. 1 (2005): 3.

131. Robinson, "Advancing Economic, Social, and Cultural Rights," 866.

132. Shultz, "Promises to Keep," 20; Ignatieff, *Human Rights as Politics,* 19; Julie A. Mertus, *Bait and Switch: Human Rights and U.S. Foreign Policy* (London: Routledge, 2004).

133. Alston, "U.S. Ratification," 372; Mertus, *Bait and Switch*, 7; Janet Poppendieck, "The USA: Hunger in the Land of Plenty," in *First World Hunger: Food Security and Welfare Politics*, ed. Graham Riches (New York: St. Martin's Press, 1997), 137.

134. Mittal and Rosset, *America Needs Human Rights*, xii.

135. Ibid.

136. Based on author's interview with a senior staff member of a U.S. social justice NGO, in June 2004.

137. Natalie Mivelaz, "Report on the First Meeting of the Working Group on an Optional Protocol to the ICESCR," *Housing and ESC Rights Law Quarterly* 1, no. 1 (2004): 10.

138. Alston, "U.S. Ratification," 383.

139. The 1996 law eliminated the Aid to Families with Dependent Children program, which acted as an entitlement for the most vulnerable populations, and replaced it with the Temporary Assistance to Needy Families program, which imposed time limits on assistance, work requirements, overall funding cuts, block grants to U.S. states, and incentives for states to reduce the number of people served. Mittal and Rosset, *America Needs Human Rights*, 82, 87, 131. See also Kenneth Neubeck, *When Welfare Disappears: The Case for Economic Human Rights* (New York: Routledge, 2006), 18.

140. Alston, "U.S. Ratification," 372–78.

141. Ibid.

142. Offenheiser and Holcombe,"Challenges and Opportunities," 6.

143. Some U.S. states and municipalities have adopted legal subsistence rights in limited form. For example, New York City has adopted a human rights law that provides wide protections against discrimination in employment and housing. (See http://www .nyc.gov/html/cchr/; accessed April 2006.) Yet the status of subsistence rights among the fifty states varies widely, and there is very little protection for subsistence rights in the U.S. Constitution, at least as it is currently interpreted in the courts.

144. Ford Foundation, *Close to Home,* 8.

145. Quoted from the author's interview with a senior staff member of a U.S. social justice NGO, in June 2004.

146. Alston, "U.S. Ratification."

147. Based on the author's interview with a senior staff member of an international human rights organization, June 2003.

148. See the comments by Keith Hansen in "Economic and Social Rights and the Right to Health," Session 3.

149. This complaint was echoed several times by various sources at the inaugural ESCR-Net Conference in Chiang Mai, Thailand on June 8–10, 2003. See also Robinson, "Advancing Economic, Social and Cultural Rights," 868; and Jaichand, "Public Interest Litigation," 128.

150. Quoted in Schulz, *In Our Own Best Interest,* 6.

151. Paul Farmer, *Pathologies of Power: Health, Human Rights, and the New War on the Poor* (Berkeley: University of California Press, 2005), 221.

152. Larry Cox, "Reflections on Human Rights at Century's End," *Human Rights Dialogue* 2, no. 1 (2000): 5.

153. Chidi Anslem Odinkalu, "Why More Africans Don't Use Human Rights Language," *Human Rights Dialogue* 2, no. 1 (2000): 3.

154. Yamin, "The Future in the Mirror," 1239.

155. Quoted from an African human rights practitioner, in a workshop on June 8, 2003 at the inaugural ESCR-Net Conference in Chiang Mai, Thailand.

156. Some examples may include positive vs. negative obligations; primary, secondary, and tertiary duties; progressive realization; maximum available resources; and minimum core content. Legal institutions and complaints procedures can also seem like an insurmountable hurdle for many organizations.

157. Cited from a Latin American human rights activist, in a workshop on June 10, 2003 at the inaugural ESCR-Net Conference in Chiang Mai, Thailand.

158. Odinkalu, "Why More Africans," 4.

159. See, for example, Merali and Oosterveld, *Giving Meaning,* 1; Edwin M. Martin, "Focus on Nutrition: Who Should Pay for What?" in *Food Policy: The Responsibility of the United States in the Life and Death Choices,* ed. Peter G. Brown and Henry Shue (New York: Free Press, 1977), 336.

160. For an elaboration of this argument within the international development field, see David Goldsworthy, "Thinking Politically about Development," *Development and Change* 19:504–30. For a description of the use of rhetoric in legitimation, see Jackson, "Relational Constructivism."

161. See, for example, Hunt, *Reclaiming Social Rights,* 208; Robinson, "Advancing Economic, Social and Cultural Rights," 868; among many others. Leonard Rubenstein argues to the contrary, that legal obligations are sufficiently clear and precise to guide legal judgments. See Rubenstein, "How International Human Rights Organizations Can Advance," 857; Leonard S. Rubenstein, "Response by Leonard S. Rubenstein," *Human Rights Quarterly* 26, no. 4 (2004): 881.

162. As I will discuss below, this is why Ken Roth believes that human rights organizations should focus their energies on the relatively clear and winnable cases such as these. See Roth, "Defending Economic, Social and Cultural Rights."

163. See COHRE, "50 Leading Cases." One right-to-food advocate noted in an interview with the author that 80–90 percent of their case work involved states' obligations to respect and protect subsistence rights. Only recently have they increasingly focused on more "positive" obligations to fulfill rights.

164. See, for example, FIAN International, "Spearheading the Right to Food," 3; Jones, *Global Justice*; and Aiken, "The Right to be Saved," 86. Others who take the maximum position cite poverty as a "violation" of subsistence rights without much attempt to identify who is responsible. See Mittal and Rosset, *America Needs Human Rights*, viii, 132.

165. Shareen Hertel and Lanse Minkler, "Economic Rights: The Terrain," in *Economic Rights: Conceptual, Measurement, and Policy Issues*, ed. Shareen Hertel and Lanse Minkler (Cambridge, U.K.: Cambridge University Press, 2007), 2.

166. For implicit arguments in this regard, see Jean Ziegler, "The Right to Food" (United Nations Commission on Human Rights, 2004), 4; Roth, "Defending Economic, Social and Culture Rights."

167. Roth, "Defending Economic, Social and Culture Rights."

168. Abbott and Snidal, "Hard and Soft Law," 433.

169. See the discussion by Philip Alston in "Economic and Social Rights and the Right to Health," Session 3.

170. This definition of legalization is drawn from Goldstein and others, "Introduction," 387.

171. Keck and Sikkink, *Activists beyond Borders*, 27.

172. See, for example, Rubenstein, "How International Human Rights Organizations Can Advance," 846; International Council on Human Rights Policy, "Duties sans Frontieres: Human Rights and Global Social Justice" (Versoix, Switzerland: International Council on Human Rights Policy, 2003), 35.

173. This is my critique of Audrey Chapman's approach to violations. See Audrey R. Chapman, "A 'Violations Approach' for Monitoring the International Covenant on Economic, Social and Cultural Rights," *Human Rights Quarterly* 18, no. 1 (1996): 48ff.

174. Robinson, "Advancing Economic, Social and Cultural Rights," 871; Roth, "Response," 874. Personally, I believe along with many human rights activists that the United States spends far too much money on its own military. However, as a movement we still have to recognize the trade-offs involved, and make a persuasive argument to cut military spending in favor of social spending in the face of political circumstances that make military spending tremendously easy to sell to the public. There are persuasive arguments to be made, but the point is that they are not inherent within the legal discourse of international human rights.

175. See Rubenstein, "How International Human Rights Organizations Can Advance," 858. A philosopher of ethics who downplays the trade-offs between rights is Henry Shue, who uses his "priority principle" to argue that basic subsistence and security rights should hold priority over other nonbasic rights and preferences. Shue, *Basic Rights*, 114. This is an attractive analytical framework. However, it does not recognize the difficulties in measuring how much of a public good like military security is necessary or existent at a particular time. As Peter Uvin notes, denial "is the most popular way of addressing the issue of prioritization and trade-offs in the human rights literature." Uvin, *Human Rights and Development*, 186.

176. See Rubenstein, "Response," 880.

177. Tomasevski, "Indicators," 401.

178. Yamin, "The Future in the Mirror," 1209.

179. David Kennedy, "The International Human Rights Movement: Part of the Problem?" *Harvard Human Rights Journal* 15, Spring (2002): 113.

180. See the discussion by Ken Anderson in "Economic and Social Rights and the Right to Health," Session 1.

181. See the discussion by Martha Minow in "Economic and Social Rights and the Right to Health," Session 1.

182. Cass R. Sunstein, *The Second Bill of Rights: FDR's Unfinished Revolution and Why We Need it More than Ever* (New York: Basic Books, 2004), 104.

183. Neil Stammers, "A Critique of Social Approaches to Human Rights," *Human Rights Quarterly* 17, no. 3 (1995): 504.

184. John Rapley, *Globalization and Inequality: Neoliberalism's Downward Spiral* (Boulder, CO: Lynne Rienner, 2004), 83.

185. Shue, *Basic Rights*, 58.

186. Brodsky, Gwen, and Shelagh Day, "Poverty Is a Human Rights Violation," The Poverty and Human Rights Project, in collaboration with the Centre for Feminist Legal Studies at the University of British Columbia, 2001; available at http://www.povnet.org/human_rights/Paper v3.pdf (accessed May 10, 2006), 8.

187. Robinson, "Advancing Economic, Social and Cultural Rights," 871.

188. Leckie, "Another Step Towards Indivisibility," 88.

189. Based on the author's e-mail communication with several human rights practitioners in 2003.

190. Tomasevski, "Indicators," 395.

191. See, for example, Beetham, "What Future," 49; Hertel and Minkler, "Economic Rights," 26.

192. See, for example, Susan Dicklitch and Rhoda E. Howard-Hassmann, "Public Policy and Economic Rights in Ghana and Uganda," in *Economic Rights: Conceptual, Measurement, and Policy Issues*, ed. Shareen Hertel and Lanse Minkler (Cambridge, U.K.: Cambridge University Press, 2007), 325. They argue that World Bank/IMF structural adjustment programs can be beneficial for developing countries in facilitating macroeconomic and institutional reforms that lead to the protection of subsistence rights. Most human rights advocates, on the other hand, tend to be extremely critical of structural adjustment programs.

193. Mitlin and Patel, "Re-interpreting the Rights-based Approach," 20.

194. Cited in Sen, *Development as Freedom*, 46, 144.

195. Alexandra N. Barrantes, "What Matters Most for Poverty Reduction? Inequality and Economic Growth in Perspective," *Swords and Ploughshares* 14, no. 1 (2004): 36.

196. Mwangi S. Kimenyi, "Economic Rights, Human Development Effort, and Institutions," in *Economic Rights: Conceptual, Measurement, and Policy Issues*, 183.

197. Ibid., 198.

198. Michael Yates, "Poverty and Inequality in the Global Economy," *Monthly Review* 55, no. 9 (2004).

199. Alston, "U.S. Ratification," 383.

200. "Poverty and Inequality: A Question of Justice?" *The Economist*, 11 March 2004; available at http://www.economist.com/opinion/displayStory.cfm?story_id=2499118 (accessed September 2005).

201. Mahmood Monshipouri and others, eds., *Constructing Human Rights in the Age of Globalization* (London: M. E. Sharpe, 2003), 272.

202. Sen, *Development as Freedom,* 111.

203. Kerry Rittich, "Feminism After the State: The Rise of the Market and the Future of Women's Rights," in *Giving Meaning to Economic, Social and Cultural Rights*, ed. Ishafan Merali and Valerie Oosterveld (Philadelphia: University of Pennsylvania Press, 2001), 96, 98.

204. Shultz, "Promises to Keep," 37.

205. Baxi, *The Future of Human Rights,* 88.

206. Rittich, "Feminism after the State," 101.

207. Ibid., 96, 98.

208. See the discussion by Ken Anderson in "Economic and Social Rights and the Right to Health," Session 1.

209. Evans, "International Human Rights Law," 1060.

210. Kennedy, "The International Human Rights Movement," 119.

211. Note that "reasonable" does not mean "accurate." I believe many of these excuses to be exactly that—excuses for failing to fulfill an obligation. However, when an actor can persuasively argue to its constituency that it is fulfilling its obligations through policies over which experts themselves disagree—then the effectiveness of human rights arguments are obviously diminished.

212. For examples of the above, see Roth, "Defending Economic, Social and Cultural Rights," 72; Graham Riches, "Hunger, Welfare and Food Security: Emerging Strategies," in *First World Hunger*, 170; Langford, "The Question of Resources," 2; Roth, "Response," 876; Stephen Uttley, "Hunger in New Zealand: A Question of Rights?" in *First World Hunger* , 95; Gary Craig and Elizabeth Dowler, "Let Them Eat Cake! Poverty, Hunger and the UK State," in *First World Hunger*, 120.

213. See, for example, Frances Moore Lappe and Joseph Collins, *Food First: Beyond the Myth of Scarcity* (New York: Ballantine Books, 1977), 4; Alston, "U.S. Ratification," 381; Poppendieck, "The USA," 134.

214. Graham Riches, "Hunger in Canada: Abandoning the Right to Food," in *First World Hunger*, 68.

215. Piovesan, "Social, Economic and Cultural," 36.

216. Roth, "Defending Economic, Social and Cultural Rights."

217. Based on e-mail communication between the author and human rights practitioners, 2003. See also Roth, "Defending Economic, Social and Cultural Rights," 66.

218. The Office of the UN High Commissioner on Human Rights argues, for exam-

ple, that explicitly adopting international law on economic and social rights would lead to "[e]asier consensus, increased transparency and less 'political baggage' in national development processes, as development objectives, indicators and plans can be based on the agreed and universal standards of the international human rights instruments . . ." See United Nations High Commissioner for Human Rights, "Rights-based Approaches: How do Rights-based Approaches Differ and What is the Value Added?" *UNHCHR Online;* available at http://www.unhchr.ch/development/approaches-07.html (accessed June 29, 2005).

219. For examples, see Otto, "Defending Women's Economic and Social Rights," 52; Thomas Nagel, "Poverty and Food: Why Charity Is Not Enough," in *Food Policy: The Responsibility of the United States in the Life and Death Choices,* ed. Peter G. Brown and Henry Shue (New York: Free Press, 1977), 58; Piovesan, "Social, Economic and Cultural," 34; Rittich, "Feminism after the State."

220. Based on the author's interview with a human rights donor/practitioner, August 2005.

221. Farmer, *Pathologies of Power,* 152.

222. Based on the author's interview with a human rights scholar, August 2005.

223. For a report on the results of one such meeting, see Radhika Balakrishnan, *Why MES with Human Rights? Integrating Macro Economic Strategies with Human Rights* (New York: Marymount Manhattan College, 2004).

224. See, for example, Roth, "Defending Economic, Social and Cultural Rights," 72.

225. Yamin, "The Future in the Mirror," 1234.

226. Stammers, "A Critique of Social Approaches," 508.

227. Rubenstein, "How International Human Rights Organizations Can Advance," 864.

228. Roth, "Defending Economic, Social and Cultural Rights," 72. See also VeneKlasen and others, "Rights-based Approaches," 24.

229. Roth, "Defending Economic, Social and Cultural Rights," 72.

230. Cited from the author's interview with a human rights donor/practitioner, September 2005.

231. Roth, "Defending Economic, Social and Cultural Rights," 72; Jochnick and Garzon, "Rights-Based Approaches," 4.

232. Based on the author's interview with a human rights donor/practitioner, September 2005. See also the Center for Economic and Social Rights website at http://cesr.org/training (accessed June 7, 2006).

233. Based on the author's interview with a former Amnesty board member, April 2004.

234. Rubenstein, "How International Human Rights Organizations Can Advance," 855.

235. Bowen, " 'Full Spectrum' Human Rights," 2.

236. Felice, *The Global New Deal,* 28.

237. See Goldstein and others, "Introduction," 387.

238. Kennedy, "The International Human Rights Movement," 121.

239. Ibid., 116.

240. Hertel and Minkler, "Economic Rights," 24.

241. Caroline Moser and others, "To Claim our Rights: Livelihood Security, Human Rights and Sustainable Development" (London: Overseas Development Institute, August 2001), 21.

242. Chris Jochnick, "Confronting the Impunity of Non-State Actors: New Fields for the Promotion of Human Rights," *Human Rights Quarterly* 21, no. 1 (1999): 60.

243. Based on the author's interview with a human rights lawyer, July 2005.

Chapter 4. Social Justice Organizations

1. Social justice movements are often perceived as an afterthought in work on economic and social rights. For example, in a recent volume on economic rights, the social justice movement received only cursory coverage from the editors because not a single contributor focused attention on their importance. See Hertel and Minkler, *Economic Rights*.

2. Neil Stammers, "Social Movements and the Social Construction of Human Rights," *Human Rights Quarterly* 21, no. 4 (1999): 986.

3. Joanna Wheeler and Jethro Pettit, "Whose Rights? Examining the Discourse, Context and Practice of Rights-based Approaches to Development" (Paper delivered at The Winners and Losers from Rights-Based Approaches to Development Conference, Manchester, U.K., February 21–22, 2005), 4.

4. I chose to narrow my research to social justice groups within the United States because of the wide range of approaches to human rights within this country, the accessibility of these groups, and the history of U.S. exceptionalism on human rights (particularly economic and social rights).

5. Doug McAdam, Sidney Tarrow, and Charles Tilly, *Dynamics of Contention* (Cambridge, U.K.: Cambridge University Press, 2001), 12, 30.

6. Marco Giugni, "How Social Movements Matter: Past Research, Present Problems, Future Developments," in *How Social Movements Matter*, ed. Marco Giugni, Doug McAdam, and Charles Tilly (Minneapolis: University of Minnesota Press, 1999), xx.

7. Doug McAdam and David A. Snow, "Social Movements: Conceptual and Theoretical Issues," in *Social Movements: Readings on their Emergence, Mobilization, and Dynamics*, ed. Doug McAdam and David Snow (Los Angeles: Roxbury, 1997), xviii.

8. As Chapter 5 will illustrate, humanitarian organizations are becoming increasingly involved in advocacy for social change, extrainstitutional protest, and capacity building for local movements. As such, their actions belong in the broad category of social movements. However, because actors within this emerging movement identify these organizations as a separate category, and because they are in many ways still analytically distinct from social justice groups, they are treated separately in this study.

9. Based on my participation in the Inaugural ESCR-Net Conference in Chiang Mai,

Thailand in June 2003. See also ESCR-Net's website at http://www.escr-net.org/EngGeneral/about_ESCR.asp (accessed April 2006).

10. While there are important differences in emphasis between the terms "social justice," "economic justice," and "antipoverty," many people in the movement use these terms interchangeably, thus for simplicity's sake I will do so as well.

11. I recognize that "social justice" or "economic justice" organizations do more than just work for better conditions for the poor. For example, they may support equality for women or gay rights. However, because my focus is on basic subsistence and an adequate livelihood, and there is a clear link between subsistence and poverty, my focus is specifically on the antipoverty social movement.

12. Farmer, *Pathologies of Power,* 157.

13. Philip Alston, "Conjuring up New Human Rights: A Proposal for Quality Control," *American Journal of International Law* 78, no. 3 (1984): 608.

14. Clifford Bob, "Constructing New Human Rights Norms: A Theoretical Framework." Paper delivered at the International Studies Association meeting, Montreal, Canada, March 2004.

15. Ford Foundation, *Close to Home,* 8.

16. Ibid., 12. For a list of organizations involved in the Poor People's Economic Human Rights Campaign, see http://www.ppehrc.org/ (accessed June 2009).

17. See Mittal and Rosset, *America Needs Human Rights,* viii.

18. Based on the author's interview with a human rights donor/practitioner, September 2005.

19. Carol Anderson, *Eyes off the Prize: The United Nations and the African American Struggle for Human Rights, 1944–1955* (Cambridge, U.K.: Cambridge University Press, 2003), 5, 276.

20. Glendon, *Rights Talk,* 3–5.

21. Based on the author's interview with a human rights donor/practitioner, September 2005.

22. Ibid.

23. Based on the author's interview with a national homeless advocate, July 2005.

24. Ford Foundation, *Close to Home,* 6.

25. Ibid., 18.

26. See http://www.citizen.org/ for more information (accessed April 2006).

27. Based on discussions with Bread for the World senior staff in 2004, attendance at two annual Bread conferences (2003 and 2005), and a review of archived documents in Bread files in 2004.

28. Mitlin and Patel, "Re-interpreting the Rights-based Approach," 7.

29. Ibid.

30. Ford Foundation, *Close to Home,* 9.

31. Based on the author's participation in the inaugural gathering of the U.S. Human Rights Network, November 2006.

32. Human rights practitioners tend to use the term "international standards" rather than "international law" to denote the fact that some international documents, such as the Universal Declaration, do not have the same binding force as other agreements. Nevertheless, for most of these practitioners, it is essential to their understanding of human rights that they are based in a tangible set of international documents, and these are essentially legal texts.

33. The reason why it is a spectrum is because there are not clearly identifiable categories of organizations; rather, there are differences in emphases in rhetoric and practice. Falling on the left side of the spectrum indicates more of a legal approach to human rights; on the right side, a moral approach.

34. Loretta J. Ross, "Beyond Civil Rights: A New Vision for Social Justice in the United States," *Human Rights Dialogue* 2, no. 1 (2000): 11.

35. Jochnick and Garzon, "Rights-Based Approaches," 5.

36. See http://www.mertzgilmore.org/www/default2.asp?section=what (a ccessed April 2006).

37. This phrase was repeated multiple times in my interviews with representatives of human rights organizations and private foundations.

38. Based on a workshop given by a social justice organization, at the inaugural conference of the U.S. Human Rights Network, November 12, 2005.

39. For more information, see http://www.economichumanrights.org/updates/oas-hearing.htm (accessed April 2006).

40. Michael McCann, *Rights at Work: Pay Equity Reform and the Politics of Legal Mobilization* (Chicago: University of Chicago Press, 1994), 6.

41. Based on discussions at the Inaugural ESCR-Net Conference in Chiang Mai, Thailand in June 2003. See also Nelson and Dorsey, *New Rights Advocacy*, 153; Hertel and Minkler, "Economic Rights," 29.

42. I witnessed this through personal attendance at a U2 concert in Philadelphia in June 2005, and a video of two concerts in San Diego in March 2005. For more information, see http://www.u2.com/tour/ (accessed July 2005).

43. Sen, *Development as Freedom*, 228.

44. Ford Foundation, *Close to Home*, 53.

45. Ibid., 67.

46. Farmer, *Pathologies of Power.*

47. "Sick in America: It Can Happen to You," *Oprah Winfrey Show*, September 27, 2007. Transcript available from http://www.oprah.com (accessed July 22, 2008).

48. Sen, *Development as Freedom*, 211. For Africans, the struggles for independence from colonial powers represents the most prominent human rights movement, even though many of them predated the Universal Declaration of Human Rights and have never been expressed explicitly in human rights terms. See Odinkalu, "Why More Africans," 3.

49. Farmer, *Pathologies of Power*, 17.

50. Roth, "Defending Economic, Social and Cultural Rights," 65; Mittal and Rosset, *America Needs Human Rights*, 3.

51. Quoted from the author's interview in July 2005.

52. Ford Foundation, *Close to Home*, 53.

53. See the comments from Troyan Brennan in "Economic and Social Rights and the Right to Health."

54. See http://www.comminit.com/experiences/pds2005/experiences-3074.html (accessed April 2006).

55. Ford Foundation, *Close to Home*, 26.

56. Glendon, *Rights Talk*, 11.

57. Ibid., 101.

58. Ignatieff, *Human Rights as Politics*, 53.

59. Quoted from the author's interview with a human rights practitioner, June 2003. See also International Council on Human Rights Policy, "Duties sans Frontieres," 25.

60. Quoted from the author's interview with a human rights donor/practitioner, September 2005.

61. Based on the author's interview with a human rights practitioner, June 2003.

62. International Council on Human Rights Policy, "Duties sans Frontieres," 4, 25; Patrick Earle, "Towards a Framework for a Human Rights Analysis of Poverty" (Bangkok, Thailand: Human Rights Council of Australia, 2003), 2.

63. Rubenstein, "How International Human Rights Organizations Can Advance," 861.

64. Offenheiser and Holcombe, "Challenges and Opportunities," 18.

65. Based on author's interview with a UN human rights staff member, June 2003.

66. Based on author's interview with a human rights lawyer/academic, June 2003.

67. Baxi, *The Future of Human Rights*, 2. Italics in the original.

68. Mittal and Rosset, *America Needs Human Rights*, xiv; Offenheiser and Holcombe, "Challenges and Opportunities," 5.

69. Riches, "Hunger in Canada," 46; Riches, "Hunger, Welfare and Food Security," 173.

70. Frances Moore Lappe, Joseph Collins, and David Kinley, *Aid as Obstacle: Twenty Questions about our Foreign Aid and the Hungry* (San Francisco: Institute for Food and Development Policy, 1980), 149.

71. Riches, "Hunger in Canada"; Mittal and Rosset, *America Needs Human Rights*, 177.

72. Aiken, "The Right to be Saved," 99.

73. Riches, "Hunger in Canada," 73.

74. Nagel, "Poverty and Food," 56.

75. Mertus, *Bait and Switch*, 9; Ignatieff, *Human Rights as Politics*, 163.

76. Shue, *Basic Rights*, 15.

77. Shultz, "Promises to Keep," 17.

78. George McGovern, *The Third Freedom: Ending Hunger in Our Time* (New York: Simon and Schuster, 2001), 13. See also the 2001 Hunger Report from Bread for the World.

79. Katarina Tomasevski, *Development Aid and Human Rights Revisited* (London: Pinter Publishers, 1993), 211.

80. Mittal and Rosset, *America Needs Human Rights*, 149; Martin, "Focus on Nutrition," 323.

81. Sachs, *The End of Poverty*, 335. Whether extreme poverty actually creates insecurity for people in developed countries is subject to debate. For example, Alan Krueger argues that terrorism is not strongly related to poverty, but to a "deep devotion to a political, social or religious cause" that cannot find nonviolent means of expression. See Alan B. Krueger, "Poverty Doesn't Create Terrorists," *New York Times*, 29 May 2003; available at http://www.jpef.net/jul03/Poverty doesnt.pdf (accessed May 10, 2006). Regardless of the accuracy of the claim, it is undeniable that since 9/11, more people are sympathetic to the argument that alleviating extreme poverty is a security interest of the United States.

82. Sachs, *The End of Poverty*, Ch. 13.

83. See Thomas Princen and Jennifer Clapp, "Food, Water, Crisis: The Normative Case for a Neo-Prudential Order" (Paper delivered at the International Studies Association meeting, Honolulu, Hawaii, March 3, 2005) .

84. Mittal and Rosset, *America Needs Human Rights*, xiii.

85. See Farmer, *Pathologies of Power* for several poignant examples in the public health field.

86. Ibid., 19.

87. Schulz, *In Our Own Best Interest*. See also David Forsythe, "The United States and International Economic Rights: Law, Social Reality, and Political Choice," in *Economic Rights: Conceptual, Measurement, and Policy Issues*, ed. Shareen Hertel and Lanse Minkler (Cambridge, U.K.: Cambridge University Press, 2007), 320.

88. See, for example, Sebastian Mallaby, "High-Profile Help for Africa," *Washington Post*, May 23, 2005, A19; available at http://www.washingtonpost.com/wp-dyn/content/article/2005/05/22/AR2005052200889.html (accessed May 10, 2006).

89. McGovern, *The Third Freedom,* 161.

90. Steven Weber, "International Organizations and the Pursuit of Justice in the World Economy," *Ethics and International Affairs* 14 (2000): 99.

91. Cited from a Poor People's Economic Human Rights Campaign public brochure, acquired in November 2005.

92. See "Poverty and Inequality: A Question of Justice?" *Economist.* 11 March 2004. Available from http://www.economist.com/opinion/displayStory.cfm?story_id=2499118; Internet; accessed September 2005.

93. See, for example, McAdam, Tarrow, and Tilly, *Dynamics of Contention;* and Sidney Tarrow, *Power in Movement: Social Movements and Contentious Politics* (Cambridge, U.K.: Cambridge University Press, 1998).

94. See Herbert Haines, "Black Radicalization and the Funding of Civil Rights: 1957–1970," in *Social Movements: Readings on their Emergence, Mobilization and Dynamics*, ed. Doug McAdam and David Snow (Los Angeles: Roxbury, 1997).

95. Devashree Gupta, "Radical Flank Effects: The Effect of Radical-Moderate Splits in Regional Nationalist Movements." Paper presented at the Conference of Europeanists, Chicago, 2002. Available at http://falcon.arts.cornell.edu/sgt2/pscp/documents/RFEgupta.pdf (accessed June 2009).

96. See, for example, "Economic and Social Rights and the Right to Health."

97. See Felice, *The Global New Deal*, 22.

98. For example, Article 12(1) of the International Covenant on Economic, Social and Cultural Rights leans heavily in this direction in promoting "the right of everyone to the enjoyment of the highest attainable standard of physical and mental health." See also Martha Nussbaum's discussion in "Economic and Social Rights and the Right to Health."

99. Arjun Sengupta, "The Right to Development as a Human Right," François-Xavier Bagnoud Center for Health and Human Rights, 2000; available at http://www.hsph.harvard.edu/fxbcenter/FXBC_WP7—Sengupta.pdf (accessed May 10, 2006; 14).

100. Oxfam International, "Towards Global Equity: Strategic Plan 2001–2004" (Oxford, U.K.: Oxfam International, 2001), 7.

101. A. Belden Fields, *Rethinking Human Rights for the New Millennium* (New York: Palgrave Macmillan, 2003), 135.

102. See a review of Sowell's book in Richard Ebeling, Review of *The Quest for Cosmic Justice* by Thomas Sowell, available at http://www.fff.org/freedom/1299h.asp (accessed August 9, 2005.

103. Ibid.

104. Farmer, *Pathologies of Power*, 240. Note that Farmer still contends that substantive equality in health care should be the standard of treatment we should aspire to. In other words, literally everyone should have access to the highest quality medical care. Farmer, however, does not examine the astronomical costs required to implement this in practice.

105. See Mandler's discussion in "Economic and Social Rights and the Right to Health."

106. Again, this gives the impression that human rights are nonnegotiable, absolute trumps rather than tools in an ongoing political debate.

107. I attended this conference in Atlanta, Georgia on November 12–13, 2005.

108. Shue, *Basic Rights*. See also Jean Carmalt and Sarah Zaidi, "The Right to Health in the United States of America: What Does It Mean?" (Brooklyn, N.Y.: Center for Economic and Social Rights, 2004), 6.

109. Weber, "International Organizations," 100.

110. Ibid., 110. There is a caveat to this argument, because as human rights theorists note, societal understandings of the minimum standard change across time and cultures, depending on society's capacity to fulfill basic needs. As capacity grows, so does the society's conception of the "minimum."

111. Sachs, *The End of Poverty*, 289.

112. Ibid.; Balakrishnan, *Why MES with Human Rights?* 21.

113. See Rubenstein, "How International Human Rights," 857; Sachs, *The End of Poverty*, 298.

114. Jack M. Balkin, "How Social Movements Change (or Fail to Change) the Constitution: The Case of the New Departure," Social Science Research Network Electronic Paper Collection, September 5, 2005; available at http://papers.ssrn.com/sol3/papers.cfm?abstract_id=847164 (accessed December 16, 2005).

115. Ibid., 3.

116. Sunstein, *The Second Bill of Rights*, 30.

117. Ibid., 56.

118. Jack M. Balkin, "Brown, Social Movements, and Social Change," Delaware Brown Symposium, 2005; available at http://www.yale.edu/lawweb/jbalkin/articles/brownsocialmovementsandsocialchange1.pdf (accessed 8 March 8, 2006), 6.

119. Balkin, "How Social Movements Change," 30.

120. Ibid., 11.

121. Cited from the author's interview with a human rights practitioner, September 2005.

122. Wapner, *Environmental Activism*.

123. Ibid., 50; Balkin, "Brown, Social Movements," 7, 12.

124. Odinkalu, "Why More Africans," 3.

125. Ellen Dorsey, "Human Rights and U.S. Foreign Policy: Who Controls the Agenda?" *Journal of Intergroup Relations* 22, no. 1 (1995): 12.

126. Cited from the author's interview with a human rights donor, July 2005.

127. Kennedy, "The International Human Rights Movement," 108.

128. Blackstock, "Using International Human Rights Law."

129. Quoted from a workshop at the inaugural conference of the U.S. Human Rights Network, Atlanta, Georgia, November 12, 2005.

130. Offenheiser and Holcombe, "Challenges and Opportunities," 26.

131. Based on the author's interviews in September 2005 and April 2006.

132. Ford Foundation, *Close to Home*, 56.

133. Ibid., 8.

134. Based on the author's interviews with human rights donors and practitioners in 2005.

135. Hans-Otto Sano, "Development and Human Rights: The Necessary, but Partial Integration of Human Rights and Development," *Human Rights Quarterly* 22, no. 3 (2000): 745.

136. See Sachs, *The End of Poverty*, 339.

137. Abbott and Snidal, "Hard and Soft Law," 422.

138. Moser and others, "To Claim Our Rights," 14.

139. Uvin, *Human Rights and Development*, 133.

140. Yamin, "The Future in the Mirror," 1212.

141. See the Americans and the World website at: http://www.americans-world.org/digest/global_issues/human_rights/HRinGen.cfm (accessed April 2006).

142. See the Global Policy Forum website at: http://www.globalpolicy.org/socecon/inequal/poll-usa.htm (accessed April 2006). Interestingly, between 1988 and 1998, an increasing number of Americans appeared to believe that the primary responsibility for ending poverty resided with the poor themselves (from 18 percent to 28 percent). Yet this proportion is still far smaller than the combined proportion of those who believe the responsibility lies with government (32 percent), the church (14 percent), or individual families (12 percent). Depending on how survey questions are worded, public support for the state's responsibility to end poverty is as high as 65 percent.

143. See the Live 8 website at http://www.live8live.com/ (accessed April 2006).

144. Sunstein, *The Second Bill of Rights*, 2, 5.

145. "Sick in America: It Can Happen to You," *Oprah Winfrey Show*, September 27, 2007.

146. Ibid.

147. See http://www.youtube.com/watch?v=zAR8K2KCiGc (accessed June 2009).

148. See Nelson and Dorsey, *New Rights Advocacy*, 142ff.

149. Rosalind Eyben, "The Rise of Rights: Rights-based Approaches to International Development" (Brighton, U.K.: Institute of Development Studies, May 2003, IDS Policy Briefing #17), 2.

150. See, for example, Mitlin and Patel, "Re-interpreting the Rights-based Approach."

151. Glendon, *Rights Talk*, 3.

152. Cox, "Reflections on Human Rights," 5.

Chapter 5. Humanitarian Organizations

1. Most global humanitarian NGOs are Western in the sense that their headquarters and main sources of support are located in Western countries. Humanitarian NGOs are those organizations whose mission involves easing human suffering, typically through delivering goods and services in the least developed areas of the world.

2. See "Definitions of a Rights-based Approach to Development" at the InterAction website: http://www.interaction.org/files.cgi/2496_Analysis_of_RBA_Definitions1.pdf, 9. Last updated August 2003, accessed November 23, 2005.

3. Sen, *Development as Freedom*.

4. United Nations Development Program, "Human Development Report 2000," 19, 20.

5. Stephen P. Marks, "The Human Rights Framework for Development: Five Approaches" (Boston: Francois-Xavier Bagnoud Center for Health and Human Rights, April 2001), 2.

6. See, for example, United Nations High Commissioner for Human Rights, "Rights-based Approaches: How Do Rights-based Approaches Differ?"

7. United Nations Development Program, "Human Development Report 2000," 20.

8. Tomasevski, "Indicators," 398.

9. Uvin, *Human Rights and Development,* 13. Uvin describes the major trends as focusing on infrastructure in the 1960s, to basic needs in the 1970s, to structural adjustment and governance in the 1980s, to human resource development in the 1990s.

10. Quoted from the author's interview with a human rights donor/practitioner, September 2005.

11. Jochnick and Garzon, "Rights-Based Approaches," 6.

12. Orla Sheehy, "The Discourse of Human Rights and Aid Policy: Facilitating or Challenging Development?" (Paper delivered at The Winners and Losers from Rights-based Approaches to Development Conference, Manchester, U.K., February 21–22, 2005), 10–12. See also Sano, "Development and Human Rights," 735.

13. Jochnick and Garzon, "Rights-Based Approaches," 6.

14. Robinson, "Advancing Economic, Social and Cultural Rights," 867.

15. Sengupta, "The Right to Development," 2.

16. Andrea Cornwall and Celestine Nyamu-Musembi, "Why Rights, Why Now? Reflections on the Rise of Rights in International Development Discourse," *IDS Bulletin* 36, no. 1 (2005): 9–15.

13; Uvin, *Human Rights and Development,* 42.

17. For details, see HRCA's website at http://www.hrca.org.au/activities. htm#Development. Last updated April 13, 2003; accessed November 28, 2005.

18. Sano, "Development and Human Rights," 734.

19. Based on the author's interview with a subsistence rights donor, September 23, 2005.

20. Oxfam International, "Towards Global Equity," 7.

21. Based on the author's interview with a senior staff member of an international humanitarian NGO, June 2003.

22. Offenheiser and Holcombe, "Challenges and Opportunities," 3.

23. See, for example, Dochas, "Application of Rights Based Approaches."

24. Tomasevski, *Development Aid and Human Rights Revisited,* 9.

25. Jochnick and Garzon, "Rights-Based Approaches," 8.

26. See, for example, Mitlin and Patel, "Re-interpreting the Rights-based Approach," 8. See also Mary McClymont's comments in InterAction, "Discussion on the Rights-based Approach to Development" (InterAction, 2003), available at http://www .interaction.org/files.cgi/2581_Notes_RBA_Meeting_December_17_2003.doc (accessed October 18, 2005).

27. Adam Roberts, *Humanitarian Action in War: Aid, Protection and Impartiality in a Policy Vacuum* (Oxford, U.K.: Oxford University Press, 1996), 34.

28. Joanna Macrae, "Purity or Political Engagement? Issues in Food and Health Security Interventions in Complex Political Emergencies," *Journal of Humanitarian Assistance,* 7 March 1998 [e-journal]; available at http://www-jha.sps.cam.ac.uk/a/a574.htm (accessed November 20, 1998).

29. Offenheiser and Holcombe, "Challenges and Opportunities," 4.

30. For examples of some of these rhetorical trends, see Moser and others, "To Claim

Our Rights," on sustainable livelihoods. On "do no harm," see Mary B. Anderson, *Do No Harm: How Aid Can Support Peace—or War* (Boulder, Colo.: Lynne Rienner, 1999).

31. Brian Pratt argues that the rights-based approach could be seen as "no more than a metaphor; a concept that catalyzes a set of values into a phrase that many people can adopt and adapt." Quoted in Laure-Helene Piron, "Rights-based Approaches and Bilateral Aid Agencies: More Than a Metaphor?" *IDS Bulletin* 36, no. 1 (2005): 19. As will be discussed below, it is also more than just an umbrella term to describe preexisting organizational values, policies, and practices.

32. Kimberly, Anita Malley, and Santiago Cornejo, "Developmental Relief: NGO Efforts to Promote Sustainable Peace and Development in Complex Humanitarian Emergencies" (Washington, D.C.: Transition Working Group, Interaction, 2001), 5.

33. Ibid.

34. See discussion from Mara Galaty at InterAction, "Discussion on the Rights-based Approach."

35. Roy McCloughry, "Rights or Wrong?" (World Vision U.K., October 2003), 16.

36. Jochnick and Garzon, "Rights-Based Approaches," 5; Michael Barnett, "Humanitarianism Transformed," *Perspectives on Politics* 3, no. 4 (2005): 728.

37. Barnett, "Humanitarianism Transformed," 728.

38. Ibid.

39. See InterAction, "Discussion on the Rights-based Approach."

40. Mary Picard and Jay Goulden, "Principles into Practice: Learning from Innovative Rights-based Programmes" (CARE International, September 2005), ii.

41. Emma Harris-Curtis, Oscar Marleyn, and Oliver Bakewell, "The Implications for Northern NGOs of Adopting Rights-Based Approaches" (Oxford, U.K.: International NGO Training and Research Centre, Occasional Paper Series No. 41, 2005), 20.

42. Ibid., 4.

43. Cecilia M. Ljungman, "Applying a Rights-based Approach to Development: Concepts and Principles" (Paper delivered at the The Winners and Losers from Rights-based Approaches to Development Conference, Manchester, U.K., February 21–22, 2005), 13.

44. NORAD, "Handbook in Human Rights Assessment: State Obligations, Awareness and Empowerment" (Oslo, Norway: Norwegian Agency for Development Cooperation, 2001), 17.

45. Marks, "The Human Rights Framework," 19.

46. For example, see United Nations High Commissioner for Human Rights, "Rights-based Approaches: How do Rights-based Approaches Differ?"

47. VeneKlasen and others, "Rights-based Approaches," 16.

48. For example, see Harris-Curtis, Marleyn, and Bakewell, "The Implications for Northern NGOs," 12–16.

49. Moser and others, "To Claim Our Rights," viii.

50. See the discussion by Bill O'Neill at InterAction, "Discussion on the Rights-based Approach." See also Offenheiser and Holcombe, "Challenges and Opportunities," 26.

51. Farmer, *Pathologies of Power*, 229.

52. Uvin, *Human Rights and Development*, 52. Uvin cites Henry Shue (*Basic Rights*, 13) in defining rights as social guarantees.

53. Offenheiser and Holcombe, "Challenges and Opportunities," 17.

54. Ibid.

55. Mary Picard, "Measurement and Methodological Challenges to CARE International's Rights-based Programming" (CARE International, November 2003), 5.

56. Tomasevski, *Development Aid and Human Rights Revisited*, xiv.

57. Picard and Goulden, "Principles into Practice," 10.

58. Ibid., ii.

59. Jochnick and Garzon, "Rights-Based Approaches," 10.

60. Based on the author's interviews with three representatives from U.S.-based private foundations that provide grants for economic and social rights work, in 2005.

61. See, for example, Theo Van Boven, "Human Rights and Development: The UN Experience," in *Human Rights and Development: International Views*, ed. David P. Forsythe (New York: St. Martin's Press, 1989), 125.

62. See, for example, Rob Williams, "Rights-based Development: How to Get There from Here," *Global Future* (Fourth Quarter 2003), 3.

63. Oxfam International, "Towards Global Equity," 13.

64. Offenheiser and Holcombe, "Challenges and Opportunities," 8.

65. See the discussion by Rob Williams at Dochas, "Application of Rights Based Approaches."

66. Offenheiser and Holcombe, "Challenges and Opportunities," 4–5.

67. Uvin, *Human Rights and Development*, 126.

68. Eyben, "The Rise of Rights," 1.

69. Jean Ziegler, "The Right to Food" (United Nations Economic and Social Council, 2003), 11. Report submitted by the Special Rapporteur on the Right to Food, in accordance with UN Commission on Human Rights resolution 2002/25, E/CN.4/2003/54.

70. Joel Oestreich, "The Human Rights Responsibilities of the World Bank," *Global Social Policy* 4, no. 1 (2004): 57.

71. Katarina Tomasevski, "International Development Finance Agencies," in *Economic, Social and Cultural Rights: A Textbook*, ed. Asbjorn Eide, Catarina Krause, and Allan Rosas (London: Martinus Nijhoff, 1995b), 405–7.

72. Ibid.

73. Tomasevski, *Development Aid and Human Rights Revisited*, xiii.

74. Wheeler and Pettit, "Whose Rights?" 10.

75. Sheehy, "The Discourse of Human Rights," 3.

76. Uvin, *Human Rights and Development*, 50.

77. Tomasevski, *Development Aid and Human Rights Revisited*, 29; Wheeler and Pettit, "Whose Rights?," 3.

78. Based on the author's e-mail communication with a senior staff member of a human rights organization, in July 2003. See also Offenheiser and Holcombe, "Challenges and Opportunities," 20.

79. Uvin, *Human Rights and Development,* 51.

80. Moser and others, "To Claim Our Rights," 33.

81. See ICCO, "Human Rights: A Matter of Decency and Dignity" (Zeist, Netherlands: Interchurch Organisation for Development Cooperation, 2003), 4; Tomasevski, *Development Aid and Human Rights Revisited,* 142.

82. Uvin, *Human Rights and Development,* 50. Uvin outlines a four-fold typology for the incorporation of rights-based approaches, beginning with the least meaningful: (1) the "rhetorical incorporation" of rights, that is, the argument that the organization has been doing rights work all along; (2) the use of rights selectively by powerful countries to impose political conditions on countries receiving aid; (3) the provision of "positive support" in specific human rights projects; and (4) a fundamental rethinking of all development practice.

83. Laure-Helene Piron and Francis Watkins, "DFID Human Rights Review: A Review of How DFID has Integrated Human Rights into its Work" (London: Overseas Development Institute, 2004), 9. See also Moser and others, "To Claim Our Rights," viii.

84. See the discussion by Rob Williams in Dochas, "Application of Rights Based Approaches."

85. Jochnick and Garzon, "Rights-Based Approaches," 10.

86. Joanna Kerr, "From 'WID' to 'GAD' to Women's Rights: The First Twenty Years of AWID" (Association for Women's Rights in Development, Occasional Paper no. 9, 2002), available at http://www.awid.org/publications/OccasionalPapers/occasional9.html (accessed October 2005).

87. June Rand, "CARE's Experience with Adoption of a Rights-based Approach: Five Case Studies" (CARE, 2002), 10; Offenheiser and Holcombe, "Challenges and Opportunities," 20; Picard and Goulden, "Principles into Practice," ii.

88. Piron and Watkins, "DFID Human Rights Review," 10.

89. Ibid.

90. Concern Worldwide, "Concern Worldwide's Human Rights Policy" (Dublin, Ireland: Concern Worldwide, 2004), 6.

91. Picard and Goulden, "Principles into Practice," iii.

92. Jochnick and Garzon, "Rights-Based Approaches," 10; ICCO, "Human Rights," 6.

93. See, for example, Oxfam International, "Towards Global Equity," 10–14.

94. See, for example, Concern Worldwide, "Concern Worldwide's Human Rights Policy," 7; ICCO, "Human Rights," 11.

95. See the discussion by Michael Rewald in InterAction, "Discussion on the Rights-based Approach."

96. ICCO, "Human Rights," 10.

97. Picard and Goulden, "Principles into Practice," 6. See also the discussion by Valerie Traore in InterAction, "Discussion on the Rights-based Approach."

98. Michael Drinkwater, "Making Rights Real: Implications of a Rights Based Approach for HLS" (CARE, 2000), 2.

99. Jochnick and Garzon, "Rights-Based Approaches," 11.

100. VeneKlasen and others, "Rights-based Approaches," 5.

101. Jennifer Chapman and others, "Rights-Based Development: The Challenge of Change and Power" (ActionAid International, Working Paper 2, 2005), 4. Normative, analytical, and operational labels in brackets are mine, based on the typology provided by Piron and Watkins.

102. John Ambler, "Rights and Development: Transformational Challenges for CARE" (CARE, September 10, 2003), 1; Sheehy, "The Discourse of Human Rights," 3; Moser and others, "To Claim Our Rights," 3.

103. Wheeler and Pettit, "Whose Rights?" 8. See also Tomasevski, *Development Aid and Human Rights Revisited*, 170.

104. Kimenyi, "Economic Rights," 199.

105. Chapman and others, "Rights-Based Development," 7.

106. Offenheiser and Holcombe, "Challenges and Opportunities," 5; Uvin, *Human Rights and Development,* 3. See also the discussion by Luis Morago in Dochas, "Application of Rights Based Approaches."

107. Offenheiser and Holcombe, "Challenges and Opportunities," 15.

108. Cornwall and Nyamu-Musembi, "Why Rights, Why Now?" 9; Tomasevski, *Development Aid and Human Rights Revisited*, xiii.

109. Cornwall and Nyamu-Musembi, "Why Rights, Why Now?" 14.

110. Based on the author's interview with a human rights donor/practitioner, August 2005. See also VeneKlasen and others, "Rights-based Approaches," 20.

111. Uvin, *Human Rights and Development,* 47.

112. See Jochnick and Garzon, "Rights-Based Approaches," 6; and the discussions by Valerie Traore and Michael Rewald in InterAction, "Discussion on the Rights-based Approach."

113. See discussion by Luis Morago in Dochas, "Application of Rights Based Approaches."

114. Picard and Goulden, "Principles into Practice," 14.

115. Ambler, "Rights and Development," 1.

116. See, for example, the critique of Oxfam in Susan Aaronson, "Is Equity in Trade an Attainable Goal?" YaleGlobal online edition, September 15, 2004 [e-journal]; available at http://yaleglobal.yale.edu/display.article?id=4518 (accessed September 20, 2005). She argues that Oxfam is well intentioned in addressing global economic policy, but would be better served by focusing on "smaller scale collaborative projects" in LDCs, as they have historically done.

117. Picard and Goulden, "Principles into Practice," 14.

118. Offenheiser and Holcombe, "Challenges and Opportunities," 20.

119. Based on the author's interview with a human rights donor, September 2005.

120. Wieteke Beernink and Harry Derksen, "Searching for the Right(s) Approach," in *Dignity and Human Rights: The Implementation of Economic, Social and Cultural Rights*, ed. Berma Klein Goldewijk, Adalid Contreras Baspineiro, and Paulo Cesar Car-

bonari (New York: Intersentia, 2002), 94; Picard and Goulden, "Principles into Practice," 14; Tomasevski, *Development Aid and Human Rights Revisited*, 177.

121. Barnett, "Humanitarianism Transformed," 732.

122. Ambler, "Rights and Development," 3. As Peter Uvin notes, the "development community must find ways to counter the necessary expansion of its mandate with an equally necessary reduction in its power." See Uvin, *Human Rights and Development*, 197.

123. Based on the author's interview with a human rights donor, July 2005.

124. Harris-Curtis, Marleyn, and Bakewell, "The Implications for Northern NGOs," 39.

125. Uvin, *Human Rights and Development*, 12.

126. See generally ICCO, "Human Rights."

127. Chapman and others, "Rights-Based Development," 36.

128. Farmer, *Pathologies of Power*, 227.

129. Ambler, "Rights and Development," 4.

130. Craig Johnson and Daniel Start, "Rights, Claims and Capture: Understanding the Politics of Pro-poor Policy" (London: Overseas Development Institute, Working Paper 145, 2001), 16.

131. Moser and others, "To Claim Our Rights," x; Mitlin and Patel, "Re-interpreting the Rights-based Approach," 18.

132. Mitlin and Patel, "Re-interpreting the Rights-based Approach," 15.

133. See the discussion by Michael Rewald at InterAction, "Discussion on the Rights-based Approach."

134. Rand, "CARE's Experience," 10.

135. Picard, "Measurement and Methodological Challenges," 7.

136. Picard and Goulden, "Principles into Practice," 15.

137. Mitlin and Patel, "Re-interpreting the Rights-based Approach," 22.

138. Cornwall and Nyamu-Musembi, "Why Rights, Why Now?" 15.

139. Ljungman, "Applying a Rights-based Approach," 16.

140. Alf Morten Jerve, "Social Consequences of Development in a Human Rights Perspective: Lessons from the World Bank," in *Human Rights in Development Yearbook 1998*, ed. Hugo Stokke and Arne Tostensen (Oslo: Nordic Human Rights Publications, 1998), 39.

141. Tomasevski, *Development Aid and Human Rights Revisited*, 157.

142. Mitlin and Patel, "Re-interpreting the Rights-based Approach," 23.

143. Ambler, "Rights and Development," 2–3.

144. Wheeler and Pettit, "Whose Rights?" 7.

145. Mitlin and Patel, "Re-interpreting the Rights-based Approach," 24. As Peter Uvin states, "the rights-based approach to development changes the nature of the game not because it edicts rights as fixed properties or legal certainties or because it somehow leads us to discover brand-new actions or services we would never have thought of beforehand." Rather, it forces humanitarian organizations to focus on legal, policy, and

structural changes, and introduces a wide range of "mechanisms of accountability" into development practice. See Uvin, *Human Rights and Development*, 129.

146. VeneKlasen and others, "Rights-based Approaches," 4.

147. Quoted in McCloughry, "Rights or Wrong?" 7.

148. Uvin, *Human Rights and Development*, 37.

149. VeneKlasen and others, "Rights-based Approaches," 3.

150. Farmer, *Pathologies of Power*, 228. See also Samuel Musyoki and Celestine Nyamu-Musembi, "Defining Rights from the Roots: Insights from Council Tenants' Struggles in Mombasa, Kenya," *IDS Bulletin* 36, no. 1 (2005): 100–109; and Mwambi Mwasaru, "Beyond Approaches and Models: Reflections on Rights and Social Movements in Kenya, Haiti and the Philippines," *IDS Bulletin* 36, no. 1 (2005): 120.

151. Cornwall and Nyamu-Musembi, "Why Rights, Why Now?" 12.

152. Williams, "Rights-based Development," 3. For example, as Peter Uvin comments, "The Geneva-based UN human rights mechanisms constitute some of the most powerless, underfunded, toothless, formulaic, and politically manipulated institutions of the UN. Even the human rights NGOs by and large neglect them. For development work to be discussed there, or for development workers to read these discussions, is about as useful to on-the-ground change as knowing the lyrics to 'We Are the World' is to ending world hunger." Uvin, *Human Rights and Development*, 140.

153. Odinkalu, "Why More Africans," 3.

154. John Samuel, quoted in Wheeler and Pettit, "Whose Rights?" 4.

Chapter 6. Using a Social Theory to Interpret NGO Efforts

1. Chris Jochnick, "Human Rights for the Next Century," Washington, D.C.: Carnegie Council on Ethics and International Affairs, 2006. Available at http://www.carnegiecouncil.org/viewMedia.php/prmID/575 (accessed March 1, 2006).

2. Wheeler and Pettit, "Whose Rights?" 7.

3. See http://www.nesri.org/ for more information (accessed June 2009).

4. Yamin, "The Future in the Mirror," 1203.

5. Ibid., 1241.

6. Finnemore and Toope, "Alternatives to Legalization," 744.

7. Sunstein, *The Second Bill of Rights*, 62.

8. Forsythe, "The United States and International Economic Rights," 312.

9. Wapner, *Environmental Activism*, 14.

10. Donnelly, "The Virtues of Legalization."

11. Farmer, *Pathologies of Power*, 219.

12. Koskenniemi, "Letter to the Editors," 358.

13. Yamin, "The Future in the Mirror," 1242. Also based on the author's interviews with human rights donors and practitioners in 2005.

14. Robinson, "Advancing Economic, Social and Cultural Rights," 872.

Bibliography

Aaronson, Susan. "Is Equity in Trade an Attainable Goal?" YaleGlobal online edition, September 15 2004. [e-journal]; available at http://yaleglobal.yale.edu/display.article?id=4518 (accessed September 20, 2005).

Abbott, Kenneth W. "International Relations Theory, International Law, and the Regime Governing Atrocities in Internal Conflicts." *American Journal of International Law* 93, no. 2 (1999): 361–79.

Abbott, Kenneth W., Robert O. Keohane, Andrew Moravcsik, Anne-Marie Slaughter, and Duncan Snidal. "The Concept of Legalization." *International Organization* 54, no. 3 (2000): 401–19.

Abbott, Kenneth W., and Duncan Snidal. "Hard and Soft Law in International Governance." *International Organization* 54, no. (3) (2000): 421–56.

Addo, Michael K. "Justiciability Re-examined." In *Economic, Social and Cultural Rights: Progress and Achievement*, ed. Ralph Beddard and Dilys M. Hill, 93–117. New York: St. Martin's Press, 1992.

Aiken, William. "The Right to Be Saved from Starvation." In *World Hunger and Moral Obligation*, ed. William Aiken and Hugh La Follette, 85–102. Englewood Cliffs, N.J.: Prentice-Hall, 1977.

Alston, Philip. "Conjuring up New Human Rights: A Proposal for Quality Control." *American Journal of International Law* 78, no. 3 (1984): 607–21.

———. "U.S. Ratification of the Covenant on Economic, Social and Cultural Rights: The Need for an Entirely New Strategy." *American Journal of International Law* 84 (1990): 365–93.

Ambler, John. "Rights and Development: Transformational Challenges for CARE." CARE, September 10, 2003; available at http://careint.test.poptel.org.uk/pn726/modules/UpDownload/store_folder/Discussion_papers,_reviews,_reports_and_articles/CARE:_applying_RBA_in_practice/RBA_and_Development—_challenges_for_CARE.pdf (accessed May 23, 2006).

Amnesty International USA. "Reframing Globalization: The Challenge for Human Rights"; available at http://www.amnestyusa.org/events/agm/agm2002/panels.html (accessed February 1, 2006).

Anderson, Carol. *Eyes off the Prize: The United Nations and the African American Struggle for Human Rights, 1944–1955*. Cambridge, U.K.: Cambridge University Press, 2003.

Anderson, Mary B. *Do No Harm: How Aid Can Support Peace—or War.* Boulder, Colo.: Lynne Rienner, 1999.

Balakrishnan, Radhika. *Why MES with Human Rights? Integrating Macro Economic Strategies with Human Rights.* New York: Marymount Manhattan College, 2004.

Balkin, Jack M. "Brown, Social Movements, and Social Change." Delaware Brown Symposium, 2005; available at http://www.yale.edu/lawweb/jbalkin/articles/brownsocialmovementsandsocialchange1.pdf (accessed March 8, 2006).

———. "How Social Movements Change (or Fail to Change) the Constitution: The Case of the New Departure." Social Science Research Network Electronic Paper Collection, September 5, 2005; available at http://papers.ssrn.com/sol3/papers.cfm?abstract_id=847164 (accessed December 16, 2005).

Barnett, Michael. "Humanitarianism Transformed." *Perspectives on Politics* 3, no. 4 (2005): 723–40.

Barrantes, Alexandra N. "What Matters Most for Poverty Reduction? Inequality and Economic Growth in Perspective." *Swords and Ploughshares* 14, no. 1 (2004): 36–47.

Bauer, Joanne. "The Challenges to International Human Rights." In *Constructing Human Rights in an Age of Globalization*, ed. Mahmood Monshipouri, Neil Englehart, Andrew J. Nathan, and Kavita Philip, 239–58. London: M. E. Sharpe, 2003.

Baxi, Upendra. *The Future of Human Rights.* Oxford, U.K.: Oxford University Press, 2002.

Beck, Robert J., Anthony Clark Arend, and Robert D. Vander Lugt, eds. *International Rules: Approaches from International Law and International Relations.* Oxford, U.K.: Oxford University Press, 1996.

Beernink, Wieteke, and Harry Derksen. "Searching for the Right(s) Approach." In *Dignity and Human Rights: The Implementation of Economic, Social and Cultural Rights*, ed. Berma Klein Goldewijk, Adalid Contreras Baspineiro, and Paulo Cesar Carbonari, 91–95. New York: Intersentia, 2002.

Beetham, David. "What Future for Economic and Social Rights?" In *Politics and Human Rights*, ed. David Beetham, 41–60. Oxford, U.K.: Blackwell Publishers, 1995.

Berlin, Isaiah. *Four Essays on Liberty.* New York: Oxford University Press, 1970.

Blackstock, Sarah. "Using International Human Rights Law for Anti-Poverty Organizing." Ottawa, Canada: National Anti-Poverty Organization, 2002; available at http://www.napo-onap.ca/en/issues/using human rights.htm (accessed May 5, 2006).

Blyberg, Ann, and Dana Buhl. *Ripple in Still Water: Reflections by Activists on Local- and National-level Work on Economic, Social and Cultural Rights.* Washington, D.C.: Institute for International Education, International Human Rights Internship Program, 1997.

Bob, Clifford. "Merchants of Morality." *Foreign Policy* (March–April 2002): 36–45.

———. "Constructing New Human Rights Norms: A Theoretical Framework." Paper delivered at the International Studies Association meeting, Montreal, Canada, March 17–20, 2004.

———. *The Marketing of Rebellion.* Cambridge, U.K.: Cambridge University Press, 2005.

Bowen, Stephen. "'Full Spectrum' Human Rights: Amnesty International Rethinks."

Open Democracy (2005). [e-journal]; available at http://www.opendemocracy.net/debates/article.jsp?id=3&debateId=52&articleId=2569 (accessed May 9, 2006).

Brodsky, Gwen, and Shelagh Day. "Poverty Is a Human Rights Violation." The Poverty and Human Rights Project, in collaboration with the Centre for Feminist Legal Studies at the University of British Columbia, 2001; available at http://www.povnet.org/human_rights/Paper v3.pdf (accessed May 10, 2006).

Çali, Basak, and Saladin Meckled-Garcia. "Human Rights *Legalized*—Defining, Interpreting, and Implementing an Ideal." In *The Legalization of Human Rights*, ed. Basak Çali and Saladin Meckled-Garcia, 1–8. London: Routledge, 2006.

Carmalt, Jean, and Sarah Zaidi. "The Right to Health in the United States of America: What Does It Mean?" Brooklyn, N.Y.: Center for Economic and Social Rights, 2004; available at http://cesr.org/ushealthright (accessed May 23, 2006).

Carnegie Council on Ethics and International Affairs. "Litigating Human Rights: Promise v. Perils." *Human Rights Dialogue* 2, no. 2 (2000): 1–3. [e-journal]; available at http://cceia.org/media/608_hrd2-2.pdf?PHPSESSID=3931f36f3d393927197aea61facc5443 (accessed May 9, 2006).

Chandhoke, Neera. "How Global Is Global Civil Society?." *Journal of World-Systems Research* 11, no. 2 (2005): 355–71.

Chapman, Audrey R. "A 'Violations Approach' for Monitoring the International Covenant on Economic, Social and Cultural Rights." *Human Rights Quarterly* 18, no. 1 (1996): 23–66.

Chapman, Jennifer, Valerie Miller, Adriano Campolina Soares, and John Samuel. "Rights-Based Development: The Challenge of Change and Power." ActionAid International, Working Paper 2, 2005.

Chayes, Abram, and Antonia Handler Chayes. "On Compliance." *International Organization* 47 (1993): 175–205.

COHRE. "50 Leading Cases on Economic, Social and Cultural Rights: Summaries." Geneva, Switzerland: Centre on Housing Rights and Evictions (COHRE), ESC Rights Litigation Programme, Working Paper No. 1, 2003; available at http://www.cohre.org/downloads/50leadingcases.pdf (accessed May 23, 2006).

Concern Worldwide. "Concern Worldwide's Human Rights Policy." Dublin, Ireland: Concern Worldwide, 2004. Available at http://www.concern.net/docs/HumanRightsPolicy.pdf (accessed May 23, 2006).

Cornwall, Andrea, and Celestine Nyamu-Musembi. "Why Rights, Why Now? Reflections on the Rise of Rights in International Development Discourse." *IDS Bulletin* 36, no. 1 (2005): 9–15.

Cox, Larry. "Reflections on Human Rights at Century's End." *Human Rights Dialogue* 2, no. 1 (2000): 5–6.

Craig, Gary, and Elizabeth Dowler. "Let Them Eat Cake! Poverty, Hunger and the UK State." In *First World Hunger: Food Security and Welfare Politics*, ed. Graham Riches, 115–33. New York: St. Martin's Press, 1997.

Dicklitch, Susan, and Rhoda E. Howard-Hassmann. "Public Policy and Economic Rights in Ghana and Uganda." In *Economic Rights: Conceptual, Measurement, and Policy Issues*, ed. Shareen Hertel and Lanse Minkler, 325–44. Cambridge, U.K.: Cambridge University Press, 2007.

Dochas. "Application of Rights Based Approaches—Experiences and Challenges." Dublin, Ireland: Dochas, 2003. Report from a Dochas Seminar on Rights Based Approaches to Development, February 12, 2003. Available at http://www.dochas.ie/Working_Groups/RBA/RBA_Seminar.pdf (accessed November 2005).

Donnelly, Jack. "The Virtues of Legalization." In *The Legalization of Human Rights*, ed. Basak Çali and Saladin Meckled-Garcia, 67–80. London: Routledge, 2006.

———. "The West and Economic Rights." In *Economic Rights: Conceptual, Measurement, and Policy Issues*, ed. Shareen Hertel and Lanse Minkler, 37–55. Cambridge, U.K.: Cambridge University Press, 2007.

Dorsey, Ellen. "Human Rights and U.S. Foreign Policy: Who Controls the Agenda?" *Journal of Intergroup Relations* 22, no. 1 (1995): 3–17.

Drinkwater, Michael. "Making Rights Real: Implications of a Rights Based Approach for HLS." CARE, 2000; available at http://careint.test.poptel.org.uk/pn726/modules/UpDownload/store_folder/Discussion_papers,_reviews,_reports_and_articles/CARE:_RBA_and_Livelihoods/100-DrinkwaterM.MakingRightsRealIplicationsofRBAforHLS.May2000.pdf (accessed May 23, 2006.

Earle, Patrick. "Towards a Framework for a Human Rights Analysis of Poverty." Bangkok, Thailand: Human Rights Council of Australia, 2003.

Ebeling, Richard. Review of *The Quest for Cosmic Justice* by Thomas Sowell. The Future of Freedom Foundation, December 1999. Available at http://www.fff.org/freedom/1299h.asp (accessed August 9, 2005).

"Economic and Social Rights and the Right to Health." Cambridge, Mass.: Harvard Law School Human Rights Program, 1995. Report from a discussion held at Harvard Law School in September 1993. Available at http://www.law/harvard.edu/programs/hrp/Publications/economic1.html(accessed February 2005).

Eide, Asbjorn. "Economic, Social and Cultural Rights as Human Rights." In *Economic, Social and Cultural Rights: A Textbook*, ed. Asbjorn Eide, Catarina Krause, and Allan Rosas, 21–40. London: Martinus Nijhoff, 1995.

Evans, Tony. "International Human Rights Law as Power/Knowledge." *Human Rights Quarterly* 27, no. 3 (2005): 1046–68.

Eyben, Rosalind. "The Rise of Rights: Rights-based Approaches to International Development." Brighton, U.K.: Institute of Development Studies, May 2003. IDS Policy Briefing 17.

Farha, Leilani. "Bringing Economic, Social and Cultural Rights Home: Palestinians in Occupied East Jerusalem and Israel." In *Giving Meaning to Economic, Social and Cultural Rights*, ed. Ishafan Merali and Valerie Oosterveld, 160–79. Philadelphia: University of Pennsylvania Press, 2001.

Farmer, Paul. *Pathologies of Power: Health, Human Rights, and the New War on the Poor.* Berkeley: University of California Press, 2005.

Felice, William. *The Global New Deal: Economic and Social Human Rights in World Politics*. Oxford, U.K.: Rowman and Littlefield, 2003.

FIAN International. "Spearheading the Right to Food: FIAN Is 15." *Hungry for What Is Right*, December 2001.

———. "From Legislative Framework to Framework Legislation: A Strategy for Implementing the Right to Food." *Right to Food Journal* 1 (July 2003): 3–5.

Fields, A. Belden. *Rethinking Human Rights for the New Millenium*. New York: Palgrave Macmillan, 2003.

Finnemore, Martha. *National Interests in International Society*. Ithaca, N.Y.: Cornell University Press, 1996.

Finnemore, Martha, and Kathryn Sikkink. "International Norm Dynamics and Political Change." *International Organization* 52, no. 4 (1998): 887–917.

Finnemore, Martha, and Stephen J. Toope. "Alternatives to 'Legalization': Richer Views of Law and Politics." *International Organization* 55, no. 3 (2001): 743–58.

Florini, Ann. "The Evolution of International Norms." *International Studies Quarterly* 40 (1996): 363–89.

Ford Foundation. *Close to Home: Case Studies of Human Rights Work in the United States*. New York: Ford Foundation, 2004. Available at http://www.fordfound.org/publications/recent_articles/close_to_home.cfm (accessed May 10, 2006.

Forsythe, David. "The United States and International Economic Rights: Law, Social Reality, and Political Choice." In *Economic Rights: Conceptual, Measurement, and Policy Issues*, ed. Shareen Hertel and Lanse Minkler, 310–24. Cambridge, U.K.: Cambridge University Press, 2007.

Franck, Thomas M. *The Power of Legitimacy Among Nations*. New York: Oxford University Press, 1990.

Freeman, Michael. "Putting Law in Its Place: An Interdisciplinary Evaluation of National Amnesty Laws." In *The Legalization of Human Rights*, ed. Basak Çali and Saladin Meckled-Garcia, 49–64. London: Routledge, 2006.

Giugni, Marco. "How Social Movements Matter: Past Research, Present Problems, Future Developments." In *How Social Movements Matter*, ed. Marco Giugni, Doug McAdam, and Charles Tilly, xiii–xxxiii. Minneapolis: University of Minnesota Press, 1999.

Glendon, Mary Ann. *Rights Talk: The Impoverishment of Political Discourse*. New York: Free Press, 1991.

Goering, Curt. "Amnesty International and Economic, Social and Cultural Rights." In *Ethics in Action: The Ethical Challenges of International Human Rights Nongovernmental Organizations*, ed. Daniel A. Bell and Jean-Marc Coicaud, 204–17. Cambridge, U.K.: Cambridge University Press, 2007.

Goldstein, Judith, Miles Kahler, Robert O. Keohane, and Anne-Marie Slaughter. "Introduction: Legalization and World Politics." *International Organization* 54, no. 3 (2000a): 385–99.

Goldstein, Judith, Miles Kahler, Robert O. Keohane, and Anne-Marie Slaughter, eds.

Legalization and World Politics. Vol. 54(3): Special Issue of *International Organization*, (2000b).

Gupta, Devashree. "Radical Flank Effects: The Effect of Radical-Moderate Splits in Regional Nationalist Movements." Paper presented at the Conference of Europeanists, Chicago, 2002. Available at http://falcon.arts.cornell.edu/sgt2/pscp/documents/RFEgupta.pdf (accessed June 2009).

Haines, Herbert. "Black Radicalization and the Funding of Civil Rights: 1957–1970." In *Social Movements: Readings on Their Emergence, Mobilization and Dynamics*, ed. Doug McAdam and David Snow. Los Angeles: Roxbury, 1997.

Harris-Curtis, Emma, Oscar Marleyn, and Oliver Bakewell. "The Implications for Northern NGOs of Adopting Rights-Based Approaches." Oxford, U.K.: International NGO Training and Research Centre, Occasional Paper Series No. 41, 2005.

Hertel, Shareen and Lanse Minkler. "Economic Rights: The Terrain." In *Economic Rights: Conceptual, Measurement, and Policy Issues*, ed. Shareen Hertel and Lanse Minkler, 1–35. Cambridge, U.K.: Cambridge University Press, 2007.

Heywood, Mark. "South Africa's Treatment Action Campaign: Combining Law and Social Mobilization to Realize the Right to Health." *Journal of Human Rights Practice* 1, no. 1 (2009): 14–36.

Hill, Dilys M. "Rights and Their Realization." In *Economic, Social and Cultural Rights: Progress and Achievement*, ed. Ralph Beddard and Dilys M. Hill, 1–21. New York: St. Martin's Press, 1992.

Hirschl, Ran. "'Negative' Rights vs. 'Positive' Entitlements: A Comparative Study of Judicial Interpretations of Rights in an Emerging Neo-Liberal Economic Order." *Human Rights Quarterly* 22, no. 4 (2000): 1060–98.

Hunt, Paul. *Reclaiming Social Rights: International and Comparative Perspectives.* Brookfield, Vt.: Dartmouth, 1996.

ICCO. "Human Rights: A Matter of Decency and Dignity." Zeist, Netherlands: Interchurch Organisation for Development Cooperation (ICCO), 2003. Available at http://www.icco.nl/documents/doc/EN Rights based approach 27 juni 2003.doc (accessed May 9, 2006).

Ignatieff, Michael. *Human Rights as Politics and Idolatry.* Princeton, N.J.: Princeton University Press, 2001.

InterAction. "Discussion on the Rights-based Approach to Development." InterAction, 2003. Available at http://www.interaction.org/files.cgi/2581_Notes_RBA_Meeting_December_17_2003.doc (accessed October 18, 2005).

International Council on Human Rights Policy. "Duties sans Frontieres: Human Rights and Global Social Justice." Versoix, Switzerland: International Council on Human Rights Policy, 2003.

Jackson, Patrick T. "Relational Constructivism: A War of Words." In *Making Sense of International Relations Theory*, ed. Jennifer Sterling-Folker, 139–55. Boulder, Colo.: Lynne Rienner, 2006.

Jaichand, Vinodh. "Public Interest Litigation Strategies for Advancing Human Rights in Domestic Systems of Law." *Sur: International Journal on Human Rights* 1, no. 1 (2004): 126–41.

Jerve, Alf Morten. "Social Consequences of Development in a Human Rights Perspective: Lessons from the World Bank." In *Human Rights in Development Yearbook 1998*, ed. Hugo Stokke and Arne Tostensen, 35–66. Oslo: Nordic Human Rights Publications, 1998.

Jochnick, Chris. "Confronting the Impunity of Non-State Actors: New Fields for the Promotion of Human Rights." *Human Rights Quarterly* 21, no. 1 (1999): 56–79.

———. "Human Rights for the Next Century." Washington, D.C.: Carnegie Council on Ethics and International Affairs, 2006. Available at http://www.carnegiecouncil.org/viewMedia.php/prmID/575 (accessed March 1, 2006).

Jochnick, Chris, and Paulina Garzon. "Rights-Based Approaches to Development: An Overview of the Field." CARE and Oxfam America, October 2002. Available at http://www.crin.org/docs/resources/publications/hrbap/RBA_Oxfam_CARE.pdf (accessed May 9, 2006).

Johnson, Craig, and Daniel Start. "Rights, Claims and Capture: Understanding the Politics of Pro-poor Policy." London: Overseas Development Institute, Working Paper 145, 2001. Available at http://www.odi.org.uk/publications/working_papers/wp145.pdf (accessed May 23, 2006).

Jones, Charles. *Global Justice: Defending Cosmopolitanism*. Oxford, U.K.: Oxford University Press, 1999.

Kahler, Miles. "Conclusion: The Causes and Consequences of Legalization." *International Organization* 54, no. 3 (2000): 661–83.

Kakwani, Nanak, and Hyun H. Son. "New Global Poverty Counts." Working paper no. 29, Brasilia, Brazil: UNDP International Poverty Centre, September 2006.

Katzenstein, Peter J., ed. *The Culture of National Security: Norms and Identity in World Politics*. New York: Columbia University Press, 1996.

Keck, Margaret E., and Kathryn Sikkink. *Activists Beyond Borders: Advocacy Networks in International Politics*. Ithaca, N.Y.: Cornell University Press, 1998.

Kennedy, David. "A New Stream of International Law Scholarship." In *International Rules: Approaches from International Law and International Relations*, ed. Robert J. Beck, Anthony Clark Arend, and Robert D. Vander Lugt, 230–52. Oxford, U.K.: Oxford University Press, 1996.

———. "The International Human Rights Movement: Part of the Problem?" *Harvard Human Rights Journal* 15 (Spring 2002): 101–25.

Kerr, Joanna. "From 'WID' to 'GAD' to Women's Rights: The First Twenty Years of AWID." Association for Women's Rights in Development, Occasional Paper no. 9, 2002. Available at http://www.awid.org/publications/OccasionalPapers/occasional9.html (accessed October 2005).

Kimenyi, Mwangi S. "Economic Rights, Human Development Effort, and Institutions." In *Economic Rights: Conceptual, Measurement, and Policy Issues*, ed. Shareen Hertel and Lanse Minkler, 182–213. Cambridge, U.K.: Cambridge University Press, 2007.

Klandermans, Bert, and Sjoerd Goslinga. "Media Discourse, Movement Publicity, and the Generation of Collective Action Frames: Theoretical and Empirical Exercises in Meaning Construction." In *Comparative Perspectives on Social Movements: Political Opportunities, Mobilizing Structures, and Cultural Framings*, ed. Doug McAdam, John D. McCarthy, and Mayer N. Zald, 313–37. Cambridge, U.K.: Cambridge University Press, 1996.

Koskenniemi, Martti. "Letter to the Editors of the Symposium." *American Journal of International Law* 93, no. 2 (1999): 351–61.

Kratochwil, Friedrich. *Rules, Norms and Decisions: On the Conditions of Practical and Legal Reasoning in International Relations and Domestic Society.* Cambridge, U.K.: Cambridge University Press, 1989.

Kratochwil, Friedrich. "Contract and Regimes: Do Issue Specificity and Variations of Formality Matter?" In *Regime Theory and International Relations*, ed. Volker Rittberger, 73–93. Oxford, U.K.: Clarendon Press, 1993.

Krueger, Alan B. "Poverty Doesn't Create Terrorists." *New York Times*, May 29, 2003. Available at http://www.jpef.net/jul03/Poverty doesnt.pdf (accessed May 10, 2006).

Langford, Malcolm. "The Question of Resources." *Housing and ESC Rights Law Quarterly* 1, no. 3 (2004): 1–4.

Leckie, Scott. "Another Step Towards Indivisibility: Identifying the Key Features of Violations of Economic, Social and Cultural Rights." *Human Rights Quarterly* 20, no. 1 (1998): 81–124.

Legro, Jeffery W. "Which Norms Matter? Revisiting the Failure of Internationalism." *International Organization* 51 (1997): 31–63.

Ljungman, Cecilia M. "Applying a Rights-based Approach to Development: Concepts and Principles." Paper delivered at The Winners and Losers from Rights-based Approaches to Development Conference, Manchester, U.K., February 21–22, 2005. Available at http://www.sed.manchester.ac.uk/idpm/research/events/february2005/documents/Ljungman_000.doc (accessed May 10, 2006).

Lutz, Ellen L., and Kathryn Sikkink. "International Human Rights Law and Practice in Latin America." *International Organization* 54, no. 3 (2000): 633–59.

Macrae, Joanna. "Purity or Political Engagement? Issues in Food and Health Security Interventions in Complex Political Emergencies." *Journal of Humanitarian Assistance*, 7 March 1998 [e-journal]; available at http://www-jha.sps.cam.ac.uk/a/a574.htm (accessed November 20, 1998).

Mallaby, Sebastian. "High-Profile Help for Africa." *Washington Post*, May 23, 2005, A19. Available at http://www.washingtonpost.com/wp-dyn/content/article/2005/05/22/AR2005052200889.html (accessed May 10, 2006).

Marks, Stephen P. "The Human Rights Framework for Development: Five Approaches." Boston: Francois-Xavier Bagnoud Center for Health and Human Rights, April 2001. Available at http://www.hsph.harvard.edu/fxbcenter/FXBC_WP6—Marks.pdf (accessed May 10, 2006).

Martin, Edwin M. "Focus on Nutrition: Who Should Pay for What?" In *Food Policy: The*

Responsibility of the United States in the Life and Death Choices, ed. Peter G. Brown and Henry Shue, 319–36. New York: Free Press, 1977.

McAdam, Doug, John D. McCarthy, and Mayer N. Zald, eds. *Comparative Perspectives on Social Movements: Political Opportunities, Mobilizing Structures, and Cultural Framings*. Cambridge, U.K.: Cambridge University Press, 1996.

McAdam, Doug, and David A. Snow. "Social Movements: Conceptual and Theoretical Issues." In *Social Movements: Readings on Their Emergence, Mobilization, and Dynamics*, ed. Doug McAdam and David Snow, xviii–xxvi. Los Angeles: Roxbury, 1997.

McAdam, Doug, Sidney Tarrow, and Charles Tilly. *Dynamics of Contention*. Cambridge, U.K.: Cambridge University Press, 2001.

McCammon, Holly, Karen Campbell, Ellen Granberg, and Christine Mowery. "How Movements Win: Gendered Opportunity Structures and U.S. Women's Suffrage Movements, 1866 to 1919." *American Sociological Review* 66 (February 2001): 49–70.

McCann, Michael. *Rights at Work: Pay Equity Reform and the Politics of Legal Mobilization*. Chicago: University of Chicago Press, 1994.

McCloughry, Roy. "Rights or Wrong?" World Vision UK, October 2003. Available at http://www.worldvision.org.uk/resources/orange paper.4.pdf (accessed May 10, 2006).

McGovern, George. *The Third Freedom: Ending Hunger in Our Time*. New York: Simon and Schuster, 2001.

Meckled-Garcia, Saladin, and Basak Çali. "Lost in Translation: The Human Rights Ideal and International Human Rights Law." In *The Legalization of Human Rights*, ed. Basak Çali and Saladin Meckled-Garcia, 11–31. London: Routledge, 2006.

Mendez, Emilio Garcia. "Origin, Concept, and Future of Human Rights: Reflections for a New Agenda." *Sur: International Journal on Human Rights* 1, no. 1 (2004): 7–19.

Merali, Ishafan, and Valerie Oosterveld, eds. *Giving Meaning to Economic, Social and Cultural Rights*. Philadelphia: University of Pennsylvania Press, 2001.

Mertus, Julie A. *Bait and Switch: Human Rights and U.S. Foreign Policy*. London: Routledge, 2004.

Mitlin, Diana, and Sheela Patel. "Re-interpreting the Rights-based Approach: A Grassroots Perspective on Rights and Development." Paper delivered at The Winners and Losers from Rights-Based Approaches to Development Conference, Manchester, U.K., February 21–22, 2005. Available at http://www.scd.manchester.ac.uk/idpm/research/events/february2005/documents/Mitlin.doc (accessed May 10, 2006).

Mittal, Anuradha, and Peter Rosset, eds. *America Needs Human Rights*. Oakland, Calif.: Food First Books, 1999.

Mivelaz, Natalie. "Report on the First Meeting of the Working Group on an Optional Protocol to the ICESCR." *Housing and ESC Rights Law Quarterly* 1, no. 1 (2004): 10.

Monshipouri, Mahmood, Neil Englehart, Andrew J. Nathan, and Kavita Philip, eds. *Constructing Human Rights in the Age of Globalization*. London: M. E. Sharpe, 2003.

Moore Lappe, Frances, and Joseph Collins. *Food First: Beyond the Myth of Scarcity*. New York: Ballantine Books, 1977.

Moore Lappe, Frances, Joseph Collins, and David Kinley. *Aid as Obstacle: Twenty Questions About Our Foreign Aid and the Hungry*. San Francisco: Institute for Food and Development Policy, 1980.

Morse, Janice M. "Designing Funded Qualitative Research." In *Strategies of Qualitative Inquiry*, ed. Norman K. Denzin and Yvonna S. Lincoln, 56–85. Thousand Oaks, Calif.: Sage Publications, 1998.

Moser, Caroline, Andy Norton, Tim Conway, Clare Ferguson, and Polly Vizard. "To Claim Our Rights: Livelihood Security, Human Rights and Sustainable Development." London: Overseas Development Institute, August 2001.

Musyoki, Samuel, and Celestine Nyamu-Musembi. "Defining Rights from the Roots: Insights from Council Tenants' Struggles in Mombasa, Kenya." *IDS Bulletin* 36, no. 1 (2005): 100–109.

Mwasaru, Mwambi. "Beyond Approaches and Models: Reflections on Rights and Social Movements in Kenya, Haiti and the Philippines." *IDS Bulletin* 36, no. 1 (2005): 120–28.

Nadelmann, Ethan A. "Global Prohibition Regimes: The Evolution of Norms in International Society." *International Organization* 44, no. 4 (1990): 479–526.

Nagel, Thomas. "Poverty and Food: Why Charity Is Not Enough." In *Food Policy: The Responsibility of the United States in the Life and Death Choices*, ed. Peter G. Brown and Henry Shue, 54–62. New York: Free Press, 1977.

Neier, Aryeh. "Perspectives on Economic, Social and Cultural Rights." Lecture given at the Washington College of Law, American University, Washington, D.C., January 19, 2006. Available at http://www.wcl.american.edu/podcast/audio/20060119_WCL_Neier.mp3?rd=1 (accessed March 1, 2006).

Nelson, Paul, and Ellen Dorsey. *New Rights Advocacy: Changing Strategies of Development and Human Rights NGOs*. Washington, D.C.: Georgetown University Press, 2008.

Neubeck, Kenneth. *When Welfare Disappears: The Case for Economic Human Rights*. New York: Routledge, 2006.

NORAD. "Handbook in Human Rights Assessment: State Obligations, Awareness and Empowerment." Oslo: Norwegian Agency for Development Cooperation (NORAD), 2001. Available from http://www.norad.no/files/Handbook.pdf (accessed May 10, 2006).

Normand, Roger. "Facing the Human Rights Abyss." *Nation*, December 10, 2003 [web-only edition]; available at http://www.thenation.com/doc.mhtml?i=20031222&s=normand (accessed August 5, 2005).

Odinkalu, Chidi Anslem. "Why More Africans Don't Use Human Rights Language." *Human Rights Dialogue* 2, no. 1 (2000): 3–4.

Oestreich, Joel. "The Human Rights Responsibilities of the World Bank." *Global Social Policy* 4, no. 1 (2004): 55–76.

Offenheiser, Raymond C., and Susan Holcombe. "Challenges and Opportunities of Implementing a Rights-based Approach to Development: An Oxfam America Perspective." Oxford, U.K.: Oxfam America, 2001.

O'Neill, Onora. *Bounds of Justice*. Cambridge, U.K.: Cambridge University Press, 2000.

Onuf, Nicholas. *World of Our Making: Rules and Rule in Social Theory and International Relations*. Columbia: University of South Carolina Press, 1989.

———. "International Legal Theory: Where We Stand." *International Legal Theory* 1, no. 1 (1995). Available at http://law.ubalt.edu/cicl/ilt/1_1_1995.doc (accessed May 10, 2006).

Otto, Dianne. "Defending Women's Economic and Social Rights: Some Thoughts on Indivisibility and a New Standard of Equality." In *Giving Meaning to Economic, Social and Cultural Rights*, ed. Ishafan Merali and Valerie Oosterveld, 52–67. Philadelphia: University of Pennsylvania Press, 2001.

Oxfam International. "Towards Global Equity: Strategic Plan 2001–2004." Oxford, U.K.: Oxfam International, 2001. Available at http://www.oxfam.org/eng/pdfs/strat_plan.pdf (accessed May 10, 2006).

Picard, Mary. "Measurement and Methodological Challenges to CARE International's Rights-based Programming." CARE International, November 2003. Available at http://www.enterprise-impact.org.uk/pdf/Picard.pdf (accessed May 10, 2006).

Picard, Mary, and Jay Goulden. "Principles into Practice: Learning from Innovative Rights-based Programmes." CARE International, September 2005. Available at http://careint.test.poptel.org.uk/pn726/modules/UpDownload/store_folder/Discussion_papers,_reviews,_reports_and_articles/CARE:_applying_RBA_in_practice/Principles_into_Practice_-_CARE_International_UK_September_2005.pdf (accessed May 10, 2006).

Picolotti, Romina. "The Right to Safe Drinking Water as a Human Right." *Housing and ESC Rights Law Quarterly* 2, no. 1 (2005): 1–5.

Pieterse, Marius. "Possibilities and Pitfalls in the Domestic Enforcement of Social Rights: Contemplating the South African Experience." *Human Rights Quarterly* 26 (2004): 882–905.

Piovesan, Flavia. "The Implementation of Economic, Social and Cultural Rights: Practices and Experiences." In *Dignity and Human Rights: The Implementation of Economic, Social and Cultural Rights*, ed. Berma Klein Goldewijk, Adalid Contreras Baspineiro, and Paulo Cesar Carbonari, 111–27. New York: Intersentia, 2002.

———. "Social, Economic and Cultural Rights and Civil and Political Rights." *Sur: International Journal on Human Rights* 1, no. 1 (2004): 20–45.

Piron, Laure-Helene. "Rights-based Approaches and Bilateral Aid Agencies: More Than a Metaphor?" *IDS Bulletin* 36, no. 1 (2005): 19–28.

Piron, Laure-Helene, and Francis Watkins. "DFID Human Rights Review: A Review of How DFID has Integrated Human Rights into its Work." London: Overseas Development Institute, 2004. Available at http://www.dfid.gov.uk/pubs/files/humrightsrevfull.pdf (accessed May 23, 2006).

Poppendieck, Janet. "The USA: Hunger in the Land of Plenty." In *First World Hunger: Food Security and Welfare Politics*, ed. Graham Riches, 134–64. New York: St. Martin's Press, 1997.

"Poverty and Inequality: A Question of Justice?" *Economist*, March 11, 2004. Available at http://www.economist.com/opinion/displayStory.cfm?story_id=2499118 (accessed September 2005).

Power, Jonathan. *Like Water on Stone: The Story of Amnesty International*. Boston: Northeastern University Press, 2001.

Princen, Thomas, and Jennifer Clapp. "Food, Water, Crisis: The Normative Case for a Neo-Prudential Order." Paper delivered at the International Studies Association, annual meeting, Honolulu, Hawaii, March 3, 2005.

Puta-Chekwe, Chisanga, and Nora Flood. "From Division to Integration: Economic, Social, and Cultural Rights as Basic Human Rights." In *Giving Meaning to Economic, Social and Cultural Rights*, ed. Ishafan Merali and Valerie Oosterveld, 39–51. Philadelphia: University of Pennsylvania Press, 2001.

Rand, June. "CARE's Experience with Adoption of a Rights-based Approach: Five Case Studies." CARE, 2002. Available at http://careint.test.poptel.org.uk/pn726/modules/UpDownload/store_folder/Case_Studies/CARE_Case_Studies:_General/final_case_studies_merged_june_24_02.pdf (accessed October 2005).

Rapley, John. *Globalization and Inequality: Neoliberalism's Downward Spiral*. Boulder, Colo.: Lynne Rienner, 2004.

Ratner, Steven R., and Anne-Marie Slaughter. "Appraising the Methods of International Law: A Prospectus for Readers." *American Journal of International Law* 93, no. 2 (1999): 291–302.

Riches, Graham. "Hunger in Canada: Abandoning the Right to Food." In *First World Hunger: Food Security and Welfare Politics*, ed. Graham Riches, 46–76. New York: St. Martin's Press, 1997.

———. "Hunger, Welfare and Food Security: Emerging Strategies." In *First World Hunger: Food Security and Welfare Politics*, ed. Graham Riches, 165–77. New York: St. Martin's Press, 1997.

Risse, Thomas, Steven C. Popp, and Kathryn Sikkink, eds. *The Power of Human Rights: International Norms and Domestic Change*. Cambridge, U.K.: Cambridge University Press, 1999.

Rittich, Kerry. "Feminism After the State: The Rise of the Market and the Future of Women's Rights." In *Giving Meaning to Economic, Social and Cultural Rights*, ed. Ishafan Merali and Valerie Oosterveld, 95–108. Philadelphia: University of Pennsylvania Press, 2001.

Roberts, Adam. *Humanitarian Action in War: Aid, Protection and Impartiality in a Policy Vacuum*. New York: Oxford University Press, 1996.

Robinson, Mary. "Advancing Economic, Social, and Cultural Rights: The Way Forward." *Human Rights Quarterly* 26, no. 4 (2004): 866–72.

Ross, Loretta J. "Beyond Civil Rights: A New Vision for Social Justice in the United States." *Human Rights Dialogue* 2, no. 1 (2000): 10–11.

Roth, Kenneth. "Defending Economic, Social and Cultural Rights: Practical Issues Faced by an International Human Rights Organization." *Human Rights Quarterly* 26, no. 1 (2004): 63–73.

———. "Response to Leonard S. Rubenstein." *Human Rights Quarterly* 26, no. 4 (2004): 873–78.

Rubenstein, Leonard S. "How International Human Rights Organizations Can Advance Economic, Social, and Cultural Rights: A Response to Kenneth Roth." *Human Rights Quarterly* 26, no. 4 (2004): 845–65.

———. "Response by Leonard S. Rubenstein." *Human Rights Quarterly* 26, no. 4 (2004): 879–81.

Rucht, Dieter. "The Impact of National Contexts on Social Movement Structures: A Cross-movement and Cross-national Comparison." In *Comparative Perspectives on Social Movements: Political Opportunities, Mobilizing Structures, and Cultural Framings*, ed. Doug McAdam, John D. McCarthy, and Mayer N. Zald, 185–204. Cambridge, U.K.: Cambridge University Press, 1996.

Ruggie, John Gerard. *Constructing the World Polity: Essays on International Institutionalization*. London: Routledge, 1998.

Sachs, Jeffrey. *The End of Poverty: Economic Possibilities for Our Time*. New York: Penguin Press, 2005.

Sano, Hans-Otto. "Development and Human Rights: The Necessary, but Partial Integration of Human Rights and Development." *Human Rights Quarterly* 22, no. 3 (2000): 734–52.

Scheinin, Martin. "Economic and Social Rights as Legal Rights." In *Economic, Social and Cultural Rights: A Textbook*, ed. Asbjorn Eide, Catarina Krause, and Allan Rosas, 41–62. London: Martinus Nijhoff, 1995.

Schulz, William. *In Our Own Best Interest: How Defending Human Rights Benefits Us All*. Boston: Beacon Press, 2001.

Schulz-Forberg, Hagen, and Aoife Nolan. "Legislation: The Homelessness (Scotland) Act 2003—An Analysis." *Housing and ESC Rights Law Quarterly* 1, no. 1 (2004): 9.

Sen, Amartya. *Development as Freedom*. New York: Alfred A. Knopf, 1999.

Sengupta, Arjun. "The Right to Development as a Human Right." François-Xavier Bagnoud Center for Health and Human Rights, 2000. Available at http://www.hsph.harvard.edu/fxbcenter/FXBC_WP7—Sengupta.pdf (accessed May 10, 2006).

Sheehy, Orla. "The Discourse of Human Rights and Aid Policy: Facilitating or Challenging Development?" Paper delivered at The Winners and Losers from Rights-based Approaches to Development Conference, Manchester, U.K., February 21–22, 2005. Available at http://www.sed.manchester.ac.uk/idpm/research/events/february2005/documents/Sheehy.doc (accessed May 10, 2006).

Shue, Henry. *Basic Rights: Subsistence, Affluence, and U.S. Foreign Policy,* 2nd ed. Princeton, N.J.: Princeton University Press, 1996.

Shultz, Jim. "Promises to Keep: Using Public Budgets as a Tool to Advance Economic, Social and Cultural Rights." Cuernavaca, Mexico: Ford Foundation and FUNDAR, January 2002. Available at http://www.internationalbudget.org/themes/ESC/FullReport.pdf (accessed May 23, 2006).

Sikkink, Kathryn. "Codes of Conduct for Transnational Corporations: The Case of the WHO/UNICEF Code." *International Organization* 40, no. 4 (1986): 815–40.

Simma, Bruno, and Andreas L. Paulus. "The Responsibility of Individuals for Human
    Rights Abuses in Internal Conflicts: A Positivist View." *American Journal of Interna-
    tional Law* 93, no. 2 (1999): 302–16.
Slaughter, Anne-Marie, and Steven R. Ratner. "The Method Is the Message." *American
    Journal of International Law* 93, no. 2 (1999): 410–23.
Smith, Jackie, Charles Chatfield, and Ron Pagnucco, eds. *Transnational Social Move-
    ments and Global Politics: Solidarity Beyond the State*. Syracuse, N.Y.: Syracuse Uni-
    versity Press, 1997.
Snow, David E., and Robert Benford. "Master Frames and Cycles of Protest." In *Frontiers
    in Social Movement Theory*, ed. Aldon Morris and Carol McClurg Mueller, 133–55.
    New Haven: Yale University Press, 1992.
Snow, David A., and Robert D. Benford. "Alternative Types of Cross-national Diffusion
    in the Social Movement Arena." In *Social Movements in a Globalizing World*, ed.
    Donatella della Porta, Hanspeter Kriesi, and Dieter Rucht, 23–39. New York: St.
    Martin's Press, 1999.
Stammers, Neil. "A Critique of Social Approaches to Human Rights." *Human Rights
    Quarterly* 17, no. 3 (1995): 488–508.
———. "Social Movements and the Social Construction of Human Rights." *Human
    Rights Quarterly* 21, no. 4 (1999): 980–1008.
Steiner, Henry J., and Philip Alston, eds. *International Human Rights in Context: Law,
    Politics, Morals*. Oxford, U.K.: Oxford University Press, 2000.
Sunstein, Cass R. *The Second Bill of Rights: FDR's Unfinished Revolution and Why We
    Need It More than Ever*. New York: Basic Books, 2004.
Tarrow, Sidney. *Power in Movement: Social Movements and Contentious Politics*. Cam-
    bridge, U.K.: Cambridge University Press, 1998.
Tedeschi, Sebastian, and Julieta Rossi. "The Villa La Dulce Case: Including the Excluded
    in Social Housing Plans." *Housing and ESC Rights Law Quarterly* 1, no. 1 (2004):
    1–4.
Tomasevski, Katarina. *Development Aid and Human Rights*. New York: St. Martin's
    Press, 1989.
———. *Development Aid and Human Rights Revisited*. London: Pinter Publishers, 1993.
———. "Indicators." In *Economic, Social and Cultural Rights: A Textbook*, ed. Asbjorn
    Eide, Catarina Krause, and Allan Rosas, 389–401. London: Martinus Nijhoff, 1995.
———. "International Development Finance Agencies." In *Economic, Social and Cultural
    Rights: A Textbook*, ed. Asbjorn Eide, Catarina Krause, and Allan Rosas, 403–13.
    London: Martinus Nijhoff, 1995.
———. "Unasked Questions About Economic, Social, and Cultural Rights from the
    Experience of the Special Rapporteur on the Right to Education (1998–2004): A
    Response to Kenneth Roth, Leonard S. Rubenstein, and Mary Robinson." *Human
    Rights Quarterly* 27, no. 2 (2005): 709–20.
United Nations Commission on Human Rights. "Question on the Realization in All
    Countries of the Economic, Social and Cultural Rights Contained in the Universal

Declaration of Human Rights and in the ICESCR, and Study of Special Problems Which the Developing Countries Face in Their Efforts to Achieve These Human Rights." 2004. Draft resolution within the 60th session, E/CN.4/2004/L.38.

United Nations Development Program. "Human Development Report 2000: Human Rights and Human Development." 2000. Available at http://hdr.undp.org/reports/global/2000/en/ (accessed May 23, 2006).

——. "Human Development Report Examines Country-by-Country Progress on Millennium Development Goals," July 24, 2002. Available at http://hdr.undp.org/reports/global/2002/en/pdf/HDR PR E4.pdf (accessed March 3, 2006).

United Nations General Assembly. "International Covenant on Economic, Social and Cultural Rights." *adopted* December 16, 1966, G.A. Res. 2200 (XXI), U.N. GAOR, 21st Sess., Supp. No. 16, U.N. Doc. A/6316 (1966), 993 U.N.T.S. 3 (*entered into force* 3 Jan. 1976).

——. "Universal Declaration of Human Rights." *adopted* December 10, 1948, G.A. Res. 217A (III), U.N. GAOR, 3d Sess. (Resolutions, pt. 1), at 71, art. 25(1), U.N. Doc. A/810 (1948).

United Nations High Commissioner for Human Rights. "Human Rights Dimension of Poverty." *UNHCHR Online*; available at http://www.ohchr.org/english/issues/poverty/index.htm (accessed December 1, 2005).

——. "Rights-based Approaches: How Do Rights-based Approaches Differ and What Is the Value Added?" *UNHCHR Online*; available at http://www.unhchr.ch/development/approaches-07.html (accessed June 29, 2005).

——. "Rights-based Approaches: What Is a Rights-based Approach to Development?" *UNHCHR Online*; available t http://www.unhchr.ch/development/approaches-04.html (accessed June 29, 2005).

Uttley, Stephen. "Hunger in New Zealand: A Question of Rights?" In *First World Hunger: Food Security and Welfare Politics*, ed. Graham Riches, 80–114. New York: St. Martin's Press, 1997.

Uvin, Peter. *Human Rights and Development*. Bloomfield, Conn.: Kumarian Press, 2004.

Vago, Steven. *Law and Society*. Upper Saddle River, N.J.: Prentice Hall, 2000.

Van Boven, Theo. "Human Rights and Development: The UN Experience." In *Human Rights and Development: International Views*, ed. David P. Forsythe, 121–35. New York: St. Martin's Press, 1989.

VeneKlasen, Lisa, Valerie Miller, Cindy Clark, and Molly Reilly. "Rights-based Approaches and Beyond: Challenges of Linking Rights and Participation." Sussex, U.K.: Institute of Development Studies, Working Paper No. 235, 2004. Available at http://www.ids.ac.uk/ids/bookshop/wp/wp235.pdf (accessed May 10, 2006).

Von Tigerstrom, Barbara. "Implementing Economic, Social and Cultural Rights: The Role of National Human Rights Institutions." In *Giving Meaning to Economic, Social and Cultural Rights*, ed. Ishafan Merali and Valerie Oosterveld, 139–59. Philadelphia: University of Pennsylvania Press, 2001.

Wapner, Paul. *Environmental Activism and World Civic Politics*. Albany, N.Y.: SUNY Press, 1996.

Weber, Steven. "International Organizations and the Pursuit of Justice in the World Economy." *Ethics and International Affairs* 14 (2000): 9–117.

Wendt, Alexander. *Social Theory of International Politics*. Cambridge, U.K.: Cambridge University Press, 1999.

Wheeler, Joanna, and Jethro Pettit. "Whose Rights? Examining the Discourse, Context and Practice of Rights-based Approaches to Development." Paper delivered at The Winners and Losers from Rights-Based Approaches to Development Conference, Manchester, U.K., February 21–22, 2005. Available at http://www.sed.manchester. ac.uk/idpm/research/events/february2005/documents/Wheeler.doc (accessed May 10, 2006).

Wickeri, Elisabeth. "Grootboom's Legacy: Securing the Right of Access to Adequate Housing in South Africa?" NYU School of Law, Center for Human Rights and Global Justice Working Paper No. 5, 2004.

Wiessner, Siegfried, and Andrew R. Willard. "Policy-Oriented Jurisprudence and Human Rights Abuses in Internal Conflict: Toward a World Public Order of Human Dignity." *American Journal of International Law* 93, no. 2 (1999): 316–34.

Williams, Rob. "Rights-based Development: How to Get There from Here." *Global Future*, Fourth Quarter 2003, 3.

Woodiwiss, Anthony. "The Law Cannot Be Enough: Human Rights and the Limits of Legalism." In *The Legalization of Human Rights*, ed. Basak Çali and Saladin Meckled-Garcia, 32–48. London: Routledge, 2006.

Yamin, Alicia Ely. "The Future in the Mirror: Incorporating Strategies for the Defense and Promotion of Economic, Social, and Cultural Rights into the Mainstream Human Rights Agenda." *Human Rights Quarterly* 97, no. 4 (2005): 1200–1244.

Yates, Michael. "Poverty and Inequality in the Global Economy." *Monthly Review* 55, no. 9 (2004).

Ziegler, Jean. "The Right to Food." United Nations Economic and Social Council, 2003. Report submitted by the Special Rapporteur on the Right to Food, in accordance with UN Commission on Human Rights resolution 2002/25, E/CN.4/2003/54.

———. "The Right to Food." United Nations Commission on Human Rights, 2004. Report submitted by the Special Rapporteur on the Right to Food, in accordance with UN Commission on Human Rights resolution 2003/25, E/CN.4/2004/10.

Index

ActionAid, 15, 108, 120–22, 154

Alston, Philip, 36, 52, 73, 172 n.60

Amnesty International, 3, 143–44; expanding their mandate, 3, 14, 21, 31–39, 132, 138; as a gatekeeper of human rights, 24, 32; Global Campaign for Human Dignity, 34, 67, 143–44; and grassroots methodologies, 34, 67, 170 n.36; International Council Meetings (ICMs), 33–34, 40; and legal approaches to rights, 42–43, 103, 138; and Secretary General Pierre Sane, 39

Anderson, Carol, 74–75

Annan, Kofi, 107

antiglobalization movement, 39, 75, 101–2

Asociacion Pro Derechos Humanos (APRO-DEH), 38, 144

Association for Women's Rights in Development, 119, 154

Balkin, Jack, 95–96

Bank Information Center, 73–74, 150

Baxi, Upendra, 62, 175 n.113

bilateral aid agencies, 109, 117–18

Bob, Clifford, 24, 73

Border Network for Human Rights, 81, 83, 150

Bread for the World, 73, 76–77, 88, 91, 150, 161 n.21

budget analysis and ESCRs, 10, 40, 57–58, 121

Bush (George W.) administration, 58, 62, 141

CARE International, 3, 15, 104–5, 108, 114–15, 119–20, 126, 137, 154

Carter administration, 8, 51, 162 n.26

case law on ESCRs, 45–46; and courts' reluctance to hear ESCR cases, 48–50, 94–96; *Grootboom v. Oostenberg Municipality*,

45–46, 49; inability to address systemic issues, 49–50, 56, 59, 128; and negative obligations, 50, 56; *People's Union for Civil Liberties (PUCL) v. India*, 45; and the reasonableness standard, 45–46, 174 n.103; *Treatment Action Campaign (TAC) v. Minister of Health*, 46. *See also* legal approaches to rights

Catholic Relief Services (CRS), 111–12, 115

Center for Economic and Social Rights (CESR), 32, 67, 147

Center for Economic Justice (CEJ), 14, 73–74, 90

Center of Concern, 73–74, 151

Centre on Housing Rights and Evictions (COHRE), 32, 147

Centro de Estudios Legales y Sociales (CELS), 38, 144

Christian Aid, 109, 120, 154

civil and political rights (CPRs): and justiciability 4–13, 18, 26–27, 131, 134–35; moral approaches to, 28, 137–39; relationship to ESCRs, ix, 4–13, 18, 26–27, 31–38, 44–48, 131; taken-for-granted status, 53, 60, 162 n.35

Coalition of Immokalee Workers (CIW), 74, 151

Coalition to Protect Public Housing, 74

Cold War, ix, 2, 108, 170 n.36; end of, 37–38, 51, 75, 132; and fear of communism in the West, 36–38, 62, 74–75; and interpretations of rights, 8–10, 17, 23, 36–38, 51, 139–40

Concern Worldwide, 116, 120, 155

constitutions: European Social Charter, 44, 145; in Northern Ireland, 44–45; in South Africa, 44–49; in the United States, 83, 95–96, 139–41, 176 n.143

constructivism, 10, 13, 19–24, 30, 163 n.38;
    and debate with rationalism, 19–21
Cox, Larry, 53, 103

development as a technical vs. political pro-
    cess, 15, 61–65, 105, 122–25, 130
distributional justice, 58, 65, 91–94
Dochas, 109
downward accountability in development
    work, 126–27

economic, social and cultural rights (ESCRs):
    legal status in relation to CPRs, ix, 4–13,
    18, 26–27, 31–38, 44–48, 131, 161 n.24;
    right to food, 33, 47, 51, 148, 177 n.163;
    Right to Food resolution, 76, 150; right
    to health, 34, 81, 100, 144–46, 149, 151,
    187 n.98; right to housing, 34, 45–47, 49,
    51, 77–79, 138, 147–57; seen as a threat to
    CPRs, 23; U.S. approach to, 35–37, 50–53,
    98–101. See also civil and political rights
Ecumenical Program on Central America
    (EPICA), 80, 90
empowerment as a goal of development, 15,
    114–16, 121–27
equality, varying definitions of, 91–94

faith-based organizations, 76–77, 88, 111
Farmer, Paul, 73, 81–82, 87–88, 125, 187
    n.104
Food First Information and Action Network
    (FIAN), 32–33, 46–47, 74, 148
Ford Foundation, 24, 39–40, 65, 76–77, 82,
    159 n.3
framing strategies, ix–x, 2–3, 14, 22–24, 30,
    52–53, 60, 69, 73–76, 83–100, 111, 129–39;
    definition, 166 n.28. See also rhetoric
full spectrum approach, 1, 33–34, 143

G8 conference, 99
gatekeepers of human rights, xi, 24, 32–36,
    78–79
Glendon, Mary Ann, 83–84, 102–3,

Habitat International Coalition, 36, 156
Honkala, Cheri, 81, 97
humanitarian NGOs, x–xi, 3–5, 13–16,
    104–30, 131–39, 142, 154–56; adoption
    of rights-based approaches, 104–13;
    advocating for policy reform, 110, 120–21,

124–25; definition, 72, 105, 189 n.1; and
    new partnerships, 125–26; normative,
    analytical and operational changes within,
    119–22; and scarce resources, 123–26. See
    also moral approaches to rights
Human Rights Council of Australia (HRCA),
    108, 145
Human Rights First, 31, 145
human rights NGOs, 3–4, 31–70; expanding
    their mandates, 31–41; interpretation of
    rights, 41–44; and legal strategies,
    44–70
Human Rights Tech, 82
Human Rights Watch, 3, 12, 24, 31, 34–37,
    39, 47, 67, 103, 145; and traditional meth-
    odologies, 12, 34–37

InterAction, 109
Inter-American Commission on Human
    Rights, 79
International Budget Partnership, 40
International Centre on Economic, Social
    and Cultural Rights (CIDESC), 32, 148
International Commission of Jurists (ICJ),
    31, 146
International Covenant on Economic, Social
    and Cultural Rights (ICESCR), 42, 52,
    60, 78; Article 2.1, 11, 55; Article 11, 6;
    Article 12, 93, 187 n.98; and the Optional
    Protocol, 47, 51
International Federation for Human Rights,
    32, 156–57
International Monetary Fund (IMF), 58, 179
    n.192
International Network for Economic, Social
    and Cultural Rights (ESCR-Net), x, 32, 45,
    72–74, 157, 159 n.1
International Committee of the Red Cross
    (ICRC), 110, 112

Jochnick, Chris, 107, 116, 137
Jubilee Network, 14, 78, 89, 137
justiciability, 40, 44–46, 49, 69; definition,
    11; and the realization of rights, 49–50;
    and the validity of rights, ix, 3–4, 9–13,
    162 n.24

Kennedy, David, 29, 68–69, 97
Kensington Welfare Rights Union (KWRU),
    73–74, 78–81, 152

legal approaches to rights, x–xi, 3–6, 11–13, 41–70, 133–36; advantages and successes, 44–47; definition, 3–4, 41–44, 172 n.71; embedded in politics and culture, 13, 68–70; and ideological controversies, 55–66; and the inaccessibility of legal discourse, 53–55, 63, 77; and U.S. opposition, 50–53; and vague legal norms, 56–59. *See also* case law on ESCRs
Legal Momentum, 74
legal theory, 17–19, 24–30; critical legal studies, 19, 28–30, 68–69, 97; feminism, 19, 29; legal positivism, 18, 26–27; New Haven school, 19, 28–29; post-positivism, 27–30
Limburg Principles, 31, 146
Lutheran World Relief, 111, 155

Mercy Corps, 111, 155
Mertz-Gilmore Foundation, 39, 159 n.3
military spending, 55, 58, 178 n. 174
Millennium Development Goals, 98
minimum core content of rights, 93, 177 n. 156, 187 n.110
Moore, Michael, 81, 100
moral approaches to rights, x–xi, 4–6, 13–16, 133–42; advantages of, 84–88, 94–103, 119–23, 136; challenges faced by, 88–94, 123–27, 136; definition, 4, 80–82, 114–15; by humanitarian NGOs, 4–5, 104–7, 113–30; by social justice NGOs, 4, 78–103

NAACP, 74–75, 91
naming and shaming techniques, 12, 43–44, 47, 66–69, 134, 140
National Economic and Social Rights Initiative (NESRI), 32, 138, 148
National Law Center on Homelessness and Poverty, 74, 78, 152
National Mobilization Against Sweatshops (NMASS), 74
Neier, Aryeh, 12, 34, 36
neoliberalism, 38, 48–49, 51, 68, 75, 101–2, 118, 123, 171 n.41. *See also* poverty and economic policy
neutrality: in international humanitarian work, 109–10, 112, 122, 137–38; in the legal process, 25, 29, 58–60, 66
New International Economic Order, 107–8

Obama administration, 52, 100–101, 138
Odinkalu, Chidi Anselm, 53–54, 96, 184 n.48
Offenheiser, Ray, 108–10
ONE Campaign, 14, 73–74, 78, 80, 88–89, 91, 153
Otto Bremer Foundation, 159 n.3
overstretching, NGOs' concerns about, 36–37, 41, 68
Oxfam International, 3, 24, 104, 108–10, 114, 116, 119–20, 137, 155

participation in development projects, x, 4, 15, 53–54, 106, 110, 115–21, 126–30
People's Union for Civil Liberties (PUCL), 45
Piron, Laure-Helene, 119-20, 194 n.101
Poor People's Economic Human Rights Campaign (PPEHRC), 73–74, 79–80, 90, 152, 157, 160 n.7, 186 n.91
positive and negative rights, 6–13, 17, 40, 50–51, 131, 142, 162 n.32, 177 n.163
positivism: *See* legal positivism
poverty: and analysis of root causes, 89–90, 105, 110, 115, 120, 125, 135; and charity, 86–87; and economic policies, 60–66, 101–2; and enlightened self-interest, 87; global statistics about, 7-8, 161 n.22; relationship to subsistence rights, ix, 6–7, 56, 178 n.164; and U.S. public opinion about, 189 n.142
principles vs. interests in motivating action, 19–21, 131–33
Programa Venezolana de Educacion y Proteccion de Derechos Humanos, 38
Public Citizen, 73-74, 76, 137, 153

radical flank effect, 91
realism in international relations and international law, 17-18
rhetoric, xi, 5, 62, 139, 193 n.82; and discourses of poverty, 84–88; and social change, 19–23, 30, 82–84, 116–18
rights-based approach to development, 104–13; suspicion about, 115–18. *See also* humanitarian NGOs
Rittich, Kerry, 62–63
Robinson, Mary, 108, 129, 142, 149
Roth, Kenneth, 12, 34–35, 177 n.162
Rubenstein, Leonard, 31, 58, 177 n.161

Samuel Rubin Foundation, 159 n.3
Save the Children, 108, 112, 156

Schulz, William, 42, 88,
Sen, Amartya, 61, 105-6, 160 n.15
Shue, Henry, 6, 93, 160 n.9, 162 nn.32-33, 178 n.175
Slum Dwellers International, 77
socialism, 37, 85, 92-93, 99
social justice, varying definitions of, 88-91
social justice NGOs, x-xi, 3-5, 13-15, 21, 54, 71-103, 131-39, 142, 149-53; definition, 72-73. *See also* moral approaches to rights
social movement theory, ix, 21-23, 29-30
social theory of human rights, 5-6, 10, 13, 16, 17-30, 68-70, 103, 112-13, 130-42
Stammers, Neil, 66, 71
Sunstein, Cass, 95, 100, 140-141

Tomasevski,Katarina, 114-15, 117

U2 (rock band), 80
United Nations: global conferences, 51, 107, 159 n.1; and mainstreaming human rights, 159 n.2
United Nations Children's Fund (UNICEF), 107, 159 n.2
United Nations Committee on Economic, Social and Cultural Rights (CESCR), 32; and General Comments, 47; and NGO participation, 36, 47
United Nations Development Program (UNDP), 7-8, 107, 159 n.2; and the Human Development Report, 105-6, 161 n.22
United Nations High Commissioner on Human Rights (UNHCHR), 7, 42, 108, 142, 149, 180 n.218
United Nations Human Rights Council, 52

United States: and the Cold War, 23, 37-38, 75; economic policy, 58, 61-62, 90, 178 n.174; legal rights within, 95, 140-41; opposition to ESCRs, ix, 4, 8-9, 50-53, 76-77, 79, 98-101, 117, 136; proliferation of rights claims within, 75; public opinion about poverty within, 87-88, 92-93, 189 n. 142; support for anti-poverty efforts, 64
United States Agency for International Development (USAID), 109, 112
United States Human Rights Network (USHRN), 52, 74, 93, 157, 159 n.6, 173 n.82
Universal Declaration of Human Rights, 2, 6, 8, 35-37, 42, 78-81, 92, 99, 159 n.2, 162 n.24, 184 n.32
Urban Justice Center, 74, 153
Uvin, Peter, 99, 118, 125, 160 n.8, 178 n.175, 190 n.9, 193 n.82, 195nn. 122, 145, 196 n.152

VeneKlasen, Lisa, 128-29
Vienna Declaration, 11-12

Wapner, Paul, 96, 141
Washington Consensus, 61
Watkins, Francis, 119-20, 194 n.101
Winfrey, Oprah, 81, 100
Women's Economic Agenda Project (WEAP), 73-74, 153
Women's International Coalition for Economic Justice (WICEJ), 73
World Bank, 117, 133, 179 n.192
World Organization Against Torture (OMCT), 31-32, 146
World Vision, 108, 111, 120

Acknowlegments

I am deeply grateful for the years of support, challenge, and intellectual stimulation that I received at the School of International Service at American University. SIS, led by Dean Louis Goodman, richly deserves its reputation as one of the elite graduate schools in international relations in the world. The faculty and staff at SIS who contributed directly or indirectly to this work are too numerous to mention, but foremost among them are Paul Wapner, whose keen insights were provided with an amazing sense of compassion; and Julie Mertus, whose guidance demonstrated her superior expertise in the field of human rights. Without their wise mentoring, this book would not have been possible.

As with any significant endeavor, this book could not have been achieved without the support of a surrounding community of scholars and friends. I am grateful for the fruitful discussions at American University I engaged in with Robin Broad, Mary Gray, Patrick Jackson, Janet Lord, Steven Silvia, and my colleagues Rebecca DeWinter, Anne-Claire Hervy, Peter Howard, Naren Kumarakulasingam, Helen McClure, Mvuselelo Ngoyu, Reina Neufeldt, and Simon Nicholson. There are many others who have enriched my thinking on these issues, and I apologize for any omission.

I am also deeply appreciative of the scholars outside of American University who dedicated their time to discuss these issues with me, including Clifford Bob, George Kent, Larissa Fast, William Felice, and Jackie Smith. I am grateful for the input from my colleagues in the political science department at Rollins College, including Dexter Boniface, Don Davison, Joan Davison, Rick Foglesong, Mike Gunter, and Tom Lairson. Early versions of two chapters of this book were presented at annual conferences of the International Studies Association, and I am grateful to fellow panelists, audience members, and anonymous reviewers for their questions, comments, and critiques. I am also thankful for the many people working on the front lines to realize freedom from poverty who spoke with me; I was inspired by their conscientious and savvy commitment to this goal: Cathy Albisa, Edwin Berry, Ann Blyberg, Larry Cox, Mario Gomez, Michael Lerner, Jim McDonald, Mario Melo, David Petrasek, Sally-Anne Way, and Mona Younis. Thank you all for sharing your struggles and insights.

Finally, I am grateful for the many late-night discussions that I have had with my brothers Dave and Jon, which have not only contributed to my personal and intellectual development, but also provided a surprisingly direct foundation for this study. And my ultimate gratitude goes to my partner for life, Amy, who has always remained faithful to the good in each of us.